SINGER®

THE COMPLETE PHOTO GUIDE TO

SEWING

3RD EDITION

Inspiring | Educating | Creating | Entertaining

Brimming with creative inspiration, how-to projects, and useful information to enrich your everyday life, Quarto Knows is a favorite destination for those pursuing their interests and passions. Visit our site and dig deeper with our books into your area of interest: Quarto Creates, Quarto Cooks, Quarto Homes, Quarto Lives, Quarto Drives, Quarto Explores, Quarto Gifts, or Quarto Kids.

First edition published in 2005
Second edition published in 2009
First published in 2018 by Creative Publishing international, an imprint of The Quarto Group,
401 Second Avenue North, Suite 310, Minneapolis, MN 55401, USA.
T (612) 344-8100 F (612) 344-8692 QuartoKnows.com

Creative Publishing international titles are also available at discount for retail, wholesale, promotional, and bulk purchase. For details, contact the Special Sales Manager by email at specialsales@quarto.com or by mail at The Quarto Group, Attn: Special Sales Manager, 401 Second Avenue North, Suite 310, Minneapolis, MN 55401, USA.

10 9 8 7 6 5 4 3 2

ISBN: 978-1-58923-897-8

Digital edition published in 2018

Library of Congress Cataloging-in-Publication Data is available

Design: Laura McFadden
Photography: Nancy Langdon
Illustration: Mattie Wells (page 13)

Printed in China

SINGER®

THE COMPLETE PHOTO GUIDE TO
SEWING

3RD EDITION **BY NANCY LANGDON**

Creative Publishing
international

Contents

Why Sew?

Take a moment to look around your environment and see how many things are made of textiles. Most likely, those things have been assembled to great degree through sewing. Now think how many of those things don't fit quite comfortably, are looking worn and dated, or don't serve the intended function.

Now, if you can sew, you can make almost any textile item look and function exactly how you want it to. Besides being very practical, sewing can be an energizing and empowering life skill. Sewing for yourself and the people in your life allows you to create garments that fit and flatter all body types and personalities. Your clothes are the "skin" you choose, one way you communicate with the world around you. Sewing allows you to wear your true you. Maybe you've returned home from a shopping trip empty handed, feeling that you've been "left out" of fashion. No need to sit at home and miss out on the fun simply because you can't find anything to wear. Sewing can be your way back into fashion. With a good sewing pattern, some knowledge on how to adjust that pattern correctly, and the right fabrics, not only will you walk confidently into a room in beautiful garments, but you'll also feel that sense of personal accomplishment that comes from having made something with your own two hands. Sewing for your living spaces will add those wonderful uniquely you touches that make a house a home. Switch up your décor style on a whim for only pennies on the dollar. Sewing also allows you to play a greater role in voting with your dollars to support textile production

techniques, farming, environmental, and labor practices that align with your own values. Finally, sewing is life-long learning activity. There will always be new fabrics, advances in technologies, and innovations in fashion design. Each project, no matter how small, will be a new experience that will add to your skill set. Sewing is a wonderful activity that marries mathematical, spatial–relational, and methodical thought processes with the free-spirited creative mind to make tangible, useful, beautiful everyday items.

The Complete Photo Guide to Sewing, 3rd Edition, owes much to its predecessor editions. This edition has been updated to reflect advances in textiles and technologies, changes in tastes, and evolving sewing practices influenced to a great degree by the vibrant, global, infinitely resourceful, and selflessly helpful online sewing communities. Although what we sew and how we sew may have changed from our mother's time, many techniques survive the centuries and create a consistent thread of knowledge to be passed along, stitch by stitch, sewist to sewist, generation to generation. This book is intended to share what was given to us.

How to Use This Book

Like any other art or craft, sewing begins with basic techniques. In addition, specialty sewing topics such as fitting, sewing activewear, and sewing home décor projects are also included.

Getting Started

This section gives you information on the sewing machine and the serger. We show you how to get the perfect stitch and tell you about special features and accessories for both machines. We also tell you about the equipment and notions you will need, plus some specialized equipment that you may find indispensible.

Also covered here is the sewing pattern. You will learn how to take your measurements, select and fit the correct size. A guide to fabric selection is included, as well as cutting and sewing tips. There is also information on how to choose and apply interfacing.

Sewing Techniques

The basic sewing techniques include seams, darts, gathering, sleeves, collars, waistbands, cuffs, and closures. Each is given an overview, followed by a step-by-step description of how to achieve excellent results. Often, several methods are presented with suggestions on which may be best to use.

Home Decorating Projects

The Home Decorating section includes project categories such as decorator fabrics, pillows, cushions, slipcovers, bed and bath, and table fashions. Four basic pillow styles are shown with variations for closures. For the bedroom, we give you instructions on how to make a duvet cover, and then the matching pillow shams and a dust ruffle. For the table, learn how to make rectangular and round tablecloths, placemats, and many variations of napkins.

For easy reference, fabric and notions required to complete many projects are included in a box labeled You Will Need. The step-by-step instructions for the home décor projects are complete, so there's no need to purchase additional sewing patterns. The photographs show you how each project should look each step of the way.

Step-by-Step Guidance

The photos add depth and dimension to the instructions, giving you a close-up look at each step. In some cases, the stitches are shown in heavier thread or a contrasting color to make them more visible. Some marking lines have also been exaggerated to show a crucial matching point.

If you are learning to sew or getting back to sewing, you may want to practice your skills on an easy project before starting a larger one. Try sewing simple placemats and napkins to practice a new edge finish. When you sew a first garment, choose a simple style that is easy to fit with few details.

Whether you are new to sewing, an experienced sewist, or a returning sewist, this book is designed to be a help and an inspiration. There are many techniques, tips, and tricks within these pages for successful results that even some very experienced sewists may not yet know. Keep this book near your sewing machine, make notes on the pages, and, most importantly, enjoy the sewing experience!

The Sewing Machine

A sewing machine is your most important piece of sewing equipment—your "vehicle" on your sewing journey—so select one with care. A sturdy, well-built machine will give you many years of sewing enjoyment.

If you are buying a new machine, there are models available to fit any budget or sewing need. Types range from a basic zigzag with one or two built-in stitches, to electronic machines that use advanced computer technology to control and select the stitching. Just like you wouldn't drive a rusty old car found in a barn out on the highway, use caution when using a machine found in a closet that hasn't been used in years. It is best to have the machine thoroughly checked and adjusted by a trusted professional before heading out on your road to creativity.

Common sewing machine features include built-in buttonholer, stitch selection, instant reverse, snap-on presser foot or shank feet, free arm for stitching small round areas (such as pant legs), built-in bobbin winder, automatic tension and pressure adjustment, automatic stitch length adjustment, and even automatic thread cutters and thread tie-offs. Embroidery machines, in addition to conventional sewing, allow the user to use digital files to make elaborate and colorful machine embroidered designs. Each feature adds to the cost of the machine, so look for a machine to match your sewing projects. Invest in a machine that satisfies your sewing needs, but don't pay for features you will rarely use. Also consider the amount and difficulty of the sewing you do and the number of people you sew for. Talk to fabric store personnel and friends who sew and read reviews of different sewing machines online. Ask for demonstrations and try out and compare several models. Look for quality workmanship and ease of operation, as well as stitching options. A heavier machine will be less likely to "dance around" your sewing table while sewing at higher speeds. Also take a look inside at the inner workings of the machine and look for metal parts: Plastic parts are subject to deformation and since sewing is a matter of tiny, tiny fractions of inches, even the very slightest variations in the gear works can have significant impacts on your machine's timing and stitch quality. However, also be wary of inexpensive machines with a lot of metal parts. It is likely that a lower quality steel was used and this lesser quality steel will allow burrs to form easily on, for example, the hook, causing threads to tangle. Also consider a machine's piercing power: Make sure the machine you choose will punch a needle through four to six layers of heavy material without bending or breaking the needle (think about hemming jeans or stitching heavy upholstery).

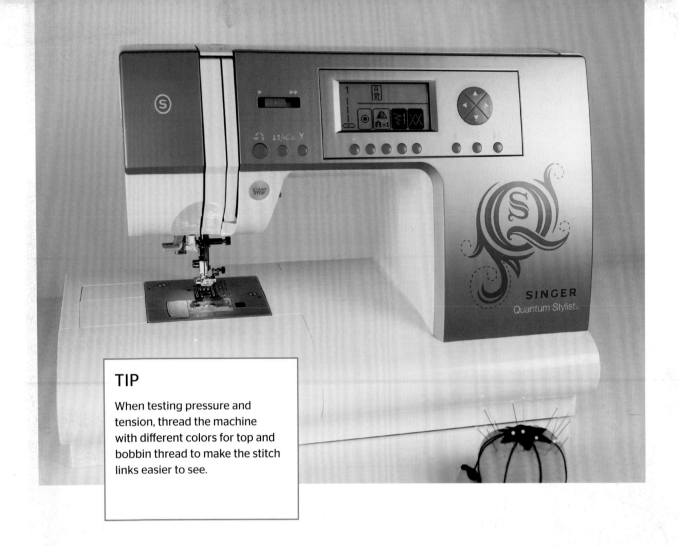

TIP

When testing pressure and tension, thread the machine with different colors for top and bobbin thread to make the stitch links easier to see.

Although sewing machines vary in capabilities and accessories, each has the same basic parts and controls. Check your manual for the specific location of these parts on your machine. Just like cars, every sewing machine is basically the same but different in several ways. It is worth investing the time to read through your sewing machine's manual and testing out each feature and function, so that using your machine becomes second nature.

Creating the Perfect Stitch

Perfect stitching is easy to achieve if you thread the machine properly and make the right adjustments in the stitch length, tension, and pressure. These adjustments depend on your fabric and the kind of stitch desired. Consult your machine manual for threading procedures and location of controls.

Either the stitch length regulator is on an inch scale from 0 to 20, a metric scale from 0 to 4, or a numerical scale from 0 to 9. For normal stitching, set the regulator at 10 to 12 stitches per inch or at the number 3 for metric scale machines. On the numerical scale, higher numbers form a larger stitch; if a shorter stitch is desired, dial a lower number. For an average stitch length, set the dial to number 5.

Older machines may have built-in bobbins, but newer machines will almost always have removable bobbins. Bobbins with a built-in case are wound in the case. Removable bobbin machines are either front loading or top loading. A front-loading machine will have the bobbin accessible from the front of the free arm. It has a removable bobbin case with an adjustable tension screw. On a top-loading machine, the bobbin is placed right in front of the needle under a clear plastic cover. Front-loading and top-loading machines have different hook systems and each has its own advantages. For example, a front-loading bobbin machine allows you to switch out a bobbin in the middle of a seam without the switch being vis-

Timing and Related Issues

When a machine's timing is affected, the result is very often missed stitches or a loose and tangled bobbin thread in the stitching line. Modern electronic machines may cease stitching altogether when a timing problem beyond normal tolerances is recognized. A timing problem most often occurs when the needle strikes a hard object, such as a pin, button, or zipper, thereby misaligning the intricate workings. Before heading to the repair shop, however, the cause may lie with something simpler, such as a bent needle or a mismatch between your thread and your fabric weight. Also, adjusting your thread tension can often resolve what appears to be a timing problem.

ible from the right side. Therefore, a front-loading machine is more practical for bobbin work. On the other hand, a top-loading machine allows you to see how much bobbin thread is left when you use clear plastic bobbins. Furthermore, you don't need to pick up the thread from below with a top-loading machine as you do with a front-loading machine when changing bobbins.

Bobbins are generally wound on the top of the machine. Always start with an empty bobbin spool. For an evenly wound bobbin, follow the threading guide for your machine. Wind the bobbin only to the point of the automatic shut off. Winding the bobbin too full may cause the bobbin to get stuck in the bobbin case and tangle within your machine.

In the ideal stitch, both top and bobbin thread are drawn equally into the fabric, and the link is formed midway between fabric layers. The stitch tension control determines the amount of tension on the threads as they pass through the machine. Too much tension results in too little thread fed into the stitch. This will cause the fabric to pucker. Too little tension produces too much thread and a weak, sloppy stitch.

Always check tension and pressure on a scrap of the fabric you will be sewing before starting to sew. Adjust the pressure regulator for light pressure on heavyweight fabrics and more pressure on light fabrics. Correct pressure ensures even feeding of the fabric layers during stitching. Some machines automatically adjust tension and pressure to the fabric.

Straight Stitch Tension and Pressure

- **Correct** tension and pressure makes stitches that are linked midway between the fabric layers. The stitches look even in length and tension on both sides. Fabric layers are fed evenly through the feed and fabric is not marred. (A)

- **Too tight** tension results in stitch links that are near the top layer of fabric. Fabric is puckered, and stitches are easily broken. Turn tension dial to a lower number. If pressure is too heavy, the bottom layer may gather up. Fabric may shift or stretch. Stitches may be uneven in length and tension. Dial pressure regulator to a lower number. (B)

- **Too loose** tension results in stitch links that are toward the bottom fabric layer. Seam is weak. Correct the problem by turning tension dial to a higher number. Too light pressure may cause skipped and uneven stitches, and may pull fabric into the feed. Dial pressure regulator to a higher number. (C)

Zigzag Stitch Tension and Pressure

- **Correct** tension and pressure in zigzag stitching produces stitches in which the interlocking link of threads falls at the corner of each stitch, midway between fabric layers. Stitches lie flat and fabric does not pucker.

- Too tight tension causes fabric to pucker. The thread link falls near the top fabric layer. To correct, decrease the tension. Incorrect pressure is not as apparent in zigzag as in straight stitching. But if the pressure is not accurate, stitches will not be of even length.

- Too loose tension causes the bottom layer to pucker and the thread link to fall near the bottom fabric layer. Increase tension to balance stitch. The zigzag stitch should be properly balanced in normal sewing. Loosen tension slightly for decorative stitches, and the top stitch pattern will become more rounded. (D)

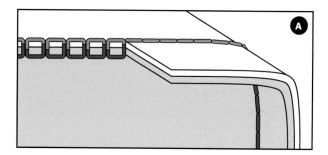

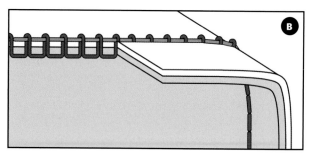

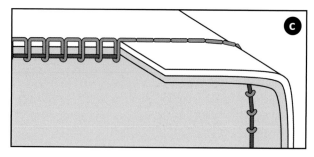

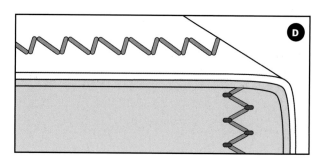

Thread comes wrapped on short thick spools, long thin spools, or cones. Read the labels carefully to find fiber content and thread weight. Sewing thread comes in different thicknesses, each having best uses and applications. As a rule of thumb, the higher the number, the thinner the thread. For example, 40 Wt is a common embroidery thread weight. The common bobbin thread used in machine embroidery is a thinner 60 Wt. For perfect tension in regular sewing, use the same size and type thread in the bobbin as you use in the needle.

Today, polyester sewing thread has replaced cotton thread for most sewing applications. Polyester has a high tensile strength, does not fray easily, can be washed at high temperatures, holds dye well, and is not very susceptible to UV or moisture damage. It is the strongest and longest lasting, given equal weight. An all-purpose polyester sewing thread is appropriate for hand and machine sewing on all fabrics: natural fibers and synthetics, wovens, and knits. Heavy thread, designed for machine stitching on denim and canvas, is usually 100% polyester for strength. Heavy thread is also used for topstitching to make the stitches more apparent as a design element. Button and carpet thread is suitable for hand sewing where extra strength is required. Button and carpet thread may not fit through the eye of a needle, but it can be used to topstitch if wound on the bobbin and the topstitching is done with the top down.

Bobbin work is one creative avenue where thread plays a starring role. By threading very heavyweight cotton or wool thread, even thin knitting yarn, onto the bobbin, you open a new world of topstitching and embellishing opportunities. Bobbin work requires you to lay the top side of your work upside down on the machine, so that the decorative bobbin thread appears on the top.

Types of Thread

Serger thread is wrapped on large cones and is usually 100% polyester. Regular serger thread is thinner than standard sewing thread to reduce bulk in multithread seams. To use a cone of thread on your conventional machine, place the cone in a glass jar or on a specially designed cone stand behind the machine as close as possible to the first thread guide.

Polyester thread is suitable for most general sewing on medium to heavy fabrics. Avoid polyester thread on lightweight and delicate fabrics, however: When seams are stressed, polyester thread can tear delicate fabrics.

Cotton thread is not as commonly used as it once was, however, it remains popular for quilting, hand sewing, and for people who prefer to sew with natural materials. Mercerized cotton thread is appropriate for sewing natural fiber woven fabrics like cotton, linen, and wool. Because cotton thread does not have much elasticity, it is a good choice for very fine fabrics, like sheer silk chiffon. Cotton thread will not pucker a fine sheer fabric and will likely break before the delicate fabric is torn. Cotton is soft and durable and adjusts well when fabrics shrink. If you would prefer not to have the sheen of rayon or polyester thread on your embroidery design, cotton thread may also be used for high-speed machine embroidery. Cotton thread, however, does not have enough stretch to use on knit fabrics.

Silk thread is slightly elastic and has a high sheen, suitable for machine embroidery. Silk thread can be used when sewing silk and synthetic silk fabrics. The delicate nature of this thread belies how very strong it is: Silk is often used in hemming and appliqué on woolens, because the silk thread will sink into the fibers of the wool and disappear. Silk thread should not be used on anything that would be bleached, as chlorine will weaken it.

Nylon thread has stretch and is a good option for sewing dance, athletic, and swimwear garments that stretch and move with the wearer. Nylon, however, has some characteristics that make it unsuitable for most other sewing. It can discolor and become brittle over time. It is also not heat resistant and cannot be ironed. There is a category of nylon thread called wooly nylon, which is often used for rolled hems on a serger. Because the nylon fibers puff out a bit and fill in the tiny gaps between stitches, including wooly nylon will make a nice, solid-looking rolled edge.

Invisible thread is a very thin, strong, clear nylon thread, that can be used alone or together with another thread, that lacks durability.

Metallic thread is not technically thread because it isn't a spun fiber. It is usually a thermoplastic core surrounded by an aluminum coil or a very thin, flat filament. It is used primarily for decorative topstitching. Sewing metallic thread requires using a metallic sewing thread needle, which has a longer eye.

Button and carpet thread is much thicker and stronger than regular sewing thread. It is used mostly in hand sewing, for example, in upholstery applications and to secure buttons onto coats.

Acrylic thread, like acrylic yarn, has some characteristics in common with wool thread. Acrylic thread is a good choice for rolled serger hems, making a nice solid edge. It is strong and flexible and is used to sew woolens and in bobbin work. Because it is fibrous like wool, it can lend an item a homespun look. Real wool thread is also available from speciality thread sellers.

Water-soluble thread is a specialty thread used in baste stitching. Once the item is washed, the stitches dissolve and disappear.

Selecting Machine Needle and Thread

Not just any needle will do: Each fabric is best sewn with the right type of thread, but also with the needle best used with that fabric and thread. Using the wrong needle can create all sorts of problems. At a minimum, the wrong needle can result in loose or puckered seams. Worse still, the needle can break and possibly damage your bobbin or hook. If a broken needle lands just right (wrong), it can throw your machine's timing off, requiring a trip to the repair shop. It is a good habit to begin a new sewing project with a fresh needle. Toss out any needle that is even slightly dull or bent.

Needles come in four basic types: Sharp, ballpoint, universal, and wedge. Each material requires the use of the correct needle. Certain sewing applications, such as embroidery or quilting, will require special needles as well. An embroidery needle, for example, will have a wider eye, so that delicate embroidery thread is subject to less friction. A needle for metallic thread will have a longer eye to accommodate the somewhat stiff nature of this thread, so it neither breaks nor tangles.

Needles are sized according to the needle diameter of the shaft below the shank (the portion that inserts into your machine) and above the scarf (the groove area around the eye). The needle size is indicated by two numbers, for example, 80/12. The larger number, 80, is the metric size. The smaller number, 12, is the traditional U.S. sizing system. In both systems, the higher the needle number, the thicker and stronger the needle will be.

Most household sewing machines use the same length sewing machine needle (H), however, some household sergers require EL (extra long) needles.

Needle manufactures also color code their different needle types on the shank. However, the color coding is not standardized across all manufacturers.

Sharp needles cut through the fibers of woven fabrics cleanly and easily. Sharps come in different thicknesses, for example, fine Microtex needles and sturdy leather needles. In addition, needles for specialty threads, such as embroidery or metallic thread, are also types of sharps that have larger eyes to reduce friction on delicate embroidery thread.

Ballpoint needles are used for knit fabrics, lingerie, and nets. They have rounded tips, which slip past the looped yarns instead of piercing them, preventing raveling along the stitching line.

A stretch needle is a ballpoint needle with a slightly modified eye (the needle's hole) and scarf (a groove around the eye). It is a good choice for very fine knits and new generation activewear fabrics. Ballpoints do not form as straight a stitch as sharps will and may cause woven fabrics to pucker, as yarns are pushed down instead of being sliced through.

Universal needles have characteristics of both sharps and ballpoint needles and can be used with many fabrics. It is a sharp needle with an ever so slightly rounded tip and is, therefore, suitable for both woven and knit fabrics. Universal needles are available in a quick-threading variation, which has a slip-in threading slot to the eye. Twin and triple needles (two or three needles connected to a single shank) are a type of universal needle that forms two or three rows of straight stitches on the top connected by a line of zigzag stitches below. Twin and triple needles are mostly used for topstitching and may also be used on knits and wovens.

Wedge needles have a flat, knifelike shape and are used to pierce leather and vinyl. A variation is a **wing/hemstitch needle**, which intentionally creates a larger hole in its wake for a decorative eyelet effect, for example, in heirloom sewing.

TIP

If your needle is dull or you are using a ballpoint needle on a woven fabric, puckers may form in your fabric as the yarns are pressed down instead of being immediately sliced by the needle.

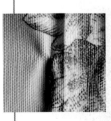

U.S. Lightest to strongest	Metric Lightest to strongest
8	60
9	65
10	70
11	75
12	80
14	90
16	100
18	110
19	120
20	125
21	130

In general, begin by testing your fabric and thread with a (A) universal needle.

If you do not like the results of the universal needle, switch to either a (B) ballpoint needle (for knits) or (C) sharp needle (for wovens).

If you do not like the results of a (K) regular ballpoint needle on your knit fabric, switch to a (L) stretch needle.

Use (M) twin needles for topstitching wovens and knits.

Select the sharp needle suitable for the weight of your fabric, which leaves the smallest hole in its wake. (D) Microtex (E) Jeans (F) Leather.

Use a (N) hemstitch wing to intentionally leave a large hole for specialty sewing effects.

Switch out the sharp or universal needle to a specialty sharp needle, for example, when using a (G) metallic thread, to (H) machine embroider, or for (I) quilting or (J) topstitching.

Feet, don't fail me now! The needle, presser foot, and feeder dogs—that's where the action is. Every sewing machine has accessories specific to it that allow you to perform a variety of special sewing tasks. There are universal accessories included with most every machine, such as the zipper foot, buttonhole attachment, and various hemming feet. Other accessories, such as a ruffler attachment, are designed to save time and effort for special types of sewing.

When adding a special accessory or foot to a machine, you must know if your machine has a high shank, low shank, or slanted shank. The shank is the distance from the bottom of the presser foot to the attachment screw. Other machine systems include the presser foot with the shank and the foot is exchanged with the shank.

The zigzag plate and the general-purpose foot come standard with virtually every sewing machine. In addition, a buttonhole foot or attachment, zipper foot, seam guide, various hemming feet, walking foot (Even Feed), or roller foot may also be included with your machine. A straight-stitch plate has a hole only wide enough for the needle to go up and down and not back and forth, as with a zigzag stitch. It is a good choice for very precise sewing of a straight stitch, for example, patchwork, edge stitching, and collar points. The machine manual explains how to attach the various accessories and achieve the best results with each. As you sew different kinds of projects and with different materials, you may want to start a collection of specialty purpose feet, such as an invisible zipper foot or a Teflon foot for "sticky" fabrics.

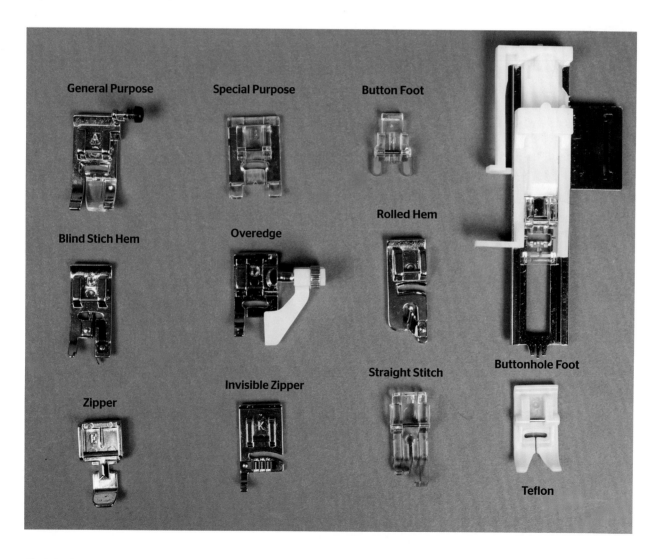

General Purpose

Special Purpose

Button Foot

Rolled Hem

Blind Stich Hem

Overedge

Straight Stitch

Buttonhole Foot

Zipper

Invisible Zipper

Teflon

Buttonhole feet allow you to stitch multiple consistent buttonholes. Some buttonhole presser feet are adjusted manually to fit your button, while others adjust the buttonhole length to fit a button you have placed in a carrier behind the foot. Older, nonelectronic straight-stitch sewing machines may have another type of buttonhole attachment, which uses metal templates of various sizes to make buttonholes.

Blindstitch hem foot positions the hem for blindstitch hemming on the machine. It has an integrated raised bit of metal, which allows for a bit of slack in the thread, allowing for enough ease for a clean and smooth turn.

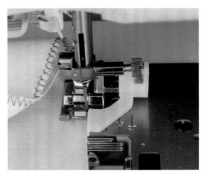

Overedge foot helps keep stitches at full width and prevents curling of flat edges when sewing overedge stitches. Stitches are formed over a hook on the inside edge of the foot.

Zipper foot is used to insert zippers, stitch cording, or stitch any seam that has more bulk on one side than the other. Some machines allow the foot to adjust to either side of a stationary needle; other machines require the needle position to be changed.

Walking (even feed) foot feeds top and bottom layers together so seams start and end evenly. It provides an extra set of feed dogs to help the top layer(s) of material feed at the same rate as the bottom layer. Use the walking foot for vinyl, pile fabrics, bulky knits, or other fabrics that tend to stick, slip, or stretch. This foot is also useful for stitching plaids, stripes, and when fabric patterns need to match exactly.

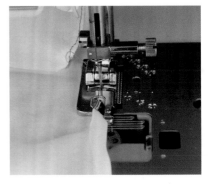

Rolled hem foot evenly turns just the very edge of the fabric over to stitch a neat rolled hem. Use this to sew rolled hems on napkins, ruffle edges, or on sheer fabrics.

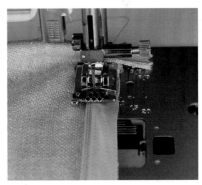

Invisible zipper foot makes it easy to attach invisible zippers very close to the coils.

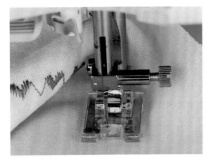

Special purpose foot has a grooved bottom that allows for thread build-up in decorative stitches. The seam guide attaches to your machine and helps keep seam allowances and hems even.

Button foot holds flat buttons in position for attaching with machine zigzag stitch. This foot saves time when sewing on several buttons.

The Serger

A serger is a special-purpose sewing machine that supplements a conventional machine. It is similar to the speed-sewing equipment used by garment manufacturers. A serger cuts sewing time considerably because it trims and overcasts raw fabric edges as it sews the seam, making self-finished narrow seams, rolled hems, and overcast edge finishes easy and fast.

Sergers form 1,500 or more stitches a minute—about twice the rate of conventional sewing machines. All fabrics feed evenly so that even traditionally difficult-to-handle fabrics, such as slippery silks and thin sheers, will not take any extra sewing time.

A serger eliminates time-consuming steps and encourages efficient sewing habits such as flat construction, pinless sewing, and continuous seaming. It also dispenses with raising the presser foot to pivot, backstitching, and filling bobbins.

Functions and Parts

A serger is the machine of choice for sewing knit fabrics, as it creates a finished and reinforced stretch stitch. The serger is also ideal for applying elastic, ribbing, and some trims. A serger also helps when sewing lace, eyelet, and other open weave materials. Adjusting the tension on different threads will allow you to gather fabric easily or create lettuce edges on knits. Use a conventional sewing machine whenever straight or zigzag stitching is necessary, such as for topstitching, inserting a zipper, or making buttonholes.

Many different models of sergers are available, each offering different types of stitches. Most household sergers sew with four or five threads, however there are models with just two or three. The name of each machine tells which stitches it offers; for example, a 4/3-thread serger can sew either a 4-thread mock safety stitch or a 3-thread overlock stitch. Each stitch type is unique and has its own purpose.

Principal Parts of the Serger

A Thread guides
B Telescoping thread guide holder
C Spool pins
D Needle, thread tension dials (1 or 2, depending on model)
E Looper thread tension dials (2 or 3, depending on model)
F Needle set screws
G Looper cover
H Stitch length regulator
I Handwheel
J Differential feed control (not on all models)
K Knives
L Presser foot
M Needle plate
N Loopers (2 or 3, depending on model)
O Stitch finger engage/disengage lever
P Stitch width regulator
Q Threading diagrams

Location of some machine parts will vary.

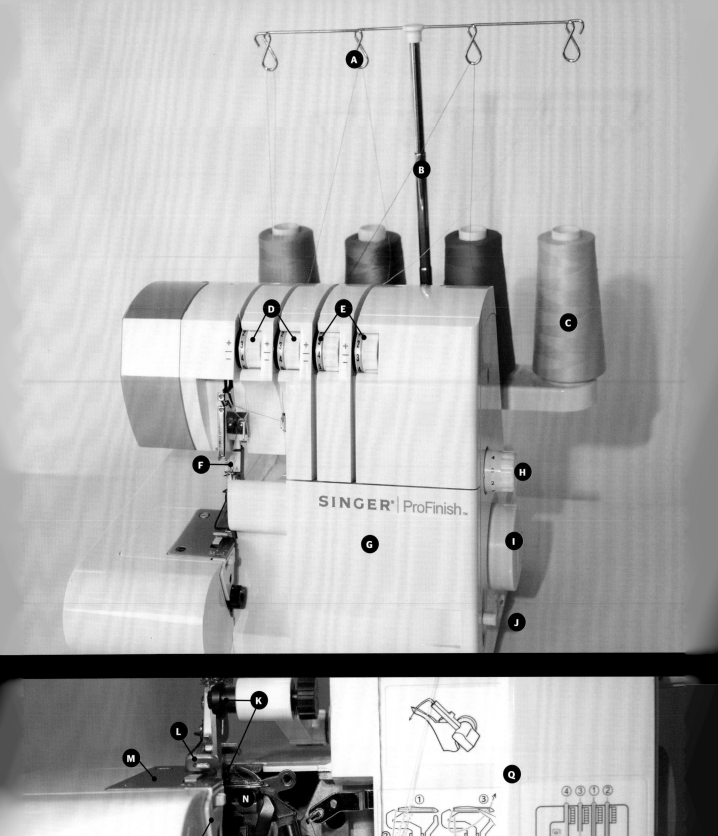
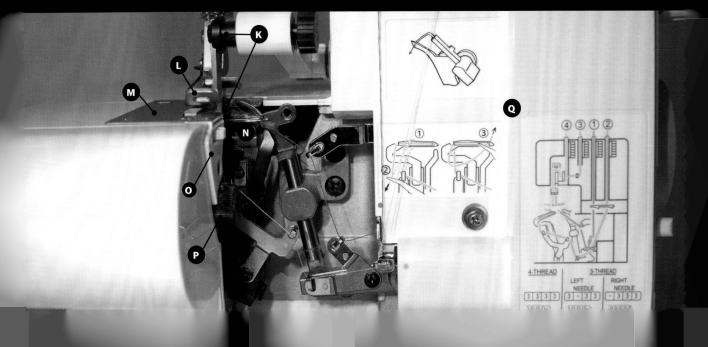

The Stitches and Their Uses

Types of Stitches

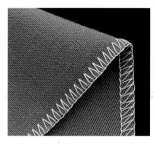

2-Thread Overedge Stitch
- lightweight seam finishes
- used for wovens

3-Thread Overlock Stitch
- stretch seams
- durable seams or seam finishes
- used for knits and wovens

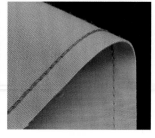

2-Thread Chainstitch
- stable basting stitch
- decorative topstitching
- used primarily for wovens

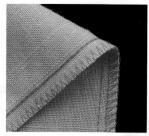

4-Thread Safety Stitch
- stable seams with light-weight seam finishes
- used primarily for wovens

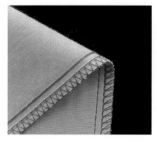

5-Thread Safety Stitch
- stable seams with durable finishes
- used primarily for wovens

3-Thread Mock Safety Stitch
- durable ultrastretch seams
- used for superstretch knits like spandex

4-Thread Mock Safety Stitch
- durable stretch seams
- used for knits and wovens

Flatlock Stitch
- flat, nonbulky stretch seams
- decorative stitching
- used primarily for knits

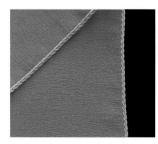

Rolled Hem Stitch
- narrow hems and seams
- decorative stitching
- used for knits and wovens

Cover Stitch
- stretch hems and seams
- decorative stitching, trims
- used primarily for knits

Serger Thread

A serger uses more thread than a conventional sewing machine, so thread companies offer thread in cones, king tubes, and compact tubes. Tubes and cones have at least 1,000 yd (920 m) of thread, and cones can have as many as 6,000 yd (5520 m).

All-purpose thread may also be used on the serger; it is available on parallel-wound or cross-wound spools. Parallel-wound spools require the use of a spool cap for even feeding. There is a wider color selection in all-purpose thread; use it for medium-weight or heavyweight fabrics when color matching is critical.

Serger threads generally have a weight of 120, which is lighter than all-purpose sewing threads. A lightweight thread is recommended for serger use, because there is more thread in a serged seam and a lighter-weight thread will better reduce a seam's bulk than an all-purpose thread. For rolled hems and lettuce edges, you may choose to include a wooly nylon or acrylic thread in the upper looper: The fibers of these specialty threads puff out a bit and fill the tiny gaps between stitches to create a more solid-looking stitching line.

Care and Maintenance

Serger machines sew at a higher rate of speed than conventional sewing machines and create more stress on the threads. Therefore, threads need to be strong and durable. Test thread for strength; poor-quality thread may break easily in some spots. Also, sergers produce more friction points on the thread and a lower-quality thread will tend to develop more lint. Hold a strand of your polyester thread against a contrasting background: If the thread looks rather fibrous and uneven, opt for a better thread. Bargain threads sometimes cause more problems than the savings are worth. Store all your thread away from direct sunlight and moisture.

Because a serger trims fabric as it sews, it creates much more lint than a conventional machine and needs to be cleaned frequently. Use a brush or special small-area attachments on your vacuum cleaner to remove lint from the looper and throat plate area. Canned air can also be used, however, be careful not to blow the lint deeper into the inner

Needles used on a serger may be an industrial type with short or long shaft. However, most household sergers use the same needle as your conventional sewing machine. Use the needle type specified for your machine. Conventional household sewing machine needles require frequent changing on your serger, as indiscernible bends and wear can affect the quality of the serger stitch. Use the finest needle possible to avoid damaging the fabric. Size 80/12 (80/11) works for most fabric weights.

Most sergers have an upper and a lower knife that work together like scissors to trim the fabric right before it is stitched. One knife is high-carbon steel and may last several years. The other knife is less durable and may require replacement much more frequently. When knives seem dull, first clean them with alcohol; then reposition and tighten the screw. Test by sewing slowly. If the problem persists, replace the less durable knife and test again. As a last resort, replace the other knife.

The tension controls on a serger are actually stitch selectors. Each thread has its own tension control. Changing one or more tension settings affects the character of the stitch, because it changes how the threads loop together. With tension adjustments, the serger can stitch a wide range of threads, fabrics, seams, hems, and decorative treatments.

A good way to become comfortable with serger tension adjustments is to thread each looper and needle with a contrasting thread color. Copy the color code used for the machine's threading diagram. Make several stitch samples, tightening and loosening the tensions in sequence. You will see the effect of each tension adjustment and learn how to use the tension controls to create a balanced stitch. Most of the stitch samples shown below and opposite were made on a 3-thread serger; stitch samples made on other models look similar and are adjusted in the same way.

Common Tension Adjustments

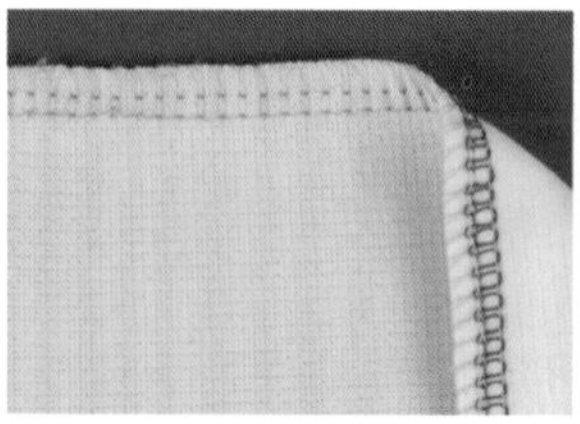

Upper looper too tight. Upper looper thread (red) pulls lower looper thread (yellow) over to the other side of the fabric. To fix, lower upper looper tension, so threads interlock right at raw edge.

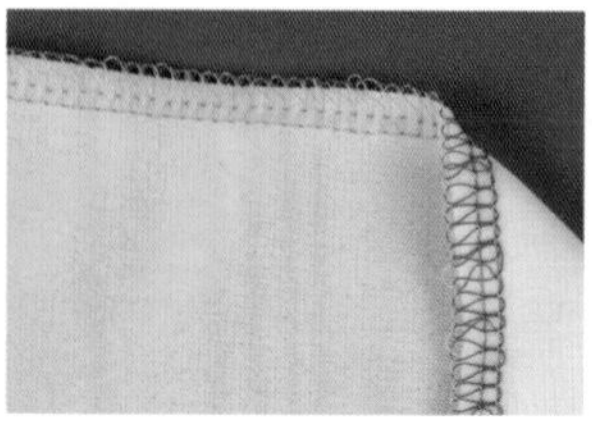

Upper looper too loose. Upper looper thread (red) interlocks with lower looper thread (yellow) either loosely over the fabric raw edge or over onto the underside. To fix, increase upper looper tension so threads interlock at raw edge.

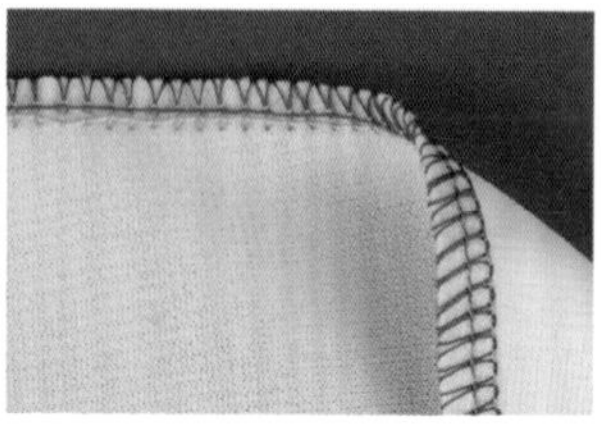

Lower looper too loose. Lower looper thread (yellow) rides loosely on top of fabric or slip over to front fabric side. To fix, increase lower looper tension until stitches lie flat and smooth on fabric and interlocks with upper looper thread right along raw edge.

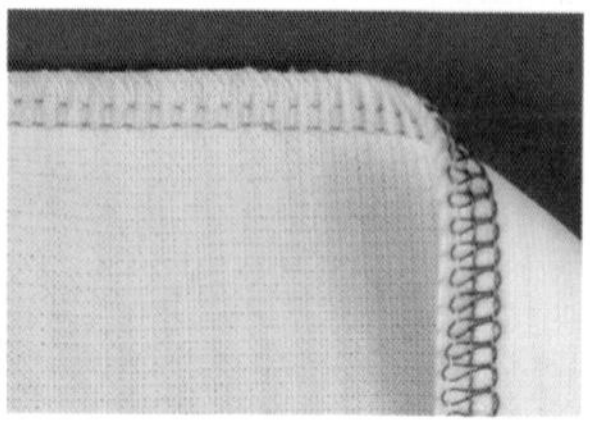

Lower looper too tight. Lower looper thread (yellow) pulls upper looper thread (red) over to underside of fabric. Stitches to interlock under fabric. To fix, decrease lower looper tension until threads interlock at right raw edge.

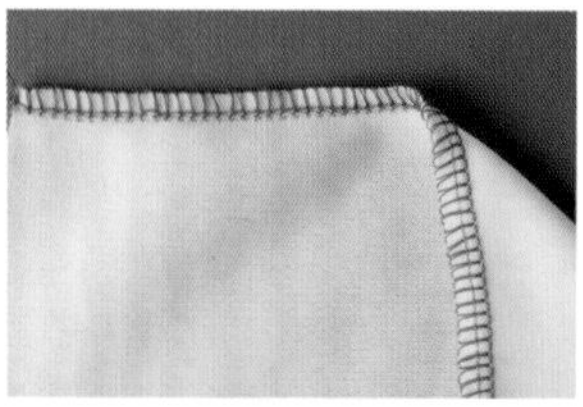

Upper and lower loopers too tight. Fabric bunches and puckers within stitches. Loosen upper and lower tensions until fabric relaxes.

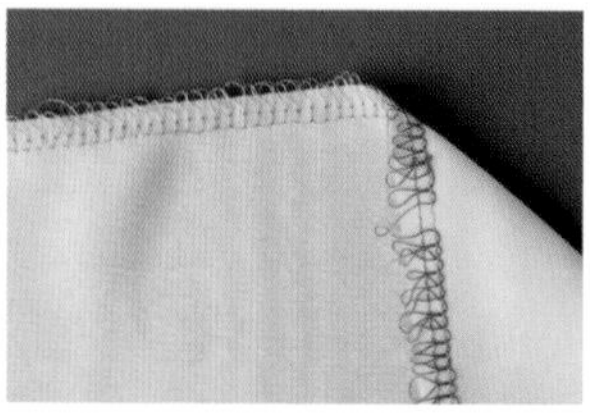

Upper and lower loopers too loose. Lower (yellow) and upper (orange) looper threads interlock beyond raw edge and form loose loops. Tighten both looper tensions so stitches hug raw edge.

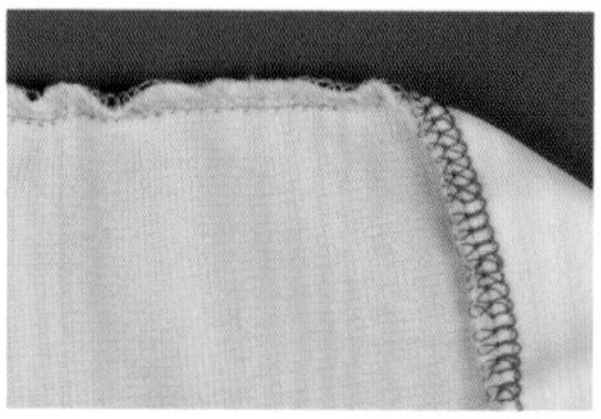

Needle too tight. Fabric puckers or draws up lengthwise when needle thread (green) is too tight **a.** Loosen needle tension until fabric relaxes. Test knits for thread breakage, loosening needle thread if necessary. On 4/3-thread machine **b.** adjust each needle thread (blue, green) individually.

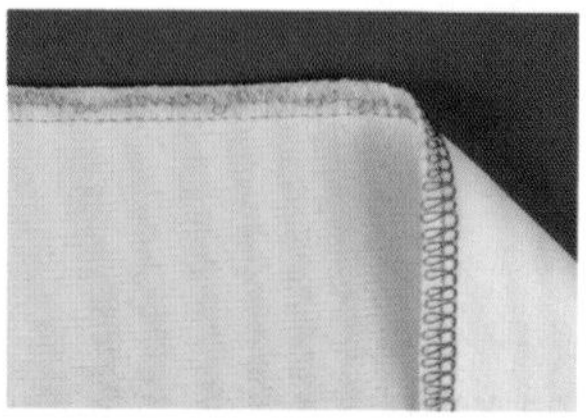

Needle too loose. Needle thread (green) forms loose loops underneath fabric **a.** Tighten needle tension for flat, smooth stitches. On 4/3-thread serger **b,** adjust each needle thread (blue, green) individually.

Correctly Balanced Tensions

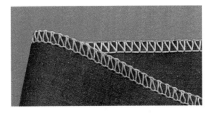

4-thread stitch is formed by two loopers and two needles. Upper looper (red) and lower looper (yellow) threads form neat, smooth interloping line right at the raw edge of the fabric. The upper looper thread (red) will be visible only on the fabric top side. The lower looper thread (yellow) will be visible only on the fabric's underneath side. Needle threads (blue and green) forms flat stitches without puckers.

3-thread stitch is formed by two loopers and one needles. Upper (red) and lower (yellow) looper threads intertwine right at the raw edge. The needle threads (green) forms flat stitches interlocking with the looper threads.

4/2-thread stitch makes double row of stitches with two loopers and two needles. Left needle thread (blue) interlocks with lower looper thread (yellow) to make neat, pucker-free chainstitch. Upper looper thread (red) and right needle thread (green) interlock over raw edge.

Differential Feed

Once seen only on higher-end models, now even most inexpensive sergers also include a differential feed. A serger has two sets of feed dogs to move the fabric along: One set pushes, the fabric, while the other set pulls it. When the differential is set to 0 or N for normal, the pushing feed dogs and the pulling feed dogs are timed the same and are moving at the same rate. For most sewing, the 0 or the normal setting is the one you will use. When the differential is adjusted, the front set of feed dogs either slow down or speed up, while the back set keeps moving at a constant pace. To work with certain fabrics, you may need to change the differential. You can also create certain effects, such as gathering or a lettuce edge, when you adjust the differential. When the differential is increased (usually to a maximum of 2) fabric is pushed faster than pulled. Conversely, when the differential is decreased (usually to 0.6) the fabric is pulled faster than pushed. When stitching stretch knits across the courses, for example, along a neckline or a shirt hem, the fabric may be stretching over the feed dogs and creating little waves in its wake. To fix this, increase the differential until the increased pushing counteracts the way the fabric is being stretched over the feed dogs. To create more waves, for example, to create a lettuce edge, decrease the differential, so that your fabric is pulled faster than pushed. A lettuce edge may be achieved only parallel to a knit fabric's courses (perpendicular to the ribs or fabric grain). Increase the differential to push fabric faster in front of the needle to achieve gathering.

To begin stitching, run the serger without fabric under the presser foot to create a chain of stitches about 2" (5 cm) long. A thread chain at the start and end of seams prevents stitches from raveling. Operating a serger without fabric does not damage the machine or break threads, because stitches are formed on the stitch fingers (prongs).

The throat plate on most sergers has one or two stitch fingers. Stitches are formed around the stitch finger so that, with the correct tension, the width of the stitch finger determines the width of the stitch. When the stitch finger is disengaged, the edge of the fabric will curl under; when the stitch length is decreased and one needle is removed, this will create a rolled hem edge. Some sergers may have a stitch finger on the presser foot, however, it is most commonly located next to the needle plate and connected to a switch to engage or disengage its use.

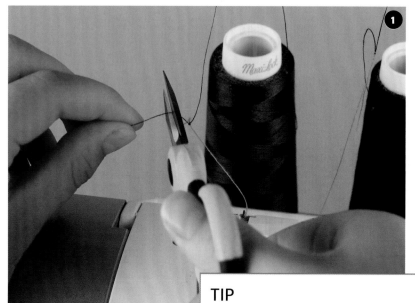

Thread Quick-change

1 **Cut each thread near cone** and remove cone. Tie new thread onto each thread in machine, using small overhand knot. Clip thread ends ½" (1.3 cm) from knot.

2 **Release tensions** or set tension controls on O. Cut needle thread in front of needle. Pull on tail chain to separate threads.

3 **Pull threads one at a time** through thread guides, upper looper, and lower looper. Pull needle thread until knot reaches needle eye. Cut off knot; thread needle with tweezers.

TIP

Each serger is threaded slightly differently, however, the basics apply to most four-thread serger machines. In general, remember to thread a machine in this sequence: "Up-Down-In-Out" or "Upper-Lower-Inner-Outer." Upper looper first, then Lower looper. Right-hand (inner) needle, then left-hand (outer) needle.

How to Clear the Stitch Fingers

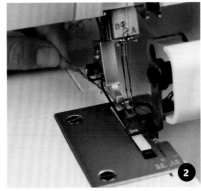

1. **Raise presser foot.** Turn flywheel to raise needle. Place left hand on thread chain behind presser foot. To slacken needle thread, pull it gently above last thread guide before needle. (Presser foot has been removed to show detail.)

2. **Pull straight back** on thread chain behind presser foot until threads separate and stitch fingers (prongs) of throat plate or presser foot are empty.

How to Start a Seam

Make thread chain. Stitch seam for one or two stitches. Raise presser foot; turn flywheel to lift needle. Clear stitch fingers. Run your fingers along thread chain to make it smooth.

Bring thread chain to the left, around and under presser foot. Place thread chain between needle and knife. Hold thread chain in position, and lower presser foot.

Stitch seam over thread chain for about 1" (2.5 cm); then swing thread chain to the right so it is trimmed off as you continue to stitch seam or trim by hand after seam is complete.

How to End a Seam

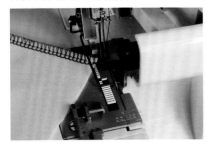

Stitch past end of seam by one stitch and stop. Raise presser foot and needle to clear stitch fingers. (Presser foot has been removed to show detail.)

Turn seam over and rotate it to align edge of seam with edge of knife. Lower presser foot. Turn flywheel to insert needle at end of seam and at left of stitch.

Stitch over previous stitches for about 1" (2.5 cm). Stitch off edge, leaving thread chain. With scissors or serger knife, trim thread chain close to edge of seam.

How to Stitch Inside Corners and Slits

Finish seams of inside corners by aligning raw edge of fabric with knife of serger. Stitch, stopping before corner.

Fold the fabric to the left to straighten edge. This may create a tuck, which will not be stitched.

With needles in up position, pivot fabric at corner. Slacken needle threads slightly. Lower needles using hand wheel at corner. Resume stitching, holding fabric in straight line.

How to Stitch Curved Edges

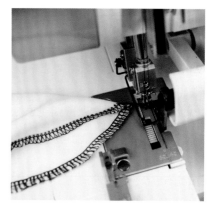

Begin cutting at an angle, until you reach the desired cutting or stitching line.

Guide fabric in front of presser foot so knives trim raw edge to curved shape. While stitching, watch knife, not needle.

Stop when stitches overlap previous stitches. Lift presser foot. Shift fabric so it is behind needle; stitch off edge so that no gradual loops form over edge of fabric. (Presser foot has been removed to show needle position.)

How to Stitch Outside Corners

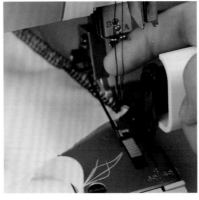

Trim off seam allowance past corner for about 2" (5 cm). If making napkins, place-mats, or similar projects, you can cut fabric to finished size and omit this step.

Sew one stitch past end of the corner, and stop. Raise presser foot and needle to clear stitch fingers and slacken needle thread slightly. (Presser foot has been removed to show needle position.)

Pivot fabric to align raw edge of trimmed seam allowance with knife. Insert needle at serged edge. Lower presser foot, and continue stitching.

How to Remove Stitches

For all serger stitches, remember that one or two threads are being punched through the fabric while other threads are being looped around those stitched threads. For best results, find the stitched thread and break those in 2–3 inch (4–6cm) increments. First, seam rip and remove the stitched threads (black), and then the looped threads (red and yellow) will easily pull away in whole sections.

Essential Equipment and Supplies

Having good tools, and the right tool for the right job, will make a good sewist better yet. Several tools can perform many tasks, while others have but one use. Nonetheless, you may find that many so-called "unitaskers" are essential for your sewing success.

Basic sewing is divided into five processes: measuring, cutting, marking, stitching by hand or machine, and pressing. For each of these tasks, there are tools to make the steps easier and the results better. Build an equipment inventory as you add to your sewing skills.

Hand Sewing Equipment

Needles and pins are available in a variety of sizes and styles for different uses. Look for rustproof needles and pins made of brass, nickel-plated steel, or stainless steel. Pins with colored ball heads rather than flat heads are easier to see in fabric and less likely to get lost. Pins with glass heads instead of plastic will not melt should they come in contact with a hot iron.

A **Sharps** are all-purpose, medium-length needles used for general sewing.

B **Milliner's needles** are long with round eyes, used for making long basting or gathering stitches.

C **Crewels** are generally used for embroidery. They are sharp and of medium length.

D **Betweens** are very short and round-eyed. They are used to help make fine stitches or for quilting.

E **Ballpoint needles** are used on knits. Instead of a sharp point, which may pierce the fabric, the rounded end pushes the knit loops apart.

F **Pin cushion** provides a safe place to store pins. Some pin cushions have an emery pack (an abrasive material) attached for cleaning pins and needles.

G **Silk pins** are used for light- to medium-weight fabrics. Size 17 is 1¹/₁₆" (2.6 cm) long; size 20 is 1¼" (3.2 cm). Both are also available with plain or glass or plastic heads. Extra fine 1¾" (4.5 cm) silk pins are easier to see in fabric because of their length.

H **Straight pins** in brass, steel, or stainless steel are used for general sewing. They are usually 1¹/₁₆" (2.6 cm) long. Straight pins with a glass head are easy to find and won't melt under the iron, should a pin be left in accidentally.

I **Quilting pins** are 1¾" (4.5 cm) long, used for heavy materials because of their length.

J **Pleating pins** are only 1" (2.5 cm) long, and are for pinning delicate fabrics in the seam allowance.

K **Ballpoint** pins are used for knits.

L **Needle threader** eases threading of hand or machine needles.

M **Beeswax** with holder strengthens thread and prevents tangling for hand sewing. It should always be used for hand sewing with cotton and silk thread. Real beeswax is available, but most commonly you find a paraffin product. For best results, after pulling your thread through the wax, press it with a warm iron between tissue paper to remove excess and seal it into the fibers of the thread.

N **Thimble** protects your middle finger while hand sewing. It is available in sizes 6 (small) to 12 (large) for individual, snug fit.

O **Wrist-pin cushion** keeps your pins always within easy reach and is especially handy in garment making while fitting.

The symbols on a pattern piece are guides for the accurate construction of the garment. Transferring these symbols from pattern to fabric is an important part construction and fitting. Different colors and types of fabrics require different marking tools and techniques, so keep a variety of marking tools handy. Make a habit of transferring all marks from the pattern sheet to the garment piece. Before sewing, read through the instructions carefully and pin small notes to your pieces to help remind you of steps or techniques with which you may be less familiar.

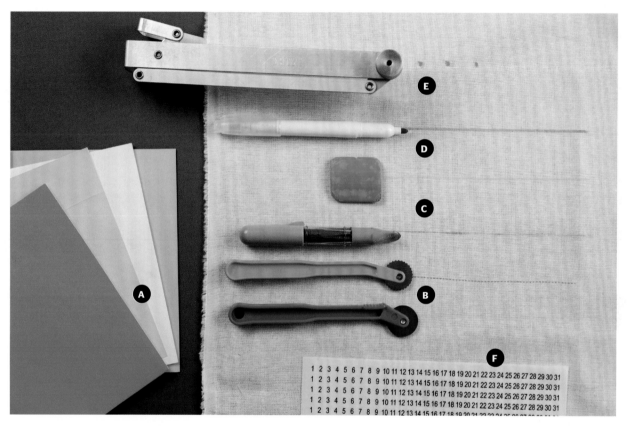

A Dressmaker's tracing paper has a colored coating that transfers the tracing wheel's line to the fabric. Choose a color close to that of the fabric, but make sure it can be seen easily. It is best to test a scrap of fabric first to make sure the color does not show through to the fabric right side.

B Tracing wheels come in two types: serrated or smooth edge. The serrated edge makes a dotted line marking, while the smooth edge makes a solid line. Tracing wheels are suitable for most fabrics but may pierce delicate ones.

C Tailor's chalk or chalk-wheel pen marks quickly and easily, directly on the fabric. Chalk rubs off quickly, so use it only when you plan to sew immediately.

D Liquid marking pens make quick work of marking tucks, darts, pleats, and pockets. One type disappears within 48 hours. The other washes out with water, so it should not be used on fabrics that show water marks. Pressing may set the marks permanently, so remove marking before pressing the area.

E Tailor tacker holds two pieces of chalk and marks the fabric from both sides at once.

F Adhesive number stickers are handy for labeling cut-out pieces of a complex pattern.

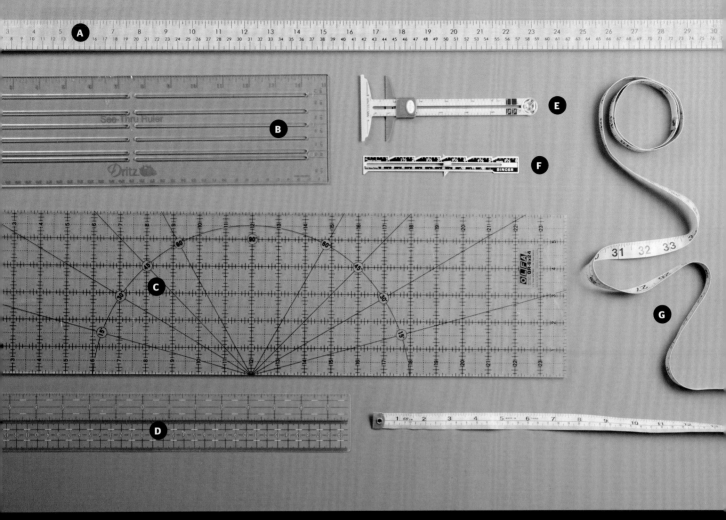

Measuring Tools

Measure twice, cut once! Accurate and careful body and pattern measurements will help ensure a beautiful fit. In addition, throughout the sewing process, you may need to measure seam allowances, symmetrical button placement, and so on. To ensure a good fit, measure often and use the best tool for the job.

A **Yardstick** is for general marking and for measuring fabric grain line when laying out the pattern. It should be made of smooth hardwood or metal.

B **See-through ruler** lets you see what you measure or mark. This ruler is used to check fabric grain line and to mark buttonholes, tucks, and pleats.

C **See-through** 24" × 6" (61 cm × 15 cm) ruler is often used with a rotary cutter to make long, straight cuts. The markings help to locate cross grains and the true bias.

D **Ruler** is for general marking. The most useful sizes are 12" or 18" (30 or 45 cm) long.

E **T-square** is used to locate cross grains, alter patterns, and square off straight edges. This T-square can also be used as a seam gauge.

F **Seam gauge** helps make quick, accurate measurements for hems, buttonholes, and pleats. It is a small, 6" (15 cm) metal or plastic ruler with a sliding marker.

G **Tape measure** has the flexibility required to take body measurements. Select a 60" (150 cm) long tape with metal tips, made of a material that will not stretch. It should be reversible, with numbers and markings printed on both sides, preferably with both Imperial and metric systems.

Buy quality cutting tools and keep them at their best with periodic professional sharpening. Scissors have both handles the same size; shears have one handle larger than the other. The best shears are joined with an adjustable screw (not a rivet) to ensure even pressure along the length of the blade. Sharp shears make clean cuts and well-defined notches. More important, they do not damage fabric. Dull shears slow the cutting process, can damage your fabric and tire your hand and wrist easily. Sewing shears should not be used for other household tasks such as cutting paper or twine. Occasionally, put a drop of oil on the screw assembly, wipe them clean with a soft dry cloth after use, and store them in a box or pouch.

A Bent-handled dressmaker's shears are best for pattern cutting because the angle of the lower blade lets fabric lie flat on the cutting surface. Blade lengths of 7" (A2) or 8" (A1) (18 or 20.5 cm) are most popular. Select a blade length that fits your hand well. Left-handed models are also available. If you sew a great deal, invest in a pair of all-steel, chrome-plated shears for heavy-duty cutting. The lighter models with stainless steel blades and plastic handles are fine for less-frequent sewing or lightweight fabrics.

B Sewing scissors have one pointed and one rounded tip for trimming and clipping seams and facings. The 6" (15 cm) blade is most practical.

C Embroidery scissors have 4" or 5" (10 or 12.5 cm) finely tapered blades. Both points are sharp for use in hand work and precision cutting.

D Seam ripper quickly rips seams, opens buttonholes, and removes stitches. Use carefully to avoid damaging the fabric.

E Thread clipper with spring-action blades is more convenient than shears for cutting notches and safer than a seam ripper for removing stitches in some instances.

F Pinking shears or scalloping shears cut a zigzag or scalloped edge instead of a straight one. These are used to finish seams and raw edges on many types of fabric, because they cut a ravel-resistant edge.

G Rotary cutter works like a pizza cutter and can be used by both left and right handers. A rotary cutter is used with a special "self-healing" plastic mat available in different sizes. The mat protects both the cutting surface and the blade. A special locking mechanism retracts the blade for safety. Rotary cutter blades are not sharpened, but replaced with new ones by easily removing an attaching screw.

H Heavy-duty craft scissors have small, precise, durable blades for cutting notches and for frequent clipping of thread ends close to the fabric.

Pressing at each stage of construction is the secret to a perfectly finished garment. Pressing goes hand-in-hand with sewing and should not be skipped. Pressing also helps manipulate the form of fabrics that respond to steam, for example, to tailor a perfectly shaped shoulder.

When possible, it helps to press several seams at once to get into the pressing habit. Stitch as much as possible at the machine, then press all the stitched areas at one time. Sometimes, however, pressing should be done between each sewing step. Your pattern directions usually tell when to press, but the general rule is: Press each stitched seam before crossing with another. Pressing does not mean ironing. In ironing, you glide the iron back and forth over the fabric. Pressing implies just that: hold the iron briefly in place and move the iron very little while it is in contact with the fabric. Use minimum pressure on the iron, press in the direction of the fabric grain, and lift the iron to move to another section.

Press on the wrong side or use a pressing cloth to prevent iron shine. Protect the iron's soleplate by removing or avoiding pins.

A Sleeve board looks like two small ironing boards attached one on top of the other. It is used when pressing seams in small or narrow areas such as sleeves, pant legs, or necklines. A sturdy cardboard tube, such as the kind used to store rolled fabrics, is a good substitute for a sleeve board.

B Steam/spray iron should have a wide temperature range to accommodate all fabrics. Invest in a dependable iron from a trusted maker. A good iron for sewing will heat quickly and shut off automatically when not in use. An iron that steams and sprays at any setting, not just the higher heat settings, is helpful for synthetic fabrics.

C Point presser/clapper is made of hardwood and used for pressing seams open in corners and points. The clapper flattens seams by holding steam and heat in the fabric. This tool is used in tailoring to achieve a flat finish and sharp edges on hard-surfaced fabrics. The top handle of the clapper may also be used as an ironing surface in hard-to-reach spaces, such as to press open the seam allowance in a collar. A clapper is especially helpful when pressing materials that cannot be ironed. To use a clapper on sensitive fabrics, burst puffs of steam from your iron over your seam or fold and then hold the clapper firmly over the area for a few seconds.

D Seam roll is a firmly packed cylindrical cushion for pressing seams. The bulk of the fabric falls to the sides and never touches the iron, preventing the seam from making an imprint on the right side of the fabric.

E Tailor's ham is used when pressing shaped areas such as curved seams, darts, collars, or sleeve caps. The ham is a firmly packed cushion with rounded curves, essential for shaping rounded garment parts, such as shoulders or hip seams. One side is cotton and the other side is covered with wool to retain more steam.

F The mitt is similar to the ham but is especially handy for small, hard-to-reach areas. It fits over your hand or onto a sleeve board. A pressing mitt is also helpful in ironing items that you cannot take to your ironing board, such as hung draperies. Just place the mitt on one hand and the hot iron in the other and gently iron the material between the two.

G Iron cleaner is a product that will remove fusible adhesive residue and other melted materials from the sole plate of your iron to keep it smooth and to prevent the transfer of residues to your fabric.

H Starch, sizing, or sizing alternative is a sprayed product that will give your finished garment a crisp feel and look. Sizing may also be used on slippery fabrics before sewing to make them easier to work with.

I Press cloth helps prevent iron shine and is always used when applying fusible interfacing. The transparent variety allows you to see if the fabric is smooth and the interfacing properly aligned.

Many kinds of special equipment and products are designed to save time and give better results in layout, construction, and pressing. As you find yourself trying different kinds of projects and using different materials, you will see the value in having a few specialized tools and products on hand. As you sew more, add new tools based on your needs. Even a one-time convenience tool can become your go-to helpmate, should you find yourself performing that task again and again.

Before using a new product or tool, read the instructions carefully and store the instructions with the items. Test any products that will adhere to your fabric on a scrap first. Here is an overview of just a handful of specialized sewing tools and products.

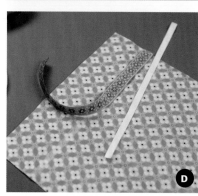

A **Table-top ironing board** is portable and saves space. It is easy to set up near your sewing machine. This ironing board keeps large pieces of fabric on the table so they do not stretch out or drag on the floor. It also helps cultivate the habit of detail pressing while you sew.

B **Liquid ravel preventer** is a colorless plastic liquid that prevents fraying by stiffening fabric slightly. It is helpful when you have clipped too far into a seam allowance or want to reinforce a pocket or buttonhole. It darkens light colors slightly, so apply cautiously.

C **Needle gripper** locks tight to hold the needle, allowing needle to be pulled through heavy fabric.

D **Basting tape** is double-faced adhesive tape that eliminates pinning and thread basting. Use it on leather and vinyl as well as on fabric. The tape is especially helpful for matching stripes and plaids, applying zippers, and positioning pockets and trims. Do not machine stitch through the tape, because the adhesive residue may stick to the needle shaft.

E **Glue substitutes** for pinning or basting by holding fabric, leather, vinyl, felt, trims, patch pockets, and zippers in place for permanent stitching. Use it for craft work as well as general sewing. Glue stick is water soluble, so it provides only a temporary bond. Liquid glue can be dotted in seam allowances to hold layers of fabric together.

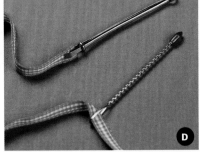

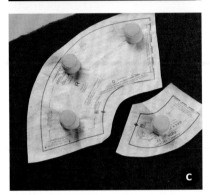

G **Point turner** pokes out the tailored points in collars, lapels, and pockets without risking a tear. Made of wood or plastic, its point fits neatly into corners. Use the point to remove basting thread and the rounded end to hold seamlines open for pressing. The rounded end can also be used as a finger presser to press, for example, seam allowances after stitching.

H **Folding cutting board** protects a table's finish from pin or shears scratches. It also prevents fabric from slipping while cutting, and holds fabric more securely. Stick pins into it for faster pinning, square off fabric against marked lines, and use grid lines as an instant measure. The folding feature makes storage easy.

A **Turning tools** are needed to turn casings or cording right side out. This plastic tube and stick system is one of a few different ways to turn a tub of fabric right side out, A loop turner is specially designed with a latch hook device at one end to grasp bias tubing or cording and turn it to the right side. Because the wire is so fine, it can be used for very narrow tubing and button loops.

B **Buttonhole cutter** makes precision cuts down the center of buttonholes. It often comes with a wooden block to place under the fabric. Otherwise, use a small cutting board to protect your work surface from the thin blade of the cutter. A buttonhole cutter is more accurate than scissors or a seam ripper and less likely to cut the buttonhole stitches.

C **Weights** hold a pattern in place, cut out time pinning and unpinning the pattern, and protect fabrics that would be permanently marked by pins. Smooth stones will also work.

D **Bodkin threads ribbon, elastic, or cord** through a casing without twisting. Some bodkins have an eye through which ribbon or elastic is threaded; others have a tweezer with a ring that slides to tighten the prongs of the pincers together to securing hold the ribbon or elastic.

E **Paper-backed fusible web** is sold on rolls, in various narrow widths. It is a timesaving product used for adhering two pieces of fabric together. Some fusible web tape is placed directly between two layers of fabric. The other kind has a protective paper backing, which is removed from one side after the other side has been heat fused to the fabric.

F **A magnetic pin catcher** keeps all-steel pins in their place. However, do not place a large magnet on or very near your computerized sewing machine, as the magnet may affect the machine's hard drive. A magnetic pin catcher is especially handy for picking up dropped pins off the floor.

Trims and Tapes

Choose trims and tapes that are compatible with your fabric and thread. Most trims and tapes can be machine stitched, but some must be applied by hand. Preshrink trims for washable garments at the same temperature as the garment fabric to prevent uneven shrinkage and puckering once stitched together.

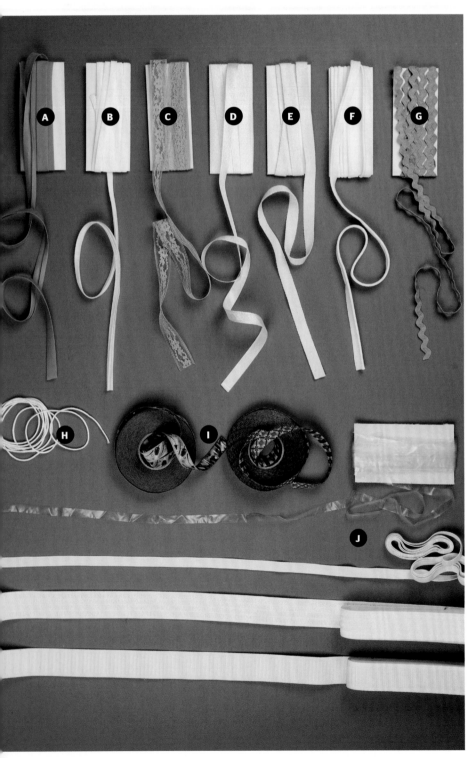

A **Single-fold bias tape,** available in ¼", ½", and ⅞" (6 mm, 1.3 cm, and 2.2 cm) widths, comes in a wide range of solid colors.

B **Double-fold bias tape** binds a raw edge. It comes in ¼" (6 mm) and ½" (1.3 cm) folded widths.

C **Lace seam binding** is a decorative, flexible lace hem finish.

D **Seam tape** is 100% polyester, ½" (1.3 cm) wide, used to stay seams and finish hems.

E **Twill tape** is used to stay seams or roll lines. It can also be used for drawstrings or ties.

F **Corded piping** is an accent trim inserted in seams to define and decorate edges.

G **Rickrack** comes in ¼", ½", and ⅝" (6 mm, 1.3 cm, and 1.5 cm) widths for accent trim and edging.

H **Braid** is rounded (soutache) or flat (middy). Use it for accent, scroll motifs, drawstrings, ties, or button loops.

I **Decorative ribbon** comes in many widths, designs, colors, and materials. Choose a ribbon with the same care guidelines as your main fabric.

J **Elastic** is inserted in casings to shape waistbands, wrists, and necklines. Knitted and woven elastics are softer than braided elastics, curl less, and can be stitched directly onto the fabric. Non roll waistband elastic has lateral ribs to keep it from twisting or rolling. Clear elastic, made of 100% polyurethane, is great for sheer fabrics, lingerie, and swimwear.

Buttons and Closures

While thoroughly functional, closures can also be fun. Closures can either be essentially invisible or a front-and-center, stand-out design element. Explore how different closure options can lend your item a new and different design aesthetic.

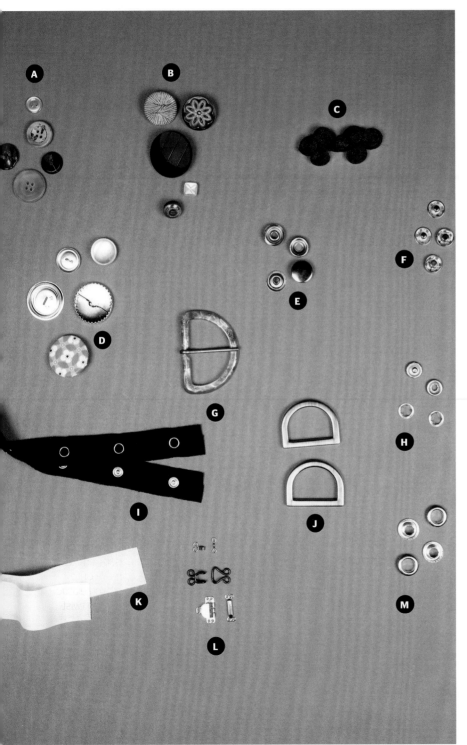

A **Sew-through buttons** are commonly used, all-purpose buttons.

B **Shank buttons** have a neck or shank underneath the button.

C **Frogs** are loop-and-ball fasteners that lend a dressy look.

D **Self-covered buttons** can be covered with the same fabric as the garment for an exact color match.

E **Gripper** snaps are hammered or squeezed onto the garment outside..

F **Sew-on snaps** are inside closures for no-stress areas such as collars.

G **Belt buckles** add a special decorative touch to those designs that can include a belt.

H **Plier-on snaps** are outside closures for low stress areas.

I **Snap tape** is often used on infant and casual clothes and home décor..

J **D rings** can be used with straps of fabric on belts and bib-front aprons and overalls.

K **Hook-and-loop fastener** (trade name Velcro) is available by the yard and as small circles. Simple and secure, hook and loop is used for closures on lapped areas of outdoor wear, handbags, and home décor.

L **Hooks and eyes** are inside closures available in various sizes for different fabric weights. Flat heavy-duty hooks and eyes are used to close waistbands on skirts or pants.

M **Grommets** are used together with cording on activewear and for laced closures.

Zippers

Zippers have metal or plastic teeth, or a synthetic coil attached to a woven tape. Both types come in all-purpose weights. Coil zippers are lightweight, flexible, heat resistant, and rustproof. Metal zippers come in heavier weights for heavy fabrics and sportswear. Although zippers are usually designed to blend into the garment, some are made to be shown off.

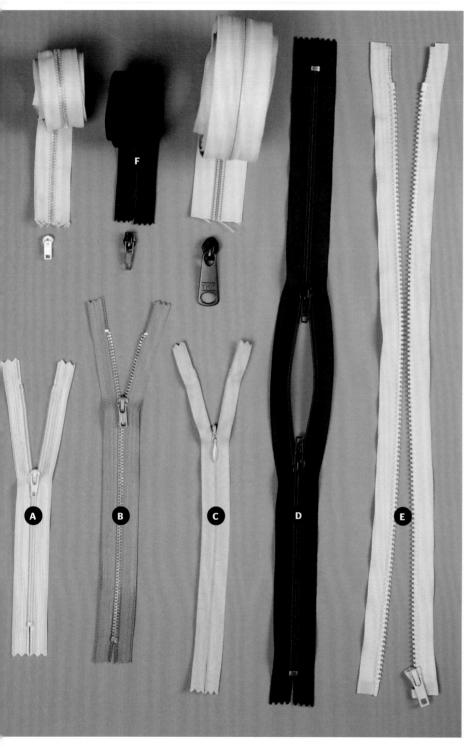

A **Polyester** all-purpose zippers are suitable for fabrics of all weights in skirts, pants, dresses, and home decorating items.

B **Metal all-purpose zippers** are strong, durable zippers for sportswear as well as pants, skirts, dresses, and home-decorating items.

C **Invisible zippers** are inserted using a special foot designed by the zipper manufacturer. Once installed, the zipper is hidden in the seam and only the slim tab shows.

D **Purse zippers** have two pulls and stops at both ends to allow for flexible opening and closing of handbags, backpacks, and travel bags.

E **Separating zippers,** available in medium and heavy metal weights, are used in jackets, sportswear, and home decorating. Reversible separating zippers have pull tabs that flip to the front and back of the zipper. Plastic molded separating zippers are lightweight yet strong and durable. Their decorative appearance makes them a natural for skiwear and outdoor wear. Two-way zippers have two sliders, so they can be opened from the top and bottom. Coil separating zippers are designed for sweaters and lightweight jackets.

F **Endless zippers** come in metal, nylon coil, and molded plastic. Endless zipper tape can be cut to any length. Pulls and stops are added, once the zipper is cut to the correct length. Endless zippers are useful for long zipper applications, such as seat cushions and sleeping bags. They can be configured to be encased, separating, or purse zippers.

The Pattern

Shopping for a sewing pattern in a catalog or online is more creative than shopping ready to wear. In a pattern catalog or online listing, you aren't limited to the fabric, color, skirt length, or buttons pictured. You can choose designs from all over the world or from any fashion era. You can choose the combination that flatters you and expresses your own personal style, fitted to your individual body.

Pattern selection has never been better. Designer styles are available in the same season that they appear in ready to wear. There are easy patterns for the sewist with limited time and advanced designs for the couture enthusiast. You will find patterns for accessories, home decoration, evening wear, men's and boys' fashions, and almost every kind of women's or children's garment. In addition, the advent of the internet has allowed a cottage industry of independent sewing pattern designers to thrive, providing access to sewing patterns from around the world, often available for immediate download.

A pattern catalog from the larger pattern publishers is divided into categories by type or fashion look. The newest fashions usually appear in the first few pages of each category. Information is given on recommended fabrics and yardage requirements. An index at the back of the catalog lists patterns in numerical order along with their page numbers. The back of the catalog also includes a complete size chart for every figure type: male, female, children, and infants. Online retailers also often include design examples, reviews submitted by other sewists and even step-by-step tutorials.

Choose a pattern with a level of sewing difficulty that matches your sewing experience. If your time or patience is limited, stay with simpler styles. If you do have the time, however, don't be afraid to stray from your comfort zone. There are no mistakes—only learning opportunities.

The number of pattern pieces listed on the back of the pattern is a clue to the complexity of the pattern. The fewer the pieces, the easier the pattern. Details like shirt cuffs, collar bands, pleats, and tucks also make a pattern more difficult to sew.

Easy-to-sew patterns feature few of these details. On the other hand, designs featuring draping tend to have fewer pieces and seams, but may require a higher degree of skill.

Pattern companies follow a uniform sizing based on standard body measurements. This is not exactly the same as ready-to-wear sizing. Furthermore, the sizing may differ from pattern manufacturer to pattern manufacturer. Also, sizing on vintage sewing patterns is much, much smaller than modern clothing ascribed those sizes.

To select the right pattern size, first take your standard body measurements. Wear your usual undergarments and use a tape measure. If you are sewing formal wear, which will be worn with specialty undergarments, such as bra inserts, be sure to measure with those undergarments. For accuracy, have another person measure you. Record your measurements and compare them with the size chart provided in the pattern catalog or online pattern description. For a woman with a larger bustline or hips, select the larger pattern sized to best fit that area.

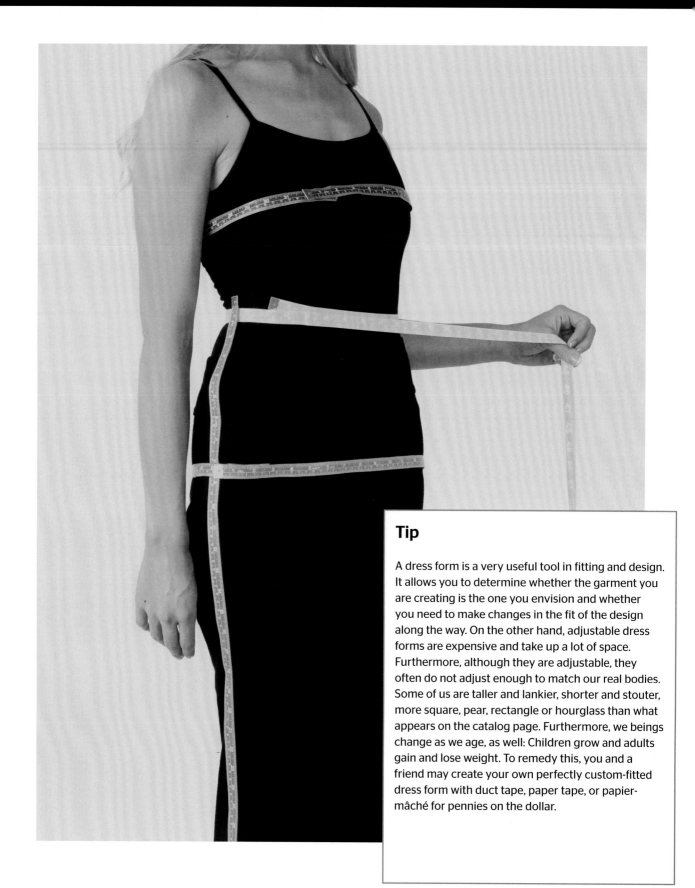

Tip

A dress form is a very useful tool in fitting and design. It allows you to determine whether the garment you are creating is the one you envision and whether you need to make changes in the fit of the design along the way. On the other hand, adjustable dress forms are expensive and take up a lot of space. Furthermore, although they are adjustable, they often do not adjust enough to match our real bodies. Some of us are taller and lankier, shorter and stouter, more square, pear, rectangle or hourglass than what appears on the catalog page. Furthermore, we beings change as we age, as well: Children grow and adults gain and lose weight. To remedy this, you and a friend may create your own perfectly custom-fitted dress form with duct tape, paper tape, or papier-mâché for pennies on the dollar.

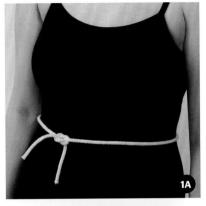

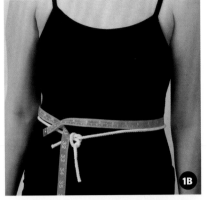

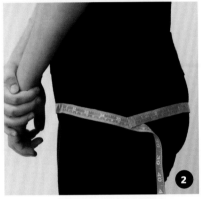

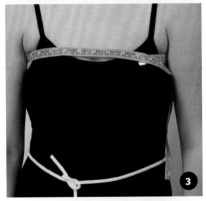

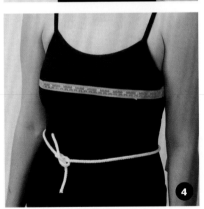

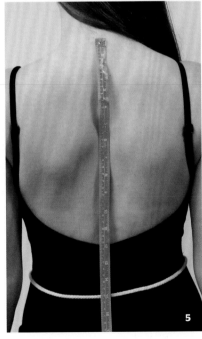

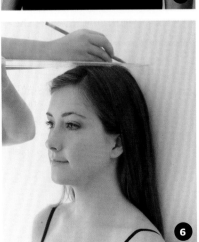

1 Waistline. Tie a string around your middle and allow it to roll to your natural waistline. (1A)

Using a string is especially helpful as your figure changes, for example, during or after pregnancy: Your waistline may be gone for a while, but the string will indicate a good place to consider as the waistline. Measure at this exact location with tape measure. (1B) Leave string in place as a reference for measuring hips and back waist length.

2 Hips. Measure around the fullest part. This is usually 7" to 9" (18 to 23 cm) below the natural waistline, depending on your height.

3 High bust. Place tape measure under arms, across widest part of back and above full bustline. Pattern size charts do not include a high-bust measurement, but this measurement should be compared with the full bust to choose the right size pattern.

4 Full bust. Place tape measure under arms, across widest part of the back and fullest part of bustline. Note: If there is a difference of 2" (5 cm) or more between high and full bust, select pattern size by high bust measurement.

5 Back waist length. Measure from middle of the most prominent bone at the base of the neck down to waistline string.

6 Height. Measure without shoes. Stand with your back against a wall. Place a ruler on top of your head and mark the wall. Measure from the mark to the floor.

The pattern envelope contains a wealth of information, from a description of the garment and number of pattern pieces to the amount of fabric and notions needed. It gives ideas for fabric and color selection, and indicates the degree of sewing difficulty with labels that indicate whether the style is a designer original, easy to sew, or suitable only for certain fabrics.

The Envelope Front

A **Style number** plus company name is essential information when communicating with others about the pattern.

B **Fashion photograph** or illustration shows the main pattern design. It suggests suitable fabric weights and designs such as solid, print or plaid. Most online retailers will welcome your email requesting fabrics. Many will send you swatches for a nominal fee.

C **Views** are alternate designs of the pattern. They may show optional trims, lengths, fabric combinations, or design details to appeal to a beginner or challenge a master dressmaker.

D **Designer** original patterns, indicated by the designer's name, often contain more difficult-to-sew details.

E **Size and figure type** ensure you select a package scaled to your figure. If the pattern is multisized, such as 8-10-12, you will find cutting lines for all three sizes on one pattern.

F **Logos or branding** may identify a pattern from a collection that has easy construction methods, is designed for timesaving sewing, has special fitting or size-related information, or shows how to handle fabrics like plaids, knits, or lace. Each pattern company has special categories and names for these designs.

G **Pattern company name** tells experienced sewers what sort of sizing, seam allowances, and style of direction to expect.

The Envelope Back

A **Body measurement** and size chart is a reference to determine if you need to make alterations. For a multi-sized pattern, compare your measurements with those in the chart to decide which cutting line to use.

B **Garment** descriptions include information on style, fit, and how the garment is constructed.

C **Notions,** such as thread, zipper, buttons, and seam binding, which are required for garment construction are listed. Purchase them at the same time as the fabric to ensure a good color match.

D **Fabric types** suitable for the garments are suggested. Use them as a general guide to fabric selection. The special advice, such as "unsuitable for stripes or obvious diagonals", alerts you to fabrics that are not appropriate.

E **Back views** show the details and style of the garments back.

F **Yardage** block tells you how much fabric to buy for the size and garment view you have selected. Yardage for lining, interfacing, and trims is also listed. To determine how much fabric you need, match the garment or view and the fabric width at the left with your size at the top of the chart. The number where the two columns meet is the number of yards to buy. Pay close attention to the fabric width indicated in the yardage. The most common fabric widths are given. If the width of your fabric is not given, be sure to check the conversion chart below or at the back of the pattern catalog, so that you purchase the correct amount of fabric. Some patterns list the extra yardage required for napped fabrics, plaids, and unidirectional prints.

G **Finished garment measurements** indicate finished length and width. You may need to make length adjustments. The width at lower edge is the measurement at the hemmed edge, indicating the fullness of the garment.

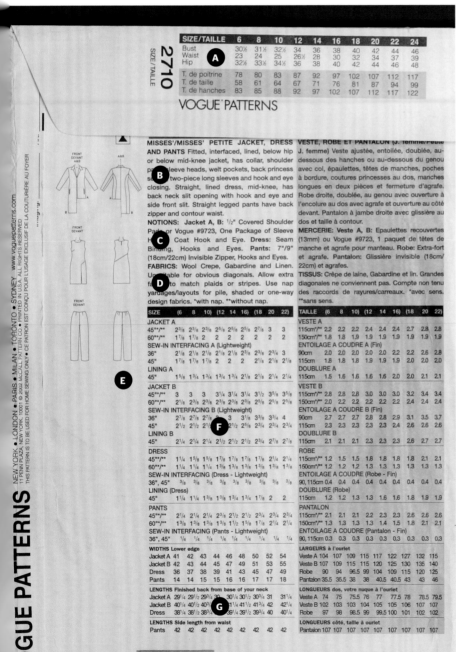

Purchasing Fabric

When purchasing fabric, remember fabric comes in several different widths and be certain to purchase the right amount. On wovens, the fabric width is the measurement across the fabric perpendicular to the selvages, without including the selvages. On knits, it is the width parallel to the courses, again, not including the selvedges. If the knit is a circular knit, the width will be double the flattened measurement of the tube.

Fabrics manufactured for the U.S. market are measured in inches, while fabrics intended for most other markets are measured in centimeters or, occasionally, in millimeters for very narrow fabrics, such as ribbing. Most material is manufactured in the widths 36"/90 cm, 45"/115 cm, 60"/150 cm, 72"/180 cm or 120"/300 cm. The width of a cut of fabric will vary depending on where you measure it. Some manufacturers allow for the variance and quote two measurements, for example, 58"/60". Most apparel fabrics come in a width of 60"/150 cm, which offers very good utilization for most common garment pattern pieces. Wider goods are usually used for home furnishings to allot for overscale designs and to reduce the number of visible seams, for example, along curtain panels or long cushions.

Fabric width yardage conversion for plain fabric

35"	YARD	1 ¾	2	2 ¼	2 ½	2 ⅜	3 ⅛	3 ⅜	3 ¾	4 ¼	4 ½	4 ¾	5
90 cm	METER	1.60	1.85	2.10	2.30	2.65	3.90	3.10	3.45	3.90	4.15	4.35	4.60
39"	YARD	1 ½	1 ¾	2	2¼	2 ½	2 ¾	3	3 ¼	3 ½	3 ¾	4	4 ¼
100 cm	METER	1.40	1.60	1.85	2.10	2.30	2.55	2.75	3.00	3.30	3.45	3.70	3.90
42"	YARD	1 ½	1 ¾	2	2 ¼	2 ½	2 ¾	2 ⅞	3 ⅛	3 ⅜	3 ⅝	3 ⅞	4 ⅛
107 cm	METER	1.40	1.60	1.85	2.10	2.30	2.55	2.65	2.90	3.10	3.35	3.55	3.80
45"	YARD	1 ⅜	1 ⅝	1 ¾	2 ⅛	2 ¼	2 ½	2 ¾	2 ⅞	3 ⅛	3 ⅜	3 ⅝	3 ⅞
115 cm	METER	1.30	1.50	1.60	1.95	2.10	2.30	2.55	2.65	2.90	3.10	3.35	3.55
50"	Yard	1 ¼	1 ½	1 ⅜	1 ¾	2	2 ¼	2 ⅜	2 ⅝	2 ¾	3	3 ¼	3 ⅜
127 cm	Meter	1.15	1.40	1.50	1.60	1.85	2.10	2.20	2.40	2.55	2.75	3.00	3.10
54"	YARD	1 ⅛	1 ⅜	1 ½	1 ¾	1 ⅞	2	2¼	2 ⅜	2 ⅝	2 ¾	2 ⅞	3 ⅛
140 cm	METER	1.05	1.30	1.50	1.60	1.75	1.85	2.10	2.20	2.40	2.55	2.65	2.90
60"	YARD	1	1 ¼	1 ⅜	1 ⅝	1 ¾	1 ⅞	2	2 ¼	2 ⅜	2 ⅝	2 ¾	2 ⅞
150 cm	METER	0.95	1.15	1.30	1.50	1.60	1.75	1.85	2.10	2.20	2.40	2.55	2.65
66"	YARD	⅞	1 ⅛	1 ¼	1 ½	1 ⅝	1 ¾	1 ⅞	2 ⅛	2 ¼	2 ½	2 ⅝	2 ¾
168 cm	METER	0.80	1.05	1.15	1.40	1.50	1.60	1.75	1.95	2.10	2.30	2.40	2.55

ADAPTED FROM COOPERATIVE EXTENTION SERVICE, RUTGERS UNIVERSITY, THE STATE UNIVERSITY OF NEW JERSEY

How to use: Find the fabric width along the left-hand side and the yardage along the rows indicated on your sewing pattern. Then follow up or down the column to the fabric width of your selected fabric. Let's say, your sewing pattern requires you to use 2 yards of 54" fabric: Find that place on the chart. The fabric you want to use measures 45" in width: Follow up the column to the 45" row. There you will see that you will need 2½ yards of your chosen fabric. This chart provides a rough estimate and it is always a good idea to purchase extra material.

Plaids and prints you want to match will require additional yardage. But how much? As a first step, you will need to look at the pattern pieces, for example on the pattern layout provided in the instructions. Then decide which and how many pieces should match up and how they should match up, for example, side by side.

Then, for all but the very largest repeats, you will need to measure the vertical and horizontal repeat and add them. Generally, you can calculate the measurement of one extra summed repeat per each major pattern piece. Let's take an example:

A garment has 4 major pattern pieces. The fabric has a vertical repeat of 4" and a horizontal repeat of 3". The summed repeat is 7" The amount of additional fabric required will be $4 \times 7" = 28"$

You may consult the table below as a general guideline. However, much depends on the garment you are sewing. It is always better to err on the side of caution and purchase an extra full repeat. Furthermore, at the cutting table, you will want to begin measuring your yardage with a full, intact repeat, which may require you to purchase a few unneeded inches at the leading edge of the bolt.

Additional fabric required to match patterns

FABRIC WIDTH (WITHOUT SELVEDGES)	3"-14" SUMMED REPEAT	15"-20" SUMMED REPEAT	21"-27" SUMMED REPEAT	8"-36" VERTICAL REPEAT	37"-43" VERTICAL REPEAT	44"-51" VERTICAL REPEAT
60"/150 CM	10%	15%	20%	25%	30%	35%
54"/140 CM	10%	15%	20%	25%	30%	35%
52"/132 CM	20%	25%	30%	35%	40%	45%
50"/127 CM	20%	25%	30%	35%	40%	45%
48"/122 CM	25%	30%	35%	40%	45%	50%
45"/115 CM	30%	35%	40%	45%	50%	55%
35"/90 CM	60%	65%	70%	75%	80%	85%

The amount of extra napped fabric required depends greatly on the design of the garment, the garment size, and the width of the material. It may be most economical to lay out the pattern on a single layer of fabric.

The printed pattern pieces and the direction sheet guide you, step by step, through the construction of the garment. Read through the direction sheet before cutting or sewing. Use it to plan and organize your sewing time and learn about the techniques you need to know as you progress.

Views of a single garment are labeled by number or letter. All pattern pieces are identified with a number and name, such as "skirt front."

Fashion drawings and views are featured prominently on the direction sheet, sketched as they appear on the front of the envelope or as detailed line drawings. Most patterns illustrate all the pattern pieces together, with a key to identify the pieces used for each garment or view.

General instructions are given up front. They usually contain tips on how to use the pattern, including information on pattern and fabric preparation; explanation of pattern markings; cutting, layout, and marking tips; and a short glossary of sewing terms.

Cutting layouts are shown for each garment view. They differ according to the width of the fabric, pattern size, and whether the fabric has nap. Layouts for interfacing and lining are also included. When the fabric is to be cut in a single thickness or on the crosswise grain, the pattern layout indicates this with a symbol, explained in the general instructions. A pattern piece, right side up, is illustrated without shading; wrong side up, it is shaded or scored. Choose the layout for the correct pattern size, fabric width, and view as a guideline. In some instances, it may be a more efficient and economical to unfold your fabric and refold the two selvedges toward the center to create two folds along which to cut. Also, pay attention to the printed design of the fabric: Border prints, for example, run along the selvedges and skirts, trousers, and blouses sewn from border print fabrics will need to be cut with the pattern piece grain line laid perpendicular to the fabric grain. Similarly, if you are us-

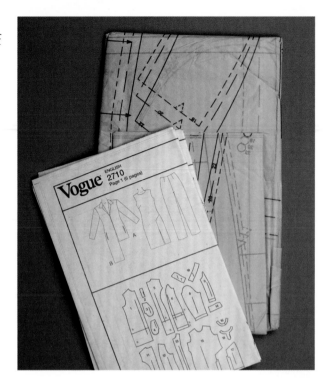

ing a fabric with a large print, arrange the pattern pieces to have the most pleasing placement of the design elements.

Sewing directions are a step-by-step guide to constructing the garment, arranged by views. Beside each instruction is a sketch illustrating the sewing technique. The right side of the fabric usually appears shaded; the wrong side, plain. Interfacing is indicated with dots or hatches. Together, the sketch and the directions give you an overview of what to do. Remember that these are only general directions. An alternative technique may be more effective for the fabric you are using.

Sewing patterns from Europe and Asia differ from U.S. sewing patterns in several ways. First off, European and Asian sewing patterns are not necessarily meant to be cut. The sewist must first trace the sewing pattern. This may be done either by placing a piece of tracing paper over the sewing pattern, tracing each piece and mark, and then using the traced pieces as you would a traditional North American sewing pattern on the fabric. Or, you may trace the pattern line and marks directly onto your fabric using a dressmaker's tracing wheel and paper. Furthermore, European and Asian sewing patterns very often do not include a seam allowance on the sewing pattern. The line indicated on the sewing pattern is the seamline, not the cutting line. Therefore, after tracing the pattern to your material or to another piece of paper, use a seam gauge to mark with dots the seam allowance all the way around your garment piece. Determine the seam allowance according to your fabric's characteristics and how you plan to sew. For example, a serged item will need a seam allowance of only 3/8" (6 mm). For very fitted items, you may want a full 1" (2.5 cm) seam allowance to allow for easier altering in the future.

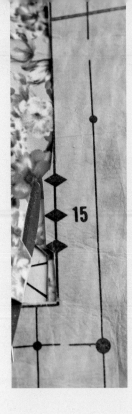

Pattern Markings

The pattern piece tissue may look like it is printed with secret symbols, but these markings are universal symbols used by all U.S. pattern companies. Different geographic regions will have different sewing pattern drafting traditions. Nonetheless, the sewing principals remain the same. Where one region, for example, may use cut notches to indicate where cut pieces should match up, in another region sewists may rely on chalk marks: The methods may be different, but the message is the same.

Pattern symbols are used from the time you start to lay out the pattern until you finish the hem or sew the last button in place, so be sure to transfer all marks from your pattern to your work in progress for best results. In addition, for sewing patterns with many pieces or unfamiliar shapes, often pinning a note to the cut fabric piece with any helpful additional information—for example, fabric direction, fabric right side, or piece name or location—can be helpful during construction.

Guide to Cutting and Marking Symbols

DESCRIPTION	SYMBOL	HOW TO USE	NORTH AMERICA	EUROPE, ASIA
GRAINLINE		Place pattern piece on fabric parallel to selvede	Heavy solid line with arrows on each end	Straight line extending down length of sewing pattern
FOLD BRACKET		Place pattern piece with arrows exactly on folded edge	Fold bracket: Long bracket with arrows on each end and/or "place on fold" instruction.	"Place on fold" or "Fold"
CUTTING LINE		Cut on this line. When more than one size is printed on the pattern, cut along the line for the size that fits best.	Heavy solid line on outer edge of pattern piece. May include a scissor symbol or "cut-off line" for different view/variation.	Often a cutting line will not be printed, only the seamline. If the pattern mentions that the cutting line is indicated, then the seamline will usually not be indicated. The cutting or seamline will be a heavy solid line, often printed in different colors to denote different sizes.
ADJUSTMENT LINE		To shorten, make a tuck in the pattern between the lines. To lengthen, cut between the lines and spread pattern apart.	Double line indicating where pattern can be lengthened or shortened before cutting.	Double or single line and "adjustment line" indicated.
NOTCHES		Cut out into margin of fabric or into seam allowance. Match like-numbered notches accurately.	Diamond shapes along the cutting line, used for matching seams, numbered in order in which seams are joined.	Diamond, triangle, stars, or other shapes, depending on the pattern maker.
FOLDLINE		Fold along this line when sewing facings, hems, tucks or pleats.	A solid line indicating where a garment is to be folded during construction.	A solid or dashed line indicating where a garment is to be folded during construction.

Construction symbols must be transferred to the fabric for accurate garment construction, but layout and cutting symbols, such as grainlines, do not need to be transferred.

To avoid confusion later, include additional information on certain garment pieces, such as the pattern piece number, "up" and "down", or fabric "W/S" ("wrong side") for fabrics where the reverse is difficult to recognize at first glance.

DESCRIPTION	SYMBOL	HOW TO USE	NORTH AMERICA	EUROPE, ASIA
SEAMLINE	– – – – –	Unless otherwise specified, stitch ⅝" (1.5 cm) from the cut edge.	Long, broken line, usually measuring ⅝" (1.5 cm) from the cut edge.	Most often, only either the seamline or the cutting line will be indicated. If only the seamline is indicated on the sewing pattern, an additional seam allowance will need to be cut. The seamline will be a heavy, unbroken line, often printed in different colors to indicste different sizes. The yardage on the pattern often indicates the seam allowance calculated, often 1 cm or 1.5 cm.
DART	•–<•–•	Mark, fold along center line and carefully match lines and dots. Stitch to a point.	Broken line and dots forming a V or a diamond shape, usually at bustline, waist, elbow or hip.	Broken, dotted or solid line, sometimes with dots forming a V or a diamond shape, usually at bustline, waist, elbow or hip.
DOTS (LARGE AND SMALL), SQUARES, OR TRIANGLES	□ ∘○ △	Areas of construction where precise matching, clipping, or stitching is essential.	Usually found along seamlines, corners, or darts.	Not usually indicated on European and Asian sewing patterns.
EASING LINE	•– –►	Easestitch larger piece; pull of stitching to match smaller piece.	Short, broken line with small dot on each end, marking area to be eased.	Short, broken line with small dot on each end or broken wavy line, marking area to be eased.
GATHERING LINES	∘ ∘	Make two rows of easestitching between marked dots; pull up stitching so dots match on smaller piece.	Two solid lines or broken lines, sometimes with dots on end, marking area to be gathered.	Two solid lines, a wavy line, or a broken wavy line, sometimes with dots on each end, marking area to be gathered.
HEMLINE	————	Turn hem up the specified amount, adjusting as necessary.	"Hemline" printed on pattern sheet.	"Hemline" printed on pattern sheet. Often indicated with a dashed line if the seamline and not the cutting line is printed.
ZIPPER PLACEMENT	⊏∷∷∷▭	Insert zipper so pull tab and bottom stop are positioned where indicated.	Parallel rows of triangles to be placed on seamline.	Parallel rows of triangles or other marking.
DETAIL POSITIONS	–⊖– – –	Mark and position detail where indicated.	Broken or solid lines indicating placement of pockets, tucks, or other details	Broken or solid lines indicating placement of pockets, tucks, or other details
BUTTON AND BUTTONHOLE PLACEMENT	✕ ⊢—–⊣	Mark and position where indicated.	Solid lines indicate length of buttonhole; "X" or illustration showing button size and placement.	Solid lines indicate length of buttonhole; "X" or illustration showing button size and placement.

Fabric Essentials

All fabrics are based on natural or man-made fibers or a combination of both. Natural fibers are those derived from plants or animals, such as cotton, wool, silk, linen, hemp, and bamboo. Man-made fibers are produced by chemical processes. They include polyester, nylon, acetate, Spandex, and many others.

Combining natural and man-made fibers produces blends, which give you the best qualities of different fibers. For example, the strength of nylon may be added to the warmth of wool, the easy care of polyester to the comfort of cotton.

There is an almost endless variety of blends available, and each one behaves differently. Check the fiber content on the bolt end for the kinds and percentages of fibers used. Care instructions are also listed. Examine the hand of the fabric—how it feels, how it drapes, whether it crushes easily or ravels, whether it stretches. Drape the fabric over your hand or arm to determine if it is as soft or crisp, heavy or light, as you need for a particular project. Vigorously rub a small corner of fabric between thumb and forefinger to see if the fabric pills with friction. Stretch knit fabrics to see how well they recover.

Fabrics are also classified by fabrication, meaning how they are made. All fabrics are woven, knit, or nonwoven. The most common woven is the plain weave construction. This is found in fabrics such as muslins, poplin, and taffeta. Denim and gabardine are diagonal weaves. Cotton sateen is a satin weave. Knits also have several classifications. Jersey is an example of a plain knit. Sweater knits can be made by the purl, patterned, or Raschel knit processes. Felt is an example of a nonwoven fabric. Laces are constructed using a variety and combination of techniques.

Selecting the right fabric for your sewing project takes a little practice. Refer to the back of the pattern envelope for suggestions, and learn to feel the hand of fabric. Quality fabric needn't be expensive. On the other hand, sewing with cheap fabric can be false economy. Remember, you are also investing your time. Better-quality fabrics will produce better results and more sewing joy. Choose quality fabric that will wear well and stay looking great after repeated washings.

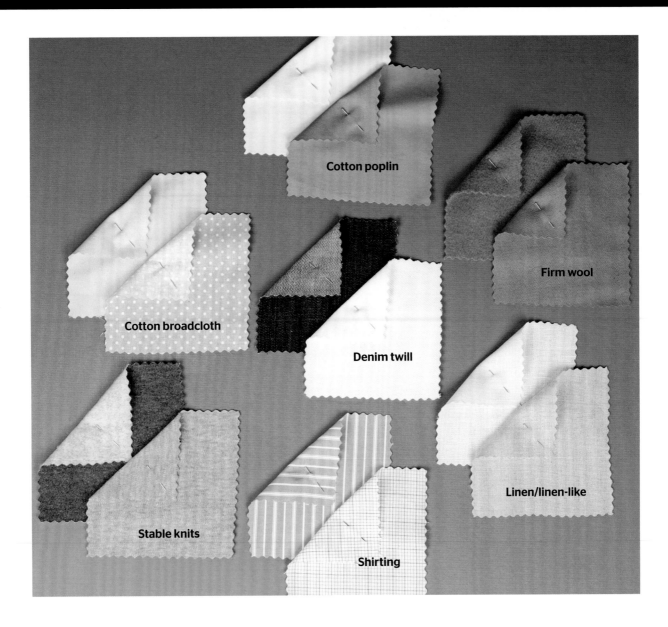

There are many fabrics that are easy and quick to sew. These fabrics are generally plain weave or firm knit, and of medium weight. Most of these fabrics do not require complicated seam finishes or special preparation and handling, since they ravel very little and maintain their grain easily.

Small overall prints, and narrow stripes and checks do not require matching at the seams. Prints, especially if they are dark, will hide most stitching imperfections.

Stable and moderate-stretch knits do not need seam finishing, and their elasticity makes fitting easy and wear easier still.

Stitching blends easily into natural-fiber fabrics, such as cottons and lightweight wools, and they respond well to heat and steam.

Handling Specific Fabrics

All fabrics, because of their design, fabrication, or content, require specific handling, construction techniques and tools. Any special handling beyond that required for the easy fabrics listed on the previous page often involves more patience than actual skill. Very often, only one extra step, such as a particular seam finish, is all that is needed for sewing success.

Guide to Fabrics and Sewing Techniques

WEIGHT	FABRIC	SPECIAL SEAMS	MACHINE NEEDLE	THREAD
SHEERS	Crisp: organdy, organza, voile Soft: batiste, lawn, chiffon, China silk, georgette, gauze	French, mock French, self-bound, double stitched	8 (60), 9 (65), or 11 (75)	Extra fine: mercerized cotton, cotton-covered polyester, long-fiber polyester, silk
LIGHTWEIGHT	Silk shirtings, broadcloth, calico, oxford cloth, chambray, lightweight linens, challis, seersucker, eyelet, charmeuse	French, mock French, self-bound, stitched and pinked or multi-zigzag, double stitched	8 (60), 9 (65), or 11 (75)	Extra fine: mercerized cotton, cotton-covered polyester, long-fiber polyester
LIGHT TO MEDIUM-WEIGHT KNITS	Tricot, interlocks, jerseys, light sweater knits, stretch terry, stretch velour	Double stitched, straight and zigzag, narrow zigzag, three-step zigzag	11 (75), 14 (90), ballpoint	All purpose: cotton/polyester, long-fiber polyester
MEDIUM WEIGHT	Wool flannel, linen types, crepe, gabardine, chino, poplin, chintz, corduroy, velvet, velveteen, velour, taffeta, double knits, fleece, sweatshirt knits, denim, quilted fabric	Welt, lapped, flat fell, mock flat fell, as well as plain seam with appropriate edge finish	11 (75), 14 (90), ballpoint for knits and fleece	All purpose: cotton/polyester, long-fiber polyester
MEDIUM- TO HEAVYWEIGHT	Heavy wool flannel, fleece, fake fur, canvas, heavy denim, heavy cotton duck, coating	Welt, lapped, flat fell, mock flat fell, stitched-and-pinked	16/100, 18/100	Heavy duty: cotton/polyester, long-fiber polyester, topstitching, buttonhole twist
NO GRAIN (NONWOVEN)	Leather, suede (natural and man made), buckskin, calfskin, reptile, plastic, felt	Welt, lapped, mock flat-fell, topstitched, plain seam	11/75, 14/90, 16/10	All purpose: cotton-wrapped, polyester, long-fiber polyester, Leather: avoid cotton-wrapped, polyester

A **Napped and pile** fabrics such as velvet, velveteen, velour, flannel, and corduroy require extra attention when laying out and cutting. Light reflects differently off the fibers when hung in one lengthwise direction or the other. These fabrics appear light and shiny when hung one way, and darker and denser when hung in the other. To prevent your garment from having a two toned look, you must follow the "with-nap" layouts on the pattern instruction sheet. Decide which way you want the nap to lie, and cut all pattern pieces with the top edges facing the same direction. If you want a richer, more intense color, cut with the nap running up. If you prefer a more subtle hue and smooth hand running down, cut your layout with the nap running down. Although satin and moiré taffeta are not napped fabrics, their surfaces reflect light differently in each lengthwise direction. Decide which effect you prefer, and use a one-way layout.

B **Sheer** fabrics look best with special seams and seam finishes. Unfinished seam allowances detract from the fragile, see-through look of voile, batiste, eyelet, or chiffon. French seams are a classic choice, but other seam finishes can also be used.

C **Twill weave** fabrics such as denim and gabardine have diagonal ridges. If these ridges are very noticeable, use a with nap layout for cutting, and avoid patterns that are not suitable for obvious diagonals. Denim ravels easily and requires enclosed or finished seams.

D **Plaids and stripes** require extra attention in layout and cutting (pages 106–109). To match plaids and large stripes at seams, you will need extra yardage. Buy ¼ to ½ yd (0.25 to 0.5 m) more than the pattern calls for, depending on the scale of the plaid.

E **One-way design** fabrics require a with nap cutting layout so the design does not go up one side of the garment and down the other. Border prints are cut on the crosswise rather than lengthwise grain of the fabric. You will likely need additional yardage when working with a border print.

F **Knits,** particularly unstable knits, must be handled gently during construction to keep them from stretching out of shape. Special stitches and seam finishes (page 62) are needed to maintain the right amount of stretch.

Not all sewing patterns are suitable for knit fabrics. Furthermore, not all knit fabrics are suitable for all knit sewing patterns. Be sure to check the amount of recommended stretch on your sewing pattern and compare that to the fabrics you are considering.

Classic Fabric Textures and Designs

Linen and linen-like fabrics are often available as a loose weave and are commonly used in home décor applications, such as curtains. Tobacco cloth is a lightweight fabric originally used to protect tobacco plants, but now comes in a variety of colors and can be used to make breezy blouses, dresses, or curtains. Raw silk (also known as silk noil) is ravel-prone because of the thick and thin crosswise yarns. Gauze fabrics, lightweight and crinkly, should be handled with sewing techniques for sheer fabrics. Wool suiting fabrics can also be loosely woven to feature the texture and variations of the fibers.

Pattern Selection for Loose Weaves

The less stable the fabric, the more loosely fitted the pattern should be. Simple styles are the best. Choose a pattern that has the potential for omitting linings, facings, and interfacings, as well as closures such as buttons and zippers. Many jacket, blouse, and skirt patterns, especially pullover or wrap styles, can be adapted this way. Test the stability of loosely woven fabrics by draping the fabric over your hand and letting a length hang freely. See how much it stretches and whether it drapes softly.

Fabric Preparation

Preshrink all loose weaves, using the care method planned for the finished garment. To prevent excessive raveling, zigzag crosswise cut ends or bind them with sheer bias tricot binding before washing. To wash, treat loose weaves like delicate fabrics. Air dry to prevent shrinkage from the heat of a dryer. Roll the fabric in towels to remove excess moisture. Spread on a flat surface and straighten the grain.

Layout, Cutting, and Marking

It is important to arrange the fabric straight and on grain for pattern layout. Any wavy grainlines will show clearly on the finished garment. When the fabric texture comes from nubby, irregular yarns, use a with-nap layout. Space pins closely to anchor the pattern pieces securely to the fabric. Keep cut pieces lying flat and avoid excessive handling, as some loosely woven fabrics will pull along the bias and loose their shape.

If you are working with a fabric that frays readily, cut out the pattern with a 1" (2.5 cm) seam allowance. Wider seam allowances are easier to handle for special seam and edge finishes, and they provide ample fabric for clean cuts on raw edges that must be trimmed. Transfer pattern markings with marking pen or thread basting.

Linen **Tobacco cloth** **Silk noil** **Gauze** **Wool suiting**

Special Seam Techniques

Plain seam with raw edges enclosed in sheer tricot bias binding is a quick, neat treatment. Use zigzag, 3-step zigzag, or long straight stitches, 10 to 12 per inch (2.5 cm).

Flat-fell seam, formed on right side of garment, makes a reversible seam which is ideal for roll-up sleeves or other areas showing both faces of seams.

Overlocked seam, sewn on 4-thread overlock machine or 3-thread machine with a row of straight stitches, covers raw edges with thread.

Special Hem Techniques

Topstitch to stabilize hem edges. This method is fast and attractive. Finish raw edge before hemming; use a zigzag stitch or a 2-thread or 3-thread overlock stitch.

Bind edge with sheer tricot bias binding. Hand hem with blind catchstitch or blind hem, worked loosely between garment and hem.

Fringe edge. Pull a thread at desired depth of fringe. Stitch on thread-pulled line (arrow); then. one by one, remove fabric yarns below stitching.

Corduroy, made from cotton or a blend of cotton and polyester fibers, comes in many forms. Corduroys are usually named according to the size and style of the ribs (wales).

Pattern Selection for Corduroys

Traditionally, corduroy is used for casual clothing and children's wear because it is durable and washable. The heavier the fabric and the bulkier the wales, the simpler the pattern style should be. Lightweight corduroys drape softly and can be used for more detailed styles, including those with gathered sections or ruffles. Midweight corduroys are often used for tailored jackets.

Fabric Preparation

Preshrink corduroy and velveteen to prepare them for pattern layout. Tumble dry to fluff up the pile. This is especially important for all-cotton types, even though prewashing fades strong colors and can make the fabric look worn sooner. Polyester/cotton types shrink less, are less likely to fade, and shed wrinkles better than all-cotton corduroy.

Stitching Tips

Pile fabrics such as corduroy, velvet, and velveteen tend to shift as you stitch. A walking (even feed) foot or roller foot helps to prevent this. It is helpful to pin seams at close intervals and to practice taut sewing, holding the fabric under tension in front of and behind the presser foot. Stitch in the direction of the nap to keep the pile fabric texture smooth.

Some sewing machine adjustments may be needed for a smooth, balanced stitch. Use a long stitch, 10 to 12 per inch (2.5 cm), on most corduroys and velveteens. On thick, bulky corduroy, decrease pressure on the presser foot. The raw edges of corduroy and velveteen may ravel, so finish them with binding or overlocking.

Grade enclosed seams to reduce bulk, but do not trim too closely. Exposed raw edges can ravel unless topstitched or treated with liquid fray preventer.

Hem bulky or heavy corduroys and velveteen by hand, or face the hem to reduce bulk. Use purchased hem facing, or cut 2" (5 cm)-wide bias strips of polyester/cotton broadcloth.

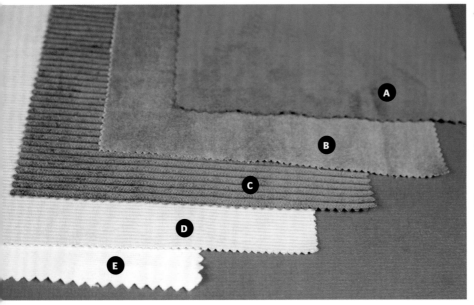

A Velveteen, like corduroy, may be all-cotton or a cotton/polyester blend, but the texture is shorter and thicker than that of corduroy. Velveteen is easier to sew and more durable than velvet.

B Ribless corduroy resembles the allover plush pile of velveteen.

C Wide wale, also called jumbo wale, is a heavyweight corduroy with as few as three ribs per inch (2.5 cm).

D Midwale corduroy is heavier than pinwale and has fewer ribs.

E Pinwale corduroy, also named baby wale or fine wale corduroy, is lightweight and has 16 ribs per inch (2.5 cm).

Sewing Techniques for Corduroy and Velveteen

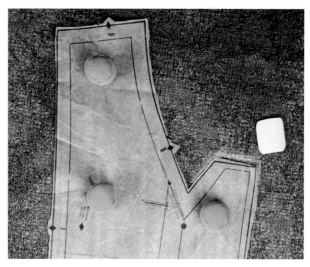

Choose nap by deciding which color shading you prefer before pattern layout. When nap runs up toward top of garment, color looks darker. When nap runs down toward garment hem, color looks lighter with a slight sheen. Corduroy wears longer when nap runs down.

Mark cutout pattern sections with chalk and pins or marking pen; mark only on wrong side of fabric layers. Do not use tracing wheel and dressmaker's carbon paper without testing; tracing wheel can mar plush textures.

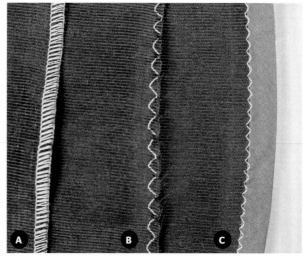

Press plush textures gently. Place self-fabric scrap, right side up, on pressing surface and place garment, right side down, on top. You may also use a wire needle board, which is a flexible surface covered in carpet of short wires, to protect the pile while pressing. Press gently to avoid flattening pile. To prevent imprints on right side, use paper strips under seam allowances, or press seams open on a seam roll.

Finish all raw edges to prevent raveling. Use either a 2-thread or 3-thread overlock using extrafine thread (a), a zigzag stitch (b), or bias binding (c).

Grade enclosed seam allowances to reduce bulk. Optional topstitching may be placed far enough in from edge to enclose raw edges of graded seam. This prevents raveling and strengthens garment edges.

Hem with catchstitch. Bind, zigzag, or overlock raw hem edge to prevent raveling. Work blind catchstitch between hem and garment, using loose stitches to prevent hem imprint.

A knit is a fabric made from interlocking looped stitches. Knits shed wrinkles well, are comfortable to wear, and are easy to sew because they do not ravel easily. Knits can be grouped into five general categories.

Firm, stable knits do not stretch significantly and are handled similarly to woven fabrics. In this group are double knits and ponte de roma, which have fine lengthwise ribs on both sides. It is difficult to tell the right and wrong side of a double knit unless the right side has a decorative design. Raschel knit is a lacy or open knit texture. The knit of a raschel knit will not stretch, because lengthwise threads are locked into some of the knitted loops. However, if the fiber content contains a stretch fiber, such as Lycra/Elastane or nylon, a raschel knit will stretch.

Lightweight single knits have fine ribs running lengthwise on the right side and loops running crosswise on the wrong side. Pull the crosswise edge of a single knit and it will roll to the right side. Unless the fiber content contains a stretch fiber, single knits such as jersey, tissue or tricot, and interlock will not stretch lengthwise, but they do have crosswise give.

Textured knits may be single or double knits, which are distinguished by a surface texture, usually on the right side. Knitted terry and velour are pile knits that look like their woven namesakes; however, they usually have a great deal of crosswise stretch. Another textured knit is the sweater knit. Patterned sweater knits have floats on the wrong side where colored yarns are carried from one motif to another. This limits their crosswise stretch. Comfortable sweatshirt fleece looks like a single knit on the right side; the wrong side has a soft, brushed surface. It is usually stable with little stretch.

Two-way stretch knits have a great degree of stretch crosswise and lengthwise and a high percentage of resilient spandex fibers. New generation activewear fabrics made of new polymers and knit constructions will wick away moisture, have antimicrobial properties, and offer higher flexibility and recovery. They are a good choice for yoga and athleticwear. Strong nylon/spandex knits are resilient, even when wet, and are usually selected for swimwear.

Ribbing is a very stretchy knit that can be used for tops and for finishing knit garments at wrists, ankles, neck, and waist. One type is tubular ribbing, which is often sold by the inch (centimeter) and must be cut open along one lengthwise rib for sewing. Another type is rib trim, which is color coordinated with sweater knits; one edge is prefinished, and the other is sewn to the garment.

Sweatshirt fleece and French terry are knit fabrics to which an additional thread is added, or "laid in"—thus the terms "laid-in thread" or "laid-in fabric." This additional thread forms loops along the courses of the knit on the fabric reverse side and adds volume and insulating properties to the material. For sweatshirt jersey, these loops are brushed, making the reverse side soft and fuzzy. The additional thread adds strength to the material, however, it makes the fabric less extensible. Because sweatshirt knits have less stretch, not all sewing patterns intended for knits will work with all sweatshirt jerseys. Consider sewing patterns that recommend stable knits when sewing with sweatshirt fleece and French terry.

Ponte de roma

Raschel

Single jersey

Tissue knit

Interlock

French Terry

Velour

Sweater knit

Sweatshirt fleece

Performance knit

Nylon/Spandex

Tubular knits, ribbing

Techniques for Knits

Patterns for knits depend on the stretch characteristics and weight of the knit. The list of suggested fabrics on the back of a pattern envelope usually includes a combination of knit and woven fabrics. If a knit is soft and lightweight, such as jersey, it is suitable for patterns that have gathers, draping, and similar features. If it is firm, such as double knit, a pattern with tailoring or a shaped, fitted silhouette is suitable. If it is bulky or textured, such as a sweater knit, a pattern with few seams and details works best to show off the knit texture.

Certain patterns, however, require knits that stretch. These are closely fitted pattern styles, such as swimsuits and dancewear, which would be too small to wear if made from a fabric without elasticity, or tops and pants that use the knit for a comfortable close-to-the-body fit. Most patterns designed for knits have a stretch gauge printed on the back of the envelope. Test the knit that you have selected against the ruler gauge. When the pattern specifies "two-way stretch knit," test the crosswise and lengthwise stretchability of the knit. Some sewing patterns for knit fabrics have "negative ease," this means that the finished garment will be smaller than your actual body measurements. Especially sewing pattern pieces for swimsuits and dancewear will be smaller than the required body measurements. It is important to choose a knit fabric with excellent stretch and recovery for sewing patterns with negative ease.

Patterns designed for knits may have ¼" (6 mm) seam allowances, because these designs are often sewn on a serger. If the pattern you have selected has ⅝" (1.5 cm) seam allowances, trim them to ¼" (6 mm) when using a serger. Similarly, if using a conventional machine and the pattern has only a ¼" (6 mm) seam allowance, cut your layout to include a ⅜" – ⅝" (1–1.5 cm) seam allowance.

Fabric Preparation

For best results, preshrink knits. Wash and dry them if they will be washed as part of their routine care. Use a bulk dry cleaner if the finished garment will be dry cleaned. It is not necessary to prewash ribbing unless using a dark-colored ribbing on a light-colored garment to remove excess dye.

If, after preshrinking, a knit still has a crease where it was folded on the bolt, steam the crease. If the crease cannot be removed by steaming, it is permanent. Refold the knit for pattern layout to prevent the crease from showing on the garment.

To straighten the ends of knits, draw a chalk line across the cut crosswise edges at right angles to the ribs. Cut the fabric on the chalk line.

Pressing

Press knits on the lengthwise ribs by lifting and lowering the iron. Use a low iron temperature setting, and raise the temperature as needed. Do not press across the ribs or handle the fabric until it is completely cooled. Either action can stretch knits out of shape.

Block sweater knits instead of pressing. To block, pat the fabric or the garment into shape on a flat surface covered with a towel or felt. Steam with a hand steamer, or hold a steam iron above the knit surface and continue to pat and gently pull until you have the correct shape. Allow the fabric to dry and cool completely before further handling.

Blocking works only on natural fibers. You may also add head and moisture to a synthetic knit to change its shape, a process known as "killing." Killing melts the fibers and, therefore, alters the shape permanently. A natural-fiber blocked item will return to its original, unblocked shape after washing; a killed synthetic item will not. A blocked item will require reblocking with each washing.

How to Use a Stretch Knit Gauge

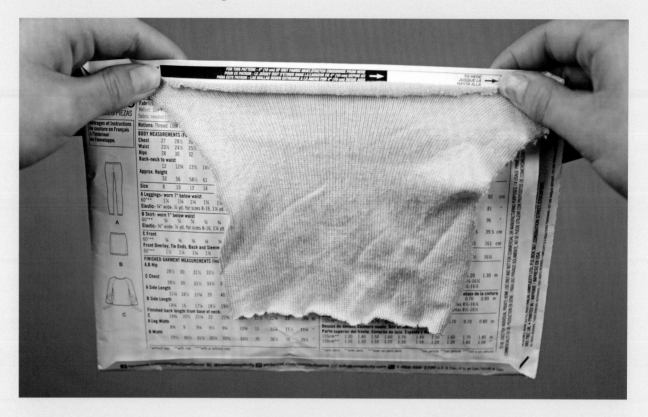

1 **Find the knit gauge** printed on the envelope of your sewing pattern. A knit fabric that is appropriate for your pattern will stretch easily to right-hand side of the knit gauge printed on pattern envelope. To test, hold your knit fabric crosswise along the courses and stretch your fabric against the gauge. The fabric should stretch to at least the end of the gauge. Knit fabrics that stretch farther than the gauge may still be used for pattern.

2 **Select a different fabric** if the fabric you are considering cannot be easily stretched to the gauge limit. Also, if the ribs of knit are distorted after stretching, and stretched edge folds over on itself because of too much stress on fabric, then this knit fabric does not have enough natural elasticity for this particular sewing pattern.

3 **Pay attention to the recovery** while checking the stretch of your fabric, also. Fabric that returns close to the 4" (10 cm) mark has good recovery and will be a good choice for garments that you would like to fit close to the body and retain their shape, such as leggings or activewear. Knit fabrics with less recovery are a good choice for more relaxed garments.

How to Calculate Stretch without a Knit Gauge

If your pattern does not include a knit gauge but does recommend a percentage of stretch, calculate the stretch of your knit fabric as follows: Hold 4" (10 cm) on the crosswise edge against a ruler and stretch the material. Subtract the original length from the maximum stretched length to find the difference, then divide the difference by the original length and multiply this by 100.

A = initial length

Subtract initial length from maximum stretched length

B = stretched length minus initial length

$[B/A] \times 100$ = the percentage of stretch of your material

For example, if 4" of your material stretches to a maximum of 6":
$6-4=2$

$[2/4] \times 100 = 50$

This material has 50% stretch

Pattern Layout

Always use a "with-nap" pattern layout on knits. Because of their looped construction, knit fabrics can have a directional quality that can be visible in the completed garment.

Stretch both crosswise edges of a knit before pattern layout to see if the knit runs. If so, the runs will occur more readily along one edge than the other. When you lay out the pattern, position the run-prone edge at the garment hemline. The hem is subject to less stress, so the knit will be less likely to run after the garment is sewn. If pinning the pattern to your material, pin the fabric using ballpoint pins.

When laying out and cutting a knit fabric, do not let it hang off the work surface. The weight of the fabric can distort the material on the work surface and pull it off grain.

On bulky or textured knits, it is easier to lay out the pattern on a single layer of fabric. Position the textured side down; pin and mark on the smoother, wrong side of the knit. Use weights instead of pins on knits with open or lacy textures.

Sewing

Many knit fabrics can be sewn with a universal needle, however, best results are achieved with a ballpoint needle. The balled tip of the needle slips past the knit loops instead of puncturing and tearing them. A ballpoint needle will eliminate or reduce the formation of holes around the stitches where the fibers have been broken.

Use a reinforcing tape along seams that carry a lot of weight or are subject to stress, such as shoulder seams. This will help the garment retain its shape through washings and wearings. Also, seam tape is recommended for all seams of lacey knits.

A four- or three-thread overedge serger stitch is preferred by many for a professional-looking seam on a knit garment. However, selecting stretch stitches on a conventional machine will also work well. On a conventional machine, a narrow, short zigzag stitch or a three-step zigzag stitch are good choices on knit fabrics, as the thread will not break as the material stretches. If your garment is loose fitting or if you practice taut sewing, then a straight stitch with a polyester sewing thread will work for sewing most knits on a conventional machine as well.

Knit items can be topstitched with a straight stitch using a twin needle, a zigzag stitch or a three-step zigzag stitch on a conventional machine or with a coverlock stitch on a coverlock machine, or variations on a flatlock seam on a serger.

Interfacings

If your knit item has details such as buttons, pockets, plackets or appliqué, you will need to stabilize the fabric with interfacing. Choose a supple interfacing that does not change the character of the knit. Two types of interfacing that work well with knits are a fusible tricot and a lightweight stretch nonwoven.

Sheer fabrics can have a soft or crisp hand; crisp sheers are easier to cut and sew. Soft sheers are batiste, chiffon, China silk, and georgette. Crisp sheers include fabrics such as organza, voile, and organdy.

The main consideration with sheer fabrics is their transparent quality. The stitches on the inside of a sheer garment show from the outside. Whether revealed clearly or as mere shadows, details such as seams, facings, and hems must be neat and narrow to look well made.

Silky fabrics are made from natural silk fibers or synthetic fibers that look like silk, such as polyester, nylon, rayon, and acetate. Most synthetic silk-like fabrics do not shrink or fade, and can be washed and dried by machine. This group of fabrics includes charmeuse, crepe de chine, lightweight jacquard weaves, lightweight satin-backed crepe, tissue faillel and silk.

Even when silk and synthetic silk-like fabrics do not have the see-through character of sheers, they do have similar fine weaves and light weights. Inner construction can show as ridges on the outside of silky garments. That is why many of the same sewing supplies and techniques are suggested for both kinds of fabrics. An additional consideration with silk and silk-like fabrics is their smooth, slick texture, which makes them slippery to handle. You will need to take special care when laying out and cutting the pattern pieces to control these fabrics.

Tissue faille

Satin-backed crepe

Charmeuse

Organdy

Lighweight jacquard weave

Chiffon

Silk

China silk

Georgette

Batiste

Organza

Guide to Sewing Sheer and Silky Fabrics

EQUIPMENT AND TECHNIQUES	Soft Sheers Batiste, chiffon, China silk, georgette Crisp Sheers Organdy, organza, voile
MACHINE NEEDLES	Size 8 (60), 9 (65), or 11 (75)
STITCH LENGTH	12 to 16 per inch (2.5 cm)
MILLIMETER STITCH SETTING	2.5 to 2
THREAD	Extra fine long staple polyester, silk, or mercerized cotton. These threads are often sold as notions for lingerie, machine embroidery, or quilting. Use finest thread possible.
HAND NEEDLES	Betweens, sizes 8 to 12
INTERFACINGS	Sheer nonwoven fusible or sew in, self fabric, organza
SPECIAL SEAMS	French, hairline, overlocked, double stitched
SPECIAL HEMS	Overlocked, rolled overlocked, hand rolled, tricot bound, hairline, narrow topstitched

Techniques for Sheer and Silky Fabrics

Keep in mind the delicate nature of sheer and silky fabrics when choosing patterns. The most suitable pattern designs are those that fit loosely and have graceful, flowing lines. Look for soft details such as gathers, ruffles, shirring, or draping. Crisp sheers, however, can be sewn from patterns with tailored, shirt-style details. Bias-cut pattern sections can be difficult to handle on silk and synthetic silk fabrics, which stretch a great deal as well as slip and slide.

For sheers, the fewer seams, darts, facings, and other details to sew, the less inside construction will show through to the right side. Also, the less time you will spend with special finishing techniques. Avoid patterns that require zippers, and omit in-seam pockets because zippers and pockets are bulky and can create an unattractive show-through on the outside of the garment.

Fabric Preparation

For best results, wash and dry sheer and silky fabrics before you begin working with them if they will be washed as part of their routine care. This preshrinks the fabric and removes resins, which can cause skipped stitches and make stitching difficult on synthetic fabrics. Follow the care instructions provided by the fabric manufacturer. Typical care instructions are to machine wash in a gentle cycle and tumble dry at a low temperature setting. Before washing, stitch along cut edges of the fabric to prevent excessive fraying.

Pure silk and silk/synthetic blend fabrics require special consideration. Silk fabrics can be dry cleaned, but hand washing may be preferred. Warm water releases a natural substance from within the silk fibers, which renews the fabric and gives it a refreshed look. It is best to wash silk with laundry soap or cationic surficant in soft water to maintain the integrity of the protein strands and natural oils.

Prewashing also frees you from worry about water spotting. The dyes in some silk fabrics may run. Hand washing is not recommended for strong colors and prints. Use a sample of your fabric as a test to see how it reacts to hand washing; then prepare the entire length of fabric accordingly.

Also preshrink other fabrics, such as interfacings and linings. Even a tiny amount of shrinkage on these inner fabrics will show up as puckers or bubbles on thin, lightweight outer fabrics.

If you dry clean your silk garment, prepare the fabric for sewing by steam pressing on the wrong side. Use a press cloth to protect the fabric. Set the iron at the lowest end of the steam setting.

Pressing

The best approach to pressing sheer and silky fabrics is to work with fabric scraps first. Determine the optimum temperature setting on your iron, beginning with a low setting and raising it as needed. Fabrics made from rayon or polyester fibers scorch easily and require a cool iron temperature. Use a press cloth to protect fragile fabrics and fibers, or use a soleplate cover on your iron. Avoid a metal-coated ironing board cover because it reflects too much heat into the fabric.

Most pure silk fabrics can be pressed at a low steam setting, but test to see if steaming leaves spots. This is a hazard especially on pure silk fabrics that have not been prewashed before pattern layout and on lustrous fabrics such as charmeuse.

Avoid overpressing. Thin, lightweight fabrics are quickly penetrated by heat and need less pressing effort than heavier fabrics. A light touch is all that is necessary. Use a hand steamer on finished garments. Finally, take your time with silk and silk-like fabrics: Your patience will reap lovely results.

How to Hand Wash Silks

Swish fabric gently in lukewarm water. Use mild detergent with a cationic surfactant, mild soap, or natural shampoo such as castile. Rinse in cool water.

Roll fabric in towel to remove excess moisture. Do not wring or twist; this causes wrinkles, which are difficult to remove.

Press on wrong side of fabric while it is still damp. Use dry iron at cool temperature, such as synthetic setting, keeping grainlines true.

Layout and Cutting

Fine, lightweight fabrics are easier to handle during pattern layout if you cover the cutting surface with a sheet, other matte-surfaced fabric, or a flannel-backed vinyl tablecloth with the flannel side up. Cardboard cutting boards and padded work surfaces also help to make slippery fabrics more controllable. Once cut, leave the pieces lying flat and avoid the temptation to drape your pieces on your dress form or otherwise move them around a great deal. If handled too much, the weave will move off grain. The pieces may also change in shape and size. Stay-stitching within the seam allowances of the piece edges of very fine silky fabrics can help the weave from slipping off grain.

TIPS

Pin your unfolded fabric between two sheets of tissue paper. Then place your pattern pieces on top of the tissue paper and cut your fabric with the tissue paper attached. You will need to cut both sides of mirror-image pieces and the opposite halves of "on fold" pieces accordingly. You may transfer marks directly onto the tissue paper instead of onto the delicate fabric. Once the pieces are cut, you may seam the pieces together with the tissue paper still attached. The tissue paper will have enough friction to move cleanly over the feeder dogs while keeping the slippery material in place. Once the seam is stitched, the tissue paper may be torn away.

To pin patterns in position, use superfine pins (0.5 mm diameter). They penetrate the fabric weave without marring it. Prepare new pins by wiping off the manufacturer's oil coating or swishing in a bit of dish soap and water and then drying to prevent leaving spots, or use the pins first on dark fabric. In spite of their name, silk pins are too coarse for these fabrics and should be reserved for use with heavier fabrics such as raw silk.

The fastest way to cut out fine fabrics is with a rotary cutter. The blade cuts fabric edges neatly and does not shift the fabric as you work. Another good cutting tool is a bent-handled dressmaker's shears. The shape of the handle allows you to rest one cutting blade on the work surface for accurate strokes that barely disturb the fabric layers. Serrated-edge shears can also be helpful. The special blades firmly grip thin and slippery fabrics, a benefit not only for initial cutting but also for trimming raw edges. Whichever tool you use, be sure it is sharp; blades of shears should be in good alignment. Also, synthetic fabrics will cause a build up of microscopic fuzz, which dulls the cutting blades. Wipe synthetic fuzz off your blades with a soft cloth.

Use a with-nap layout for all fabrics that have luster or shine. This one-way pattern layout guarantees uniform color shading in the finished garment. Some fabrics look lighter or brighter in one direction than the other; study the fabric before pattern layout and decide which shading you prefer.

Tips for Working with Silky, Slippery, and Shear Fabrics

It takes about 2,500 cocoons to make a pound of silk. Each cocoon takes about three days to make. Looking at it that way, a pound of silk takes twenty silk-worm years to make. Keep that in mind as you work with silk and silk fabrics. Take the time to prepare the fabric for cutting. Make the effort to hand baste before machine stitching. Be patient with the quirks of silky fabrics and beautiful results will follow.

For washable slippery and very sheer fabrics, you may try spraying the material with a light starch or sizing while the material is laid flat. The sizing or starch will help stabilize the material during cutting and sewing. Allow your fabric to dry completely before cutting. Do not hang the fabric to dry, but let it remain laying flat to maintain the integrity of the grain. You may also consider fusing a water soluble stabilizer to your washable material. The stabilizer will wash out once the garment is complete. Very often, the first washing will result in your sheer or slippery material having a spotty appearance: it will likely take more than one washing for the stabilizer to wash out completely. Be sure to test the starch, sizing, or stabilizer on a scrap of fabric first.

Layout Techniques for Slippery Fabrics

Fold fabric right side out so less-slick wrong sides face each other. Pick up fabric along folded edge, and let fabric fall naturally to ensure accuracy of crosswise grain.

Push pins straight down through pattern seam allowance, fabric, and padded, cork-, flannel- or felt-covered work surface to secure slippery layers. If using cardboard cutting board, avoid using superfine pins because cardboard dulls them quickly.

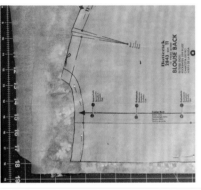

Sandwich extremely slippery or thin fabrics between two layers of tissue paper for better control. Place tissue paper on cutting board; place fabric on top and another sheet of tissue paper

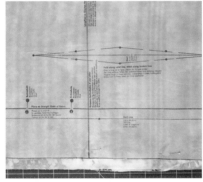

on top of that. Place pattern on top and pin through all layers. Pin only in seam allowances. Transfer marks to the tissue paper.

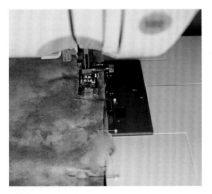

Stitch right through the tissue paper on the material when sewing.

Tear away the tissue paper gently once the primary seam is sewn. Finish the seam into a French seam or other appropriate seam as desired.

TIP

Silk and silk-like fabrics can be sewn with silk, polyester, or cotton thread. However, for delicate, sheer silks, your best choice may be cotton thread: When subject to stress, silk and polyester threads may have more tensile strength than the silk fabric, thereby causing the fabric to tear before the thread. A cotton thread will have less strength and elasticity and will likely break before the costly silk fabric itself tears. Furthermore, polyester thread has more stretch, which may produce puckers on very fine fabric. It is a good idea to test a few threads on a scrap of your material to see which is best suited for your silk fabric.

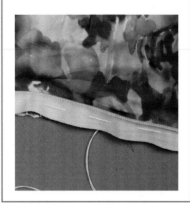

The lustrous surface of special-occasion fabrics can come from the weave of the fabric, as is true for satin, or from fibers with sheen, such as silk and acetate. Special finishes also create surface luster, or metallic yarns or sequins can be added to give an ordinary fabric glamorous sparkle.

Techniques for Lustrous Fabrics

Many fabrics fit into the lustrous category, and some have unique sewing requirements. However, all of these fabrics are alike in two ways: A "with-nap" pattern layout is used for uniform color shading in the finished garment, and the less handling, the better. Keep handling to a minimum by choosing patterns in simple styles with few seams and darts. Avoid buttoned closings and details such as shaped collars and welt pockets. Use a simple pinked finish on plain seams, or treat raw edges with liquid fray preventer instead of using elaborate dressmaker techniques. Take special care when pressing, using a light touch and covering the pressing surface with a scrap of self fabric so nap faces nap. To prevent ridges when pressing seams, press over a seam roll or place strips of heavy brown paper between seam allowance and garment.

Handling Lustrous Fabrics

Pin only in seam allowances to prevent pin marks. Use extrafine silk pins for finely woven fabrics such as satin and taffeta. Shears must be sharp or strokes will chew raw edges of fabric. Cut directionally for smoothest edges. Always use "with-nap" layout for fabrics with luster.

Use plain seams with a simple edge finish. Raw edges can be pinked, overlocked, or finished with three-step zigzag. If fabric frays easily, apply thin coat of liquid fray preventer to raw edges. Slip envelopes between seam allowances and garment to protect garment from stray drops.

Guide to Sewing Lustrous Fabrics

EQUIPMENT AND TECHNIQUES	Medium-weight Crepe-backed satin, lamé, satin, satin peau, silk, taffeta, moiré	Heavily textured brocade, sequined fabrics
MACHINE NEEDLES	Size 11 (75)	Size 14 (90) or 16 (100)
STITCH LENGTH	8 to 12 per inch (2.5 cm)	8 to 12 per inch (2.5 cm)
MILLIMETER STITCH SETTING	3.5 to 2.5	3.5 to 2.5
THREAD	All purpose cotton or cotton/polyester, silk for silk fabric	All purpose cotton or cotton/polyester
HAND NEEDLES	Betweens, size 7 or 8	Betweens, size 7 or 8
INTERFACINGS	Sew-in nonwoven or woven	Sew-in nonwoven or woven
SPECIAL SEAMS	Plain seam: pinked, overedge, three-step zigzag, or liquid fray preventer finish	Plain seam or lined to edge
SPECIAL HEMS	Catchstitched, topstitched, horsehair braid, faced	Faced

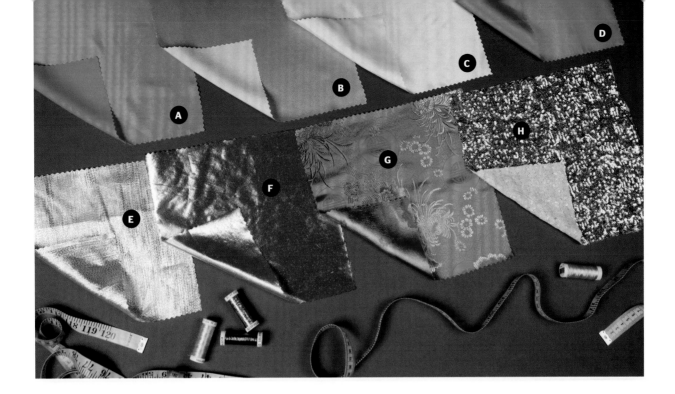

A **Satin** is a weave that produces a shiny surface texture from floating yarns. The combination of this distinctive weave with fibers such as silk, rayon, or polyester makes the fabric likely to waterspot; protect the fabric with a press cloth, and use a dry iron when pressing. Use superfine pins to avoid snagging surface yarns.

B **Crepe-backed satin** is also called satin-backed crepe because the fabric is reversible; one face has the matte, pebbly texture of crepe, and the other face has the smooth, shiny texture of satin. One side may be used as a binding or trim for the other.

C **Satin peau** is a satin with a firm twill weave on the right side. Some peaus are double faced, with fine crosswise ribs on both sides. Because pins and ripped-out stitches can leave marks, pin only in seam allowance; test fit to avoid ripping stitches.

D **Taffeta** has a crisp hand and drapes stiffly. Test sewing techniques on scraps, because pins and ripped-out stitches can leave marks. When the fiber content includes acetate, steam can leave spots. Moiré taffeta is passed between heated rollers to give it a watermarked surface texture.

E **Metallic fabrics** have metallic yarns woven or knit into them. Most are sensitive to heat and discolor when steam is used. Finger press seams with a thimble or blunt end of a point turner or use a cool, dry iron.

F **Lamé** is a smooth, shiny metallic fabric, either knit or woven. Knit metallics drape and ease better than the wovens. Besides gold, silver, and copper tones, lame is available in iridescent colors.

G **Brocade** comes in all weights, from light to heavy, and has raised tapestry-style motifs. The motifs should be balanced on major garment sections and matched at prominent seams. Most brocades are woven, but some are knit. Careful pressing on a padded surface preserves the surface texture. When brocades have shiny metallic threads, set the iron at a low temperature for pressing. To make metallic brocades more comfortable, underline with batiste.

H **Sequined fabrics** have a knit or sheer woven base. A simple pattern style is especially important for these fabrics. Or use sequined fabric for only a part of the garment, such as the bodice.

TIP

The little undulations that form naturally along a stitching line may be more pronounced on a shiny satin fabric and look like puckers. To reduce this puckering effect, practice taut sewing: While stitching, hold the material both behind the needle and in front of the needle with thumb and forefinger and gently hold the fabric very straight. Do not pull the fabric through the machine: Guide and hold the material firmly as the machine stitches.

Laces look fragile and delicate but are actually easy to sew. True laces have a net or mesh background, which has no grainline and does not ravel. You can cut into the fabric freely for creative pattern layouts, seams need no time-consuming edge finishes, and hemming requires little more than trimming close to the edges of prominent motifs. While most laces do not have a grain in the true sense, very often the woven or embroidered design will determine the orientation of your cutting layout.

The openwork designs of lace fabrics have rich histories. Some laces still bear the names of the European localities where they were once made by hand from silk, cotton, or linen fibers. Today, many laces are made by machine from easy-care cotton blends, polyester, acrylic, or nylon.

Guide to Sewing Laces

EQUIPMENT AND TECHNIQUES	Delicate Chantilly, point d'esprit	Embroidered eyelet, Schiffli	Textured Alençon, Cluny, Venice
MACHINE NEEDLES	Size 8 (60) or 9 (65)	Size 9 (65) or 11 (75)	Size 11 (75)
STITCH LENGTH	12 to 16 per inch (2.5 cm)	10 to 12 per inch (2.5 cm)	10 to 12 per inch (2.5 cm)
MILLIMETER STITCH SETTING	2.5 to 2	3 to 2.5	3 to 2.5
THREAD	Extrafine	All purpose	All purpose
HAND NEEDLES	Betweens, size 7 or 8	Betweens, size 7 or 8	Betweens, size 7 or 8
INTERFACINGS	Omit	Omit	Omit
SPECIAL SEAMS	Lapped, overlocked, double stitched	Overlocked, double stitched	Lapped, double stitched
SPECIAL HEMS	Self-hem, appliquéd	Self-hem	Self-hem, appliquéd, horsehair braid

A **Alençon** lace has filled-in motifs outlined by soft satin cord on a sheer net background. One or both lengthwise edges usually have a finished border.

B **Chantilly** lace has delicate floral motifs worked on a fine net background and outlined with silky threads. A popular bridal fabric, Chantilly lace usually has an allover pattern.

C **Eyelet** is a finely woven cotton or polyester/cotton fabric embroidered with a satin-stitched openwork design. Even though eyelet embroideries are not true laces, they require pattern layout and pressing techniques similar to those for laces.

D **Peau d'orange** is a form of Chantilly lace made with a flossy yarn to give it a soft texture.

E **Venice** lace is made from heavy yarns and unique stitches that give it a three-dimensional texture. Picot bridges join the motifs. Venice lace does not have the net background that is typical of most laces.

F **Cluny** lace is made from heavy cotton-like yarns and looks hand-crocheted. It usually has paddle or wheel motifs and may have raised knots as part of the design.

G **Schiffli** is an embroidered sheer or semisheer fabric decorated on a Schiffli machine, which imitates hand-embroidered stitches.

H **Ribbon** embroidered lace is a modern variation of Alençon lace that, uses instead a flat ribbon to empahsize the detail.

Techniques for Sewing Lace and Embroidered Fabrics

Select a pattern that suits the texture and weight of the lace fabric. Patterns for bridal and evening gowns that are illustrated in lace fabrics may require specific forms of lace, such as edgings of specific widths or a wide allover lace. Check the back of the pattern envelope for the garment requirements.

When considering a pattern that is not illustrated in laces, select a pattern with sections sized to fit the fabric width. If planning to use a bordered lace on sleeves, you may have to use a short-sleeved pattern if the lace is not wide enough for long sleeves or place the lace at the lower edge of an organza sleeve. Because lace has no grainline, it is possible to turn the pattern pieces to use an edge or border as a finished edge.

Fabric Preparation

Lace rarely requires any preparation for sewing. Most laces must be dry cleaned. Although shrinkage is rare, if the care label on a lace fabric indicates it is washable, and you are combining it with other fabrics and trims to make a washable garment, then you should preshrink the lace. Add it to the other components of the garment as you preshrink them.

Facings, Interfacings, and Underlinings

Facings and interfacings are not used on lace garments. Finish outer edges with lace trim, lace borders, or sheer tricot bias or French binding. Cut collars and cuffs as single layers, and finish the outer edges with lace trim or appliqué. Use a narrow seam to join them to the garment.

If you need to add body or support to lace, line the lace with tulle netting. The tulle netting adds strength without showing through or changing the character of the lace.

Layout and Cutting

Pattern layout is an important preliminary step for lace fabrics. Begin by studying the details of the lace design. Unfold the fabric fully on the work surface, laying contrasting fabric underneath, if necessary, to make the design easier to read.

Note the placement of prominent motifs, the spacing of the repeats, and the depth of any borders. The most noticeable motifs should be matched at the seams and centered or otherwise balanced on major garment sections, just like large fabric prints. If the design has one-way motifs, use a "with-nap" pattern layout.

Plan how to use the motifs creatively. Some laces have large primary motifs and smaller secondary motifs or borders that can be cut out and used as appliqués. To use borders as hems, determine the finished skirt and sleeve lengths before pattern layout. If you plan to trim the border from the fabric and sew it to the garment as a decorative edging, you do not need to determine lengths in advance so precisely.

Before cutting, decide which seam treatment you will be using. Allover laces can be sewn like sheer fabrics, with narrow seams. However, if you are working with a reembroidered lace or a special heirloom lace with a large motif, lapped seams may be better. They will not interrupt the flow of the lace design around the garment because the seam is nearly invisible. With this method, pattern sections must be pinned in place and cut out one by one in sequence. You may use a combination of seams in one garment, with lapped seams at shoulder and side seams and narrow zigzag or double stitched seams for set-in sleeves.

Once lace is cut, there is little margin for fitting changes. Fit the pattern before layout to avoid ripping out stitches later.

Pressing

Avoid overhandling lace with pressing. If a light touch-up is needed, press with right side down on a well-padded surface to avoid flattening the lace texture. Use a press cloth to prevent the tip of the iron from catching or tearing the net background. If you are working with lace made from synthetic fibers, such as polyester or nylon, use a low temperature setting on the iron. Finger press seams, darts, and other construction details. If further pressing is necessary, steam lightly, then finger press.

Lace Appliqués

Lace appliqués, either purchased as single medallions or cut from lace fabric, make elegant trims on special-occasion garments. These trims are often used as accents on bridal and evening gown bodices when the skirt is cut from lace fabric. They can also be used as details on silky lingerie and blouses.

To stitch appliqués in place, use either the hand or machine method. Another quick technique is securing appliqués with fusible web. This method is suitable for laces and background fabrics that are not sensitive to heat and steam.

Lace Appliqué Options

Start with lace fabric. Clip around lace motif. Leave one or two rows of net around edges to give motif definition and to keep reembroidered lace cordings from raveling. You can also purchase lace appliqué.

Fuse. Position garment, right side up, on covered pressing surface. Place appliqué on garment. Slip circles of fusible web under appliqué. Cover with paper towels or absorbent press cloth. Fuse, following manufacturer's directions.

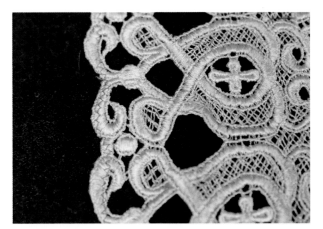

Machine stitch. Use a narrow zigzag or short straight stitch ¼" (6 mm) inside edges. Under the motif, trim fabric close to zigzag stitching for sheer effect. (Contrasting thread is used to show detail.)

Hand stitch. Use short running stitches ¼" (6 mm) from appliqué edges. Keep stitches loose so background fabric stays smooth and appliqué is not flattened. (Contrasting thread is used to show detail.)

Natural pelts can be used to add a luxury detail to jackets and coats. Depending of the fur used, the pile will usually have a direction for which a "with-nap" pattern layout may be required.

Synthetic fur has a pile texture on the right side, which imitates the coloring and texture of natural pelts, or a synthetic fur fabric can have a novelty texture and coloring. Synthetic furs can be machine washed and dried. Most have a knitted or non-woven backing.

Synthetic suede (such as Ultrasuede®) is a nonwoven, softly napped polyester/polyurethane fabric that closely resembles genuine sueded leather but can be washed and dried by machine. Lightweight synthetic suedes drape softly and do not require special patterns. Medium-weight types are more like real suede.

While natural and synthetic leathers and pelts don't ravel, you may need to take extra finishing steps, such as fusing the seam allowances and topstitching the edges because suedes are difficult to press flat with conventional pressing techniques. Or you can use flat construction techniques, such as lapped seams and faced hems.

Like suedes, vinyls have different weights. Lightweight, supple vinyls have a knitted or woven backing. They require many of the same methods used for synthetic suedes, except vinyls are damaged by heat and steam so they cannot be pressed.

Carefully test stitch lengths to be sure you aren't weakening the material with too close perforations. Needle and pinholes are permanent so fit carefully so you don't rip seams and use clothespins or clips in place of pinning.

Guide to Sewing Synthetic Fur, Suede, Vinyl, and Leather

EQUIPMENT AND TECHNIQUES	SYNTHETIC FUR	SYNTHETIC SUEDE	SYNTHETIC LEATHER/VINYL
MACHINE NEEDLES	Size 14 (90) or 16 (100)	Size 11 (75); 16 (100) for topstitching	Size 14 (90)
STITCH LENGTH	10 to 12 per inch (2.5 cm)	8 to 10 per inch (2.5 cm)	8 to 10 per inch (2.5 cm)
MILLIMETER STITCH SETTING	3 to 2.5	3.5 to 3	3.5 to 3
THREAD	All purpose polyester or polyester/cotton; topstitching/two strands of All purpose or heavy duty		
INTERFACINGS	Omit	Fusible	Sew in
SPECIAL SEAMS	Butted	Lapped, topstitched, welt	Topstitched, welt
SPECIAL HEMS	Faced or lined to the edge	Topstitched, faced, fused	Topstitched

Natural nappa leather

Natural sheepskin

Synthetic fur with knit backing

Natural suede leather

Synthetic leather with knit backing

Faux hide on woven backing

Synthetic fur with microfiber backing

Synthetic knit fur

Natural fur pelt

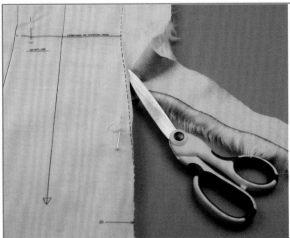

TIP

To cut, turn your fur pelt or synthetic fur over and pin or temporarily adhere your pattern pieces to the fabric's wrong side. Using shears, cut only the leather or knit backing using very short strokes. This will keep the pile intact. Pattern pieces of fur must be cut individually, and not on folded fabric. If the pattern piece you need to cut from fur is an on-fold piece, make a full pattern piece by using shears or a razor blade to cut it from a piece of folded paper.

As you plan your sewing project, you form a vision of what the final outcome will look like, what statement the item should make. While color, texture, pattern, fabric weight, accents, and embellishments comprise those parts of the design we can see, there is another component—the interlinings and interfacings—which, though they may remain unseen, contribute significantly to the look, functionality, and stability of your project.

You might consider the interlinings and interfacings to be the bones and cartilage around which the sewn garment takes form, allowing the item to flex and move while still retaining its shape. For each category of fabric and for each desired effect, there is a wide array of specific interlining and interfacings in sheer, light, medium, and heavy weight, each of which needs to be considered and selected to make the end result the one you envision. Interfacing is also required for creative uses, such as for stabilizing fabrics for appliqué or machine embroidery, and strengthening stress points, say, around buttonholes. While interfacing and interlining add to the item's structure, tear-away and water soluble interfacings aid in stitching, for example, by preventing fabric from puckering during embroidery and appliqué to helping move silky, slippery fabric over the feeder dogs and under the presser foot while sewing. Fusible webs and tapes aid in construction. Webs are generally

sheets or tapes comprised of heat-activated adhesive and are used to fuse the fibers of two fabrics together to make construction easier.

There are two types of interfacing: Sew in and fusible. Sew-in interfacings, as the name suggests, are held in place with stitches, either with baste stitches or within the seams. Today, sew-in interfacings are used infrequently and most sewists only use sew-in interfacings for rather specific fabrics, for example, fabrics that cannot be ironed or fabrics that would lose their specific appearance if the interfacing were to adhere to the fibers. Fabrics that are Teflon coated, laminated, vinyl, faux leather, crinkle, and seersucker are examples of materials for which a sew-in interfacing would be useful.

Fusible interfacings are those interlinings that have a heat-activated polymer adhesive. These interfacings bind permanently to the fabric fibers to lend your material stability or perhaps a different structure or character.

Consider the character of the item you are sewing and how it should function and appear. Unless you are specifically seeking to have a very stiff item, for example, a hat brim or formal shirt collar, choose an interfacing that has a weight and flexibility similar to your fabric.

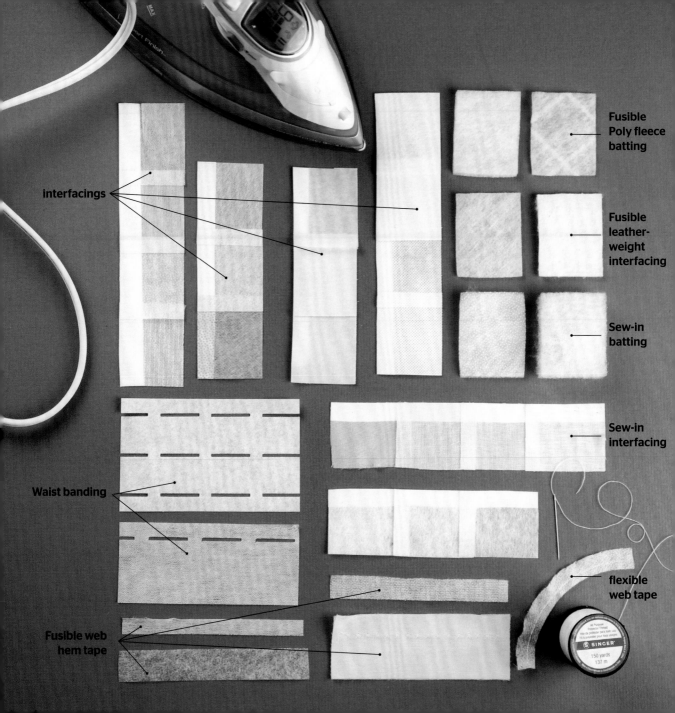

interfacings

Fusible Poly fleece batting

Fusible leather-weight interfacing

Sew-in batting

Sew-in interfacing

Waist banding

flexible web tape

Fusible web hem tape

How to Apply Fusible Interfacing

1 **Position interfacing on warm fabric.** resin side down; smooth into place. Lightly mist interfacing with water, or steam shrink. Position press cloth and dampen with liberal misting, even when using steam iron.

2 **Start at center** of large or long pieces of interfacing, and work toward each end to fuse. Do not slide iron from one position to the next, but lift and press, lift and press. To ensure complete coverage, overlap the area with the iron.

3 **Use extra, two-handed pressure.** for recommended time—10 to 15 seconds for most fusible interfacings. Otherwise, bond will not be permanent and will eventually separate from fabric. Once cooled, try to gently pull the interfacing from the fabric to see if fusing was successful.

4 **Press from right side** of fabric over the fused area for additional bonding. Use a press cloth or iron soleplate guard to protect fabric surface from iron shine and the iron's soleplate from exposure to the adhesive. Cool and dry fused fabrics flat before moving them; interfacing can be easily reshaped or distorted while warm.

When applying a fusible interfacing or web to your fabric, keep the following mind:

• Different fusible interfacings and webs require different temperature settings in order to activate the polymer. Refer to your fabric's care label and choose a fusible interfacing that will adhere at an iron temperature that will not damage your fabric. It is always a good idea to first test your fusible interfacing on a scrap of your fabric.

• Apply your fusible interfacing on a very flat ironing surface. Very often, on a metal ironing board, the padded ironing board cover loses thickness through use and the surface will become uneven. A wooden cutting board covered with layers of cloth makes a good surface for applying fusible interfacing.

• For best results, once you have adhered the interfacing to your material, allow the material to cool completely for 20 to 30 minutes to allow the fused materials to set.

Common Uses for Interfacings, Interlinings, and Webs

FORM	TYPE	DESCRIPTION	PURPOSE	USAGE
TAPES	Hem web tape	A strip of fusible web that comes on a roll.	To hold the hem in place without pins before stitching	One side is pressed to your material through the protective paper layer. Once that side is adhered, pull off paper, fold over the corresponding fabric or opposite side of hem, and press.
	Flexible web tape	A strip of fusible web that will bend and curve.	Helps prevent puckering along curved areas during sewing and helps curved areas retain shape and resist stretching out.	Used around curved areas, such as necklines, pocket openings and armholes.
	Waistbanding	A fusible fiber strip that is easily folded to make a tailored waistband. Includes perforations for stitching or folding.	To lend the waistband a very tailored, stiff structure.	In recent years, the use of waistbanding in women's apparel has fallen out of favor, as current fashions trend toward more tapered waistlines. Waistbanding, however, can be used in other applications, for example, to make stiff fabric handles for handbags.
INTERFACINGS	Nonwoven and woven interfacing	Many different materials with or without fusible adhesives	Used to stabilize fabric and add sturdiness for tailoring, as well as strengthen stress points.	For light- and medium-weight fabrics, choose an interfacing similar in weight to the fabric.
	Water-soluble and tear away interfacings	A sew-in or pin-on interfacing	Used to stabilize fabrics and prevent puckering in appliqué and machine embroidery.	Can also be used to help move difficult fabrics along the feeder dog.
INTERLININGS	Stretch Interfacings	A fusible interfacing for use on stretch materials	To give stretch fabrics stability and strength where needed.	Elastic Interfacings come in several weights. Very lightweight interfacings in a skin tone are a good choice for sheer fabrics.
	Leather-weight interfacing	A strong and flexible bonding interfacing that has similar malleability as leather	Used in hat brims, belts, handles, storage totes, handbags, and handbag accessories.	Lightweight leather-weight interfacings may be included in the seam allowance. Heavyweight interfacing needs to fit within the stitched area.
VOLUME	Fusible poly fleece batting	A layer of poly batting treated with heat-activated adhesive on the back.	Used to add volume to placemats, table accessories, totes, handbags, handbag accessories, and wall hangings.	Not recommended for blankets and quilts, as the adhesive may add unwanted structure.
	Sew-in batting	Non fusible batting is made from both natural-fiber and synthetic materials	Used for blankets and quilts and to make quilted materials. Easily delaminated for specific needs.	Lightweight natural-fiber battings are suitable for clothing; heavier ones are best for home décor and bedding.

Fitting Patterns

Pattern adjustments change the measurement and shape of standard pattern pieces to fit your figure. To streamline the entire fitting process, make as many fitting changes as you can before you cut. Step-by-step instructions for specific adjustments are given on the following pages.

Press pattern pieces with a warm, dry iron before you start to remove wrinkles in the tissue paper. Pin-fit the pattern to preview how well the fashion style fits your figure. Adjust the pattern on your body, or decide how extensively you need pattern adjustments. If you need many adjustments, reconsider your choice of pattern style. Another style may fit your figure with fewer adjustments. Also, pin-fit after making pattern adjustments as a fast check of their accuracy.

Work in a logical order, completing lengthening or shortening pattern adjustments first. Then work from the top of the pattern down to make additional adjustments. Watch for chain reactions. Adjustments on one pattern piece usually require matching adjustments on adjoining pattern sections. If you change the neckline seam, for example, you must change the neck facing to match. Sometimes, a compensating rather than a matching adjustment is necessary. For example, if you lower the shoulder seams to fit sloping shoulders, you must also lower the underarm seam to retain the armhole size.

Maintain the original grainline as printed on the pattern pieces, so the finished garment hangs properly. Extend the grainline from one edge of the pattern piece to the other before cutting. This helps preserve grainline as you make adjustments.

Blend the adjusted stitching and cutting lines back into the original lines. When adjustments are blended correctly, the original shape of the pattern piece will not be distorted.

To blend a seam, draw a continuous line where one has become broken during pattern adjustment. To blend a straight line, use a ruler or straight edge, connecting the beginning and end of the new line. To blend a curved line, use a curved ruler to reconstruct the original curve of the pattern, blending to each end from a point halfway between the broken seamline.

Blend the seamline first, then the cutting line. On multiple-sized patterns where no seamlines are marked, blend the cutting line only, and stitch the specified seam allowance, usually $5/8$" (1.5 cm). When there is a dart in the seamline, fold the dart out before blending the line. Be sure to mark all notches and darts on the new blended seamline.

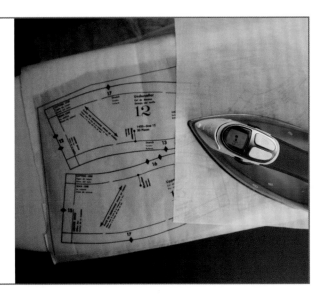

Choosing an Adjustment Method

Wherever possible, two methods are given for the most common pattern adjustments: the minor, or in-seam, method and the major, or cut-and-slide, method. Choose one method or the other, depending on how much of an adjustment you need to make.

Minor in-seam pattern adjustments are quick and easy, because you can mark them directly on the printed pattern within the seam allowance or on the pattern tissue margin. In-seam methods have narrow limitations. Usually you can add or subtract no more than $3/8$" to $½$" (1 to 1.3 cm).

Consider using a contrasting tissue paper to differentiate between the original pattern and your adjustment.

Major cut-and-slide pattern adjustments allow you to add or subtract greater amounts than in-seam methods and to make adjustments exactly where they are needed to fit your figure. Cut-and-slide methods also have limits, usually to a maximum of 2" (5 cm). The specific amount is stated in the step-by-step instructions. Do not attempt to adjust beyond the stated maximums or you will distort the shape of the pattern pieces and cause the finished garment to hang off grain. It will also be more difficult to make matching or compensating adjustments on adjoining pattern sections.

If you need a greater adjustment than cut-and-slide methods allow, consider working with another pattern size. Or distribute the adjustment over additional pattern seams and details instead of concentrating the adjustment in one area.

Before making any other pattern adjustments, adjust the length of pattern pieces to fit your personal length proportions. If your figure is close to average, basic length adjustments may be the only changes needed.

Basic length adjustments are made in two areas: above and below the waist. Use your back waist length measurement to determine the correct pattern length above the waist. To determine the correct pattern length below the waist, measure from the waist in back to the proposed hemline. Make these length adjustments using the adjustment lines printed on the pattern pieces.

Adjustments for Special Figures

If your bust point does not match the placement on the pattern, it may be necessary to adjust the length above the bust or to adjust the darts so that they point to the fullest part of the bust. If you have a full bust, adjust the front pattern length above the waist, as on page 90.

For petite figure types, reduce the pattern length proportionately, by dividing the total adjustment into smaller amounts. Shorten the pattern at the chest and sleeve cap and at the hip adjustment line, in addition to using the printed adjustment lines above the bust and waist. Length may also be adjusted at the hemline.

Standard pattern-shortening adjustments for petite are to remove ¼" (6 mm) at chest, ¾" (2 cm) above waist, 1" (2.5 cm) at hip adjustment line, and 1" (2.5 cm) at hem to shorten pattern by 3" (7.5 cm). Standard adjustments for women's petite are similar, but the chest adjustment is omitted because armhole size does not need to be reduced. Customize standard length adjustments to suit your own proportions.

How to Determine Length Adjustments

1 **Above the waist.** Measure back waist length from prominent bone at back of neck to natural waistline. Compare with back waist length measurement for your pattern size given on pattern envelope to determine how much to adjust bodice front and back patterns.

2 **Below the waist.** Measure at center back from waist to proposed garment hemline, or use a garment of correct length to determine this measurement. Compare with finished garment length given on back of pattern envelope to determine how much to adjust skirt front and back patterns.

How to Shorten Patterns

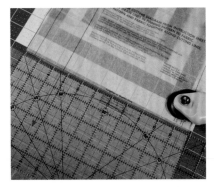

Cut on the printed adjustment lines. If skirt pattern provides no adjustment lines, cut off excess length at bottom edge.

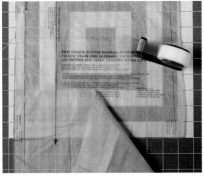

Overlap cut sections. Overlap equals total amount the pattern must be shortened. Tape sections together, keeping grainline straight.

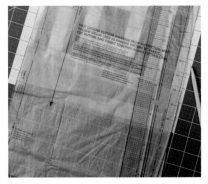

Blend stitching and cutting lines. Make matching adjustments on back and front pattern pieces.

How to Lengthen Patterns

How to Shorten Patterns for Petites

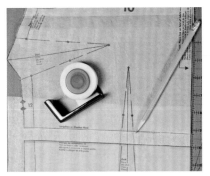

Cut on the printed adjustment lines. Spread cut sections by the amount needed. Place paper underneath to bridge gap. Tape sections in place, keeping grainline straight. Blend stitching and cutting lines. Make matching adjustments on back and front patterns.

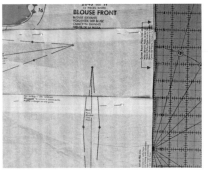

Pin-fit or measure pattern to determine how much length to remove across chest above armhole notches, at adjustment line above waist, at hipline, and at adjustment line below waist. Draw adjustment lines on front and back, midway between armhole and shoulder seam notches. Draw similar line across sleeve cap. Draw hip adjustment line 5" (12.5 cm) below waist on skirt front and back.

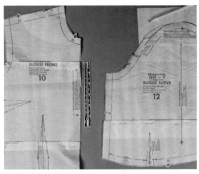

Cut pieces on each adjustment line. Lap to shorten or fold the pattern at the adjustment lines and pin. Shorten back and front patterns equally. Shorten sleeve cap by same amount removed from bodice at chest.

When fitted correctly, the bodice of a garment drapes smoothly over the bust without pulling, and the waistline of the garment lies at the natural waistline and is parallel to the floor. Adjust bodice back length according to back waist length measurement. Make similar adjustments on bodice front. In addition, front bodice seams or darts may need to be adjusted to fit your bust size and shape.

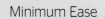

If your bust is rather fuller, you may need to add additional length and width to the bodice front pattern. Keep in mind that bodice front and backside seam lengths must match. If you have selected a pattern featuring loose or oversized fit, you can use some of the design ease in the pattern to fit a full bust and make a lesser adjustment.

For an average or small bust, pin-fitting will determine whether it is necessary to raise or lower darts. Repositioning the darts may be all that is needed to improve pattern fit.

If you make bust adjustments on the pattern beyond simply raising or lowering darts, you may want to test your adjustments by making a bodice fitting shell from the adjusted pattern. Many fitting solutions are easier to visualize in fabric, and this extra step can save time in the long run.

Ease, or extra room, is necessary for comfort at the bustline. Add the minimum amount of ease to your bust measurement, as shown in the chart below, before comparing with the pattern to judge whether pattern adjustments are needed.

The ease amounts given in the chart are general guidelines. At times, you may want to fit with more or less ease. For example, thick fabrics require more ease than lightweight ones. Knits require less ease than wovens, and very stretchy knits require no ease at all or even negative ease for form-fitting garments.

Minimum Ease

GARMENT	MINIMUM BUST EASE
Blouse, dress, jumpsuit	2½" to 3" (6.5 to 7.5 cm)
Unlined jacket	3" to 4" (7.5 to 10 cm)
Lined jacket	3½" to 4½" (9 to 11.5 cm)
Coat	3½" to 4½" (9 to 11.5 cm)

On pattern: Measure pattern front and back at bustline (red tape). Measure bodice front pattern from midpoint of shoulder, over bust point, to waist (blue tape). Note any differences to decide if pattern length must be adjusted above waist or bust (page 88). Measure side seam of bodice front pattern from underarm to waist. Note any differences to decide if pattern length must be adjusted.

On figure: Measure bust at fullest part, keeping tape measure parallel to floor (red tape). Add minimum ease to bust measurement. Measure the front waist length from midpoint of shoulder, over bust point, straight down to waist (blue tape). Measure the side length from 1" (2.5 cm) below underarm to waist (yellow tape).

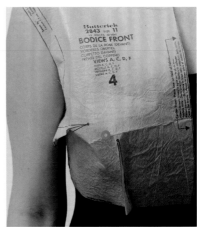

Pin-fit pattern to mark the bust point. Note if bust shaping or darts on the pattern should be raised or lowered for good fit. Compare pattern measurement with body measurement plus minimum ease to determine how much width to add for full bust or how much to remove for small bust.

How to Raise or Lower Darts

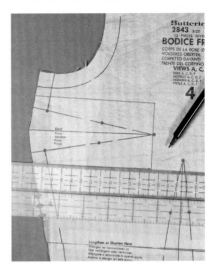

Draw horizontal lines on the pattern ½" (1.3 cm) above and below the underarm dart, at a right angle to grainline. Connect the lines with a vertical line through dart point. Cut out dart on marked lines. Mark new dart point on pattern.

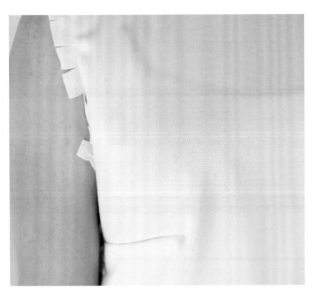

High Bust

Poor fit, when the bust is higher than average, shows in pulls across the fullest part of the bust and in wrinkles under the bust. Dart does not point to fullest part of curve. Underarm dart must be raised; dart from the waistline (if any) needs to be lengthened.

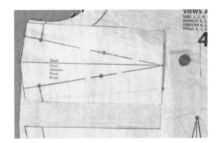

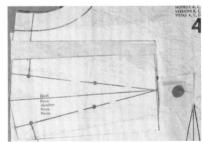

Raise or lower dart by the amount needed for a high or low bust. Position dart so that it points to the new bust point (dot) or fullest part of figure. Place paper under pattern. Tape cut edges in place, keeping edges even. Redraw side seam.

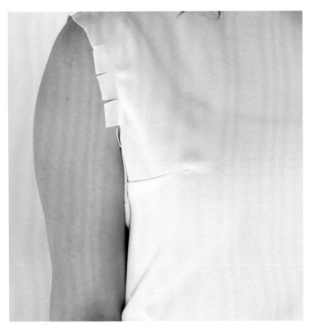

Low Bust

Poor fit, when the bust is lower than average, shows in pulls across the fullest part of the bust and in wrinkles above the bust. Darts are too high and need to be lowered and shortened.

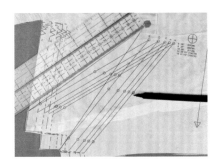

A diagonal dart requires a change in direction so that it points to bust point. Mark bust point on pattern. Mark new dart point on pattern. Redraw dart, connecting side seam ends of the dart and new dart point. On a multisize pattern, be sure to use the dart markings for the size you are sewing.

How to Fit a Full Bust without Darts

Accommodate full bust on less closely fitted pattern styles by making an adjustment that does not create a dart. This method can be used to increase the pattern a limited amount. Exceeding the maximum adjustment distorts the fabric grain at the lower edge of the garment. This adjustment is not appropriate on plaids, checks, or stripes.

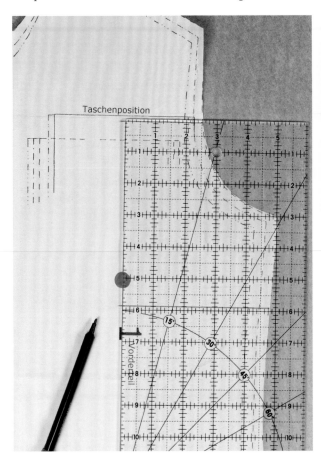

Mark bust point. Draw line across bodice front midway between armhole notch and shoulder seam, at right angle to grainline. Draw second line 2" to 4" (5 to 10 cm) below armhole or 1" below bust point, if lower, at right angle to grainline. Draw third line through bust point, parallel to grainline to connect first two lines; extend line to lower edge.

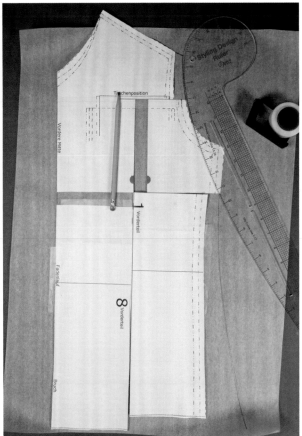

Cut pattern on adjustment lines. Slide armhole portion out a maximum of ¾" (2 cm) to add total of 1½" (3.8 cm) to bodice width. Slide center front waist section down no more than 2" (5 cm) to add bodice length. Tape to paper. Blend stitching and cutting lines at armhole and side seams. Use curved ruler to blend lower cutting line from the center front, tapering back to the original side seam.

Although a waistband or waistline should fit snugly, it must be slightly larger than your waist for good fit. For wearing comfort, a finished waistband should be from ½" to 1" (1.3 to 2.5 cm) larger than your actual measurement. In addition, allow ½" (1.3 cm) of ease from pattern waist measurement to waistband. Apply the same fitting guidelines to garments with faced waistlines. If garment has a waistline seam and no band, allow the total amount, 1"to 1½" (2.5 cm to 3.8 cm), for basic ease.

One indication of good waist fit is the way the side seams hang. They should hang straight, visually bisecting the body, without being pulled to the front or the back. Figure and posture variations may cause distortion of the side seams and require separate adjustment of skirt front and back. For example, a body with a full abdomen will need additional width and length in front, while a person with swaybacked posture may need to shorten the skirt pattern at center back. Adjustments for full abdomen and swayback should be determined and made at the same time as the waist width adjustment is made.

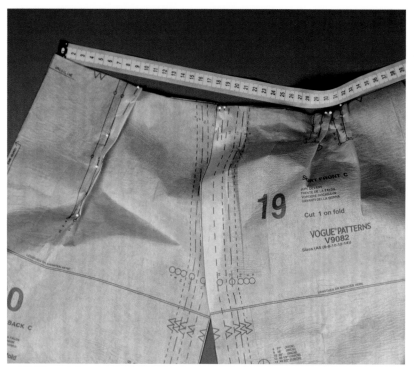

How to Determine Pattern Adjustments

1 **Measure your waist.** Compare with the waist measurement for your pattern size. Minimum wearing ease is included in the pattern, so adjust the pattern accordingly, enlarging or reducing as needed.

2 **Pin out waistline darts,** tucks, or pleats to measure pattern to compare with body measurements plus ease. Measure at the waistline seam; on a garment without a waistline seam, measure at the waistline mark at the narrowest part of the waistline area. Double the pattern measurement to compare with your waist measurement.

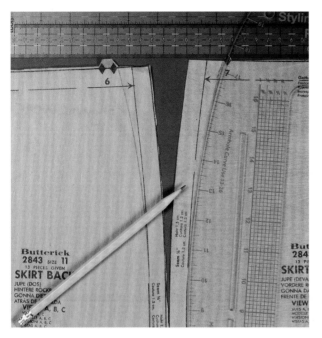

Small Waist

Poor fit has waistline or waistband that is too large, although garment fits at hips and bust. A dress with a waistline seam is baggy, with loose vertical folds at the waist. On a skirt or pants, waistband stands away from waist and tends to slide down.

MINOR ADJUSTMENT

Remove one-fourth the amount needed at each seam—maximum of ⅜" (1 cm) per seam from sizes smaller than 16; ⅝" (1.5 cm) from size 16 and larger. Blend stitching and cutting lines, using curved ruler. On dart-fitted skirts or pants, do not make darts deeper to reduce waistline unless additional garment contouring is needed to fit broad curvy hips or full round seat. Adjust width on adjoining pattern pieces.

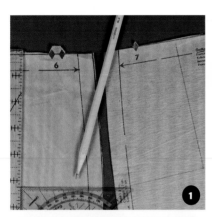

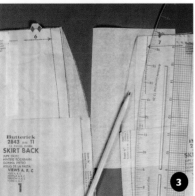

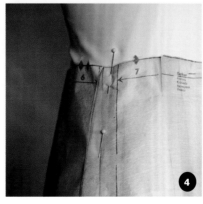

Major Adjustment

1 **Draw a line** 5" (12.5 cm) long, parallel to lengthwise grainline, between side seam and dart on the back piece. Draw a second line from bottom of first line to side seam, at right angle to grainline. Draw the same lines on the corresponding front piece.

2 **Cut out** pattern sections along lines on both pieces.

3 **Slide cut-out sections** in to remove up to 1" (2.5 cm) from waist seam front and back. Tape paper underneath. Blend stitching and cutting lines. Make matching adjustment on back, removing up to 2" (5 cm) from each seam for a total reduction of 4" (10 cm).

4 **Pin-fit pattern** to check position of waistline darts. It may be necessary to reshape or move the darts closer to center front and back for good fit. Make a corresponding width adjustment to adjoining waistband, facing, or bodice pattern.

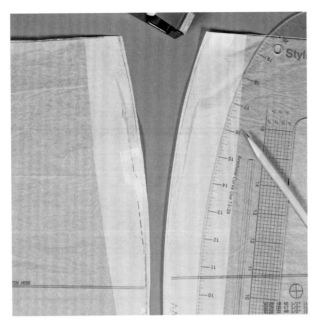

Large Waist

Poor fit is indicated by horizontal wrinkles near the waist, which cause the waistline of a dress to rise. A waistband on skirt or on pants creases from strain. Wrinkles fan out from waist or form horizontal folds below waistband.

MINOR ADJUSTMENT

Add one-fourth the amount needed at each seam, adding up to ⅜" (1 cm) per seam allowance for total of ¾" (2 cm) per seam. On dart-fitted skirts, each dart can be reduced up to ¼" (6 mm) to enlarge waistline. Blend stitching and cutting lines, using curved ruler. Make corresponding width adjustment to adjoining waistband, facing, or bodice patterns.

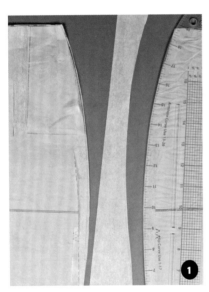
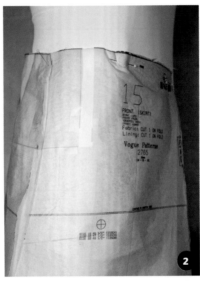

MAJOR ADJUSTMENT

1   **Draw adjustment lines and cut** pattern as in step 1 for small waist (page 95). Slide section out up to 1" (2.5 cm). Tape paper underneath. Blend stitching and cutting lines to waist, using curved ruler, and to hem, using straightedge. Make matching adjustment on back pattern, adding up to 2" (5 cm) per seam for total of 4" (10 cm).

2   **Pin-fit pattern** to check position of waistline darts. It may be necessary to reshape darts or move them closer to the side seams for a better fit. Make a corresponding width adjustment to adjoining waistband, facing, or bodice sections.

Prominent Abdomen

Poor fit is indicated by horizontal wrinkles across the front below the waistline. Diagonal wrinkles from abdomen to sides pull side seams forward. Waistline and hemline may ride up. Extra length and width are needed at center front.

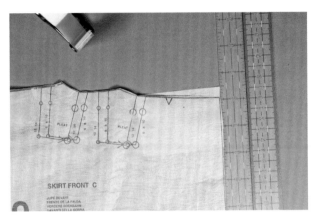

MINOR ADJUSTMENT

Raise waist stitching line on front skirt or pants pattern up to ⅜" (1 cm) at center front to add more length. Fold out darts, and blend stitching and cutting lines, using curved ruler. Add up to ½" (1.3 cm) at side seam of the front pattern piece. Remove same amount from back pattern piece to maintain the waist circumference. To further improve fit, convert front darts to gathers or unpressed pleats.

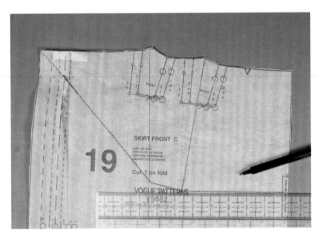

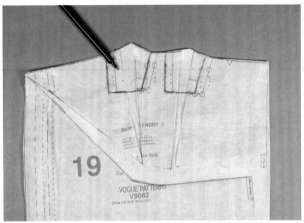

MAJOR ADJUSTMENT

Draw diagonal adjustment lines on pattern from intersection of side seam and waistline seam through dart points, extending at right angle to center front. Cut on line. Cut on dart foldline to, but not through, dart point.

Slide center section up by the amount needed and out half the amount needed, opening darts and diagonal slash. Extend center front line from new position to hemline. Darts can also be converted to gathers or unpressed pleats. Blend stitching and cutting lines at waistline.

Flat Abdomen

Poor fit is indicated by vertical wrinkles and excess fabric at center front. Hipbones may protrude. Darts are poorly located and are too deep for flat abdomen contour.

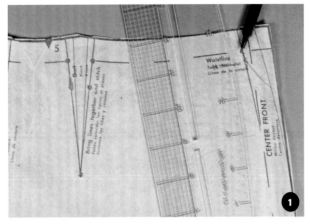

ADJUSTMENT

1 Redraw shallower darts by removing an equal amount on each side of dart foldline. To restore the original waistline measurement, remove the same amount from side seam, blending from a point on waistline seam to hipline with curved ruler.

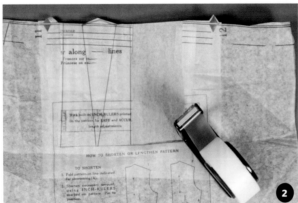

2 Move darts closer to side seam for prominent hipbones. Cut out dart as for raising or lowering bust dart (page 92), and slide it to correct position after pin-fitting pattern. Fold out dart, and blend waistline stitching and cutting lines using a curved ruler.

Swayback

Poor fit is caused by posture variation; area directly beneath waist in back does not fit smoothly, or skirt bags in seat area, indicating that garment is too long at center back. Diagonal wrinkles form, indicating that dart width or length is wrong for body shape. Pin out excess to determine amount to shorten at center back.

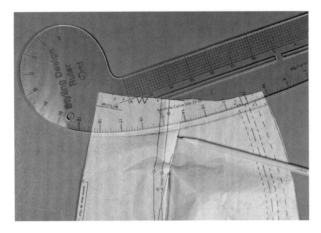

ADJUSTMENT

Adjust darts, if necessary, to accommodate protrusion of seat. If dart width is changed, make corresponding width adjustment at side seam to maintain waist size. Lower the waist stitching line on the back skirt pattern the amount needed. Fold darts toward center and blend stitching and cutting lines using a curved ruler.

When garments fit well at the hipline, they feel comfortable whether you are standing or sitting. They also look smooth, without strained wrinkles or excess fabric folds.

Before adjusting for width, make any basic lengthening or shortening adjustments below the waistline. Length adjustments may eliminate the need for adjusting pattern hip circumference. If you have one hip higher than the other, it may be necessary to make a copy of the pattern and adjust a separate pattern piece for each side of the body. If your hips are fuller or slimmer than the average, adjust the pattern to include the right amount of ease. For wearing comfort, there must be a minimum of 2" (5 cm) ease, or extra room, at the hipline of the garment for sizes smaller than 16. For size 16 or larger, there must be at least 2½" (6.5 cm) of ease. You may need more than minimum ease for good fit if you have full hips or are using a thick fabric. You may need less if you are working with a knit.

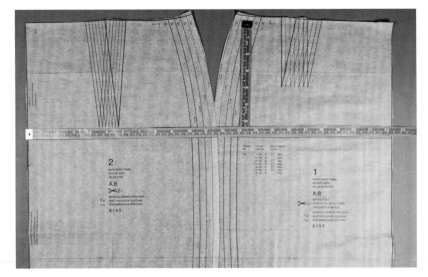

HOW TO DETERMINE PATTERN ADJUSTMENTS

On figure: Measure hips, as viewed from the side, where seat protrudes most, keeping tape measure (red) parallel to floor. Determine where hipline falls by measuring vertically (purple) at side seam from waist to fullest part of hips. Add 2" to 2½" (5 to 6.5 cm) minimum ease to hip measurement.

On pattern: Mark pattern side seam at point where fullest part of hipline falls. Lap the back and front pattern pieces at mark. Measure hipline from center front to center back at this position. Double this measurement to arrive at total finished circumference. Compare with hip measurement plus ease to determine if adjustment is needed.

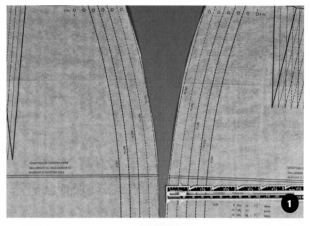

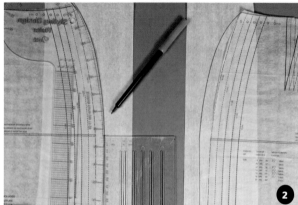

Full Hips

Poor fit causes horizontal wrinkles across hips. Skirt cups under seat in back. Skirt tends to ride up, because there is not enough width at hip level to fit full hips. Pattern needs enlarging at hipline.

MINOR ADJUSTMENT

1 **Mark hipline** at side seam of back and front patterns. Add one-fourth the amount needed at each side-seam, next to mark. Add maximum of ⅜" (1 cm) per seam allowance for total of ¾" (2 cm) per seam.

2 **Blend stitching and cutting lines** from hip to waist with curved ruler. Mark new stitching and cutting lines from hip to hem with straightedge.

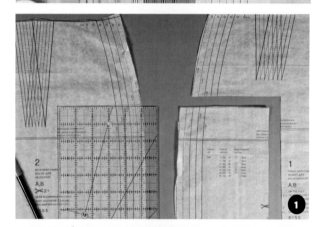

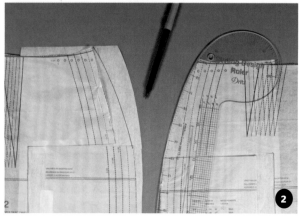

MAJOR ADJUSTMENT

1 **Draw a line** parallel to the hipline approximately 5" (12.5 cm) below the waistline on both front and back. Draw a second line parallel to length-wise grainline from end of first line to hem. Cut on lines.

2 **Slide sections** outward to add one-fourth the amount needed. Add maximum of 1" (2.5 cm) to sizes under 16 for total of 2" (5 cm) per seam and 1½" (3.8 cm) to sizes 16 and above for total of 3" (7.5 cm) per seam. Blend stitching and cutting lines from hip to waist with curved ruler. Mark the hip area to the hem with a straightedge.

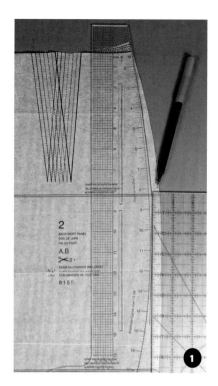

Small Hips

Poor fit causes excess fabric to drape in folds and look baggy. Skirt hipline is too broad for figure with slender hips. Pattern width needs reduction at hipline, and darts may have to be reduced. If darts are reduced, side waist seam must be decreased equal amount, as on page 95.

MINOR ADJUSTMENT

1   **Mark hipline** at side seam on back and front patterns. Remove one-fourth the amount needed at each side seam, next to mark. Remove up to ⅜" (1 cm) per seam allowance for total of ¾" (2 cm) per seam. Mark new stitching and cutting lines as in step 2 (opposite, top).

MAJOR ADJUSTMENT

Draw adjustment lines and cut as shown for major adjustment for full hips, step 1, opposite. Slide section inward to remove one-fourth of the extra width at the hipline. Blend stitching and cutting lines from waist to hip area with curved ruler. Mark hip area to hem with straightedge. Reduce dart size as needed.

Uneven Hips

Poor fit causes diagonal wrinkles on one side. Fabric is off grain in hip area. One hip may be fuller, slimmer, or higher than other hip. Make necessary width adjustments in darts and side seam.

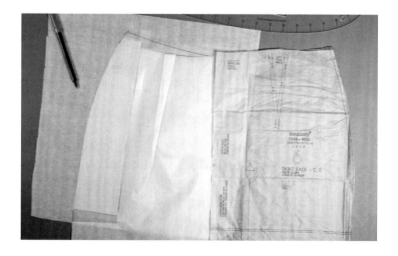

ADJUST FOR ONE HIGH HIP

Trace front and back skirt pattern pieces, flip and join at centers. Label right and left sides. Draw adjustment line on poor fit side parallel to lengthwise grainline, beginning midway between side seam and dart. Draw a second line at right angle from bottom of first line to side seam. Cut on adjustment lines.

Slide adjustment section upwards to add necessary length for fitting high hip. Tape paper underneath. Adjust skirt back and front to match. Fold darts or tucks as they will be pressed. Blend stitching and cutting lines at waist and side seams.

Layout, Cutting, and Marking

Once you have chosen the pattern and fabric and assembled the proper equipment, you're ready to start creating your garment. Before you cut, make sure the fabric is properly prepared and the pattern is correctly laid out.

Much of fabric preparation and layout has to do with the fabric grain. Grain is the direction in which the fabric warp threads run. Most of the time, the grain goes unnoticed on a garment. Until, that is, the garment begins to twist around the body or hang oddly. That is when one recognizes that the material is off grain.

Woven fabrics consist of lengthwise threads intersecting crosswise threads. When these threads cross one another at perfect right angles, the fabric is on grain. If the intersection of lengthwise and crosswise threads does not form a right angle, the fabric is off grain. Also, the material may be woven at right angles, however, the print may be slightly off: this fabric is also considered off grain. It is essential that your fabric be on grain before cutting. If fabric is cut off grain, the garment will never hang or fit correctly.

The direction of the lengthwise threads is called the lengthwise grain a. This grainline runs parallel to the selvage, a narrow, tightly woven border that runs along both lengthwise sides of the fabric. Because lengthwise threads are stronger and more stable than crosswise threads, most garments are cut so the lengthwise grain runs vertically. The crosswise threads form the crosswise grain b, which runs at right angles to the selvage. In most fabrics, it has a slight amount of give. Fabrics with border prints are often cut on the crosswise grain so the border will run horizontally across the garment.

Any diagonal line intersecting the lengthwise and crosswise grains is called a bias. Fabric cut on the bias has more stretch than fabric cut on the grainline. A true bias is formed when the diagonal line is at a 45-degree angle to any straight edge. Strips cut on the true bias are often used to finish curved edges such as necklines and armholes. Plaids and stripes can be cut on the bias for an interesting effect. Garments cut on the true bias usually drape softly.

To determine if a woven fabric is on grain, pull one weft yarn (a thread that is perpendicular to the selvedge) from the material and remove it. Using a T-square, check to see if where the yarn was removed is at right angles to both selvedges. If not, your material is off grain. If the material is not too far off grain, the fabric may be pressed or blocked back on grain. To press the material back to grain, fold your material in half lengthwise, fabric right sides together, and pin the selvedges together along the correct grain. Vigorously steam iron in the direction you want the material to pop. If the material cannot be brought on grain with an iron, you may try blocking, which is pulling and stretching the material from opposite corners along the bias. For fabrics that were printed or milled considerably off grain, it may be best to use that material as an accent fabric and not as your main garment or décor fabric. Woven fabrics with some stretch content (Lycra/Elastane) are very difficult to block it they are off grain.

Knit fabrics are formed by interlocking loops of yarn that form horizontal courses and vertical ribs.

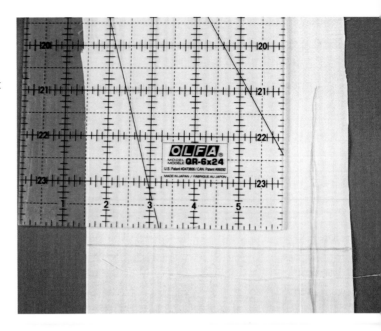

The ribs run parallel to the lengthwise sides of the fabric. Their direction can be compared to the lengthwise grain of woven fabrics. The courses are comparable to the woven crosswise grain. Knits have no bias and, generally, no selvage. If a knit has gone through a printing process, there may be tentering holes along lengthwise edges. These perforated edges that look like a selvege, but do not represent true lengthwise grain. Other knits are made in a tubular shape; these can be cut open along a lengthwise rib if a single thickness is needed for layout. Because of their circular manufacture, tubular knits can "yaw" over time and twist around the wearer. Knits have the most stretch in the crosswise direction, and are cut with the crosswise grain running horizontally around the body for maximum comfort.

Before laying out the pattern, take the necessary steps to prepare the fabric for cutting. The label on the bolt tells if the fabric should be washed or dry cleaned and how much, if any, the fabric will shrink. If the fabric has not been preshrunk by the manufacturer, or if the label says it will shrink more than 1 percent, it is best to preshrink the fabric before cutting. It is often advisable to preshrink knits, since this removes the sizing that sometimes causes skipped stitches. Zippers and trims may also need preshrinking. Fabrics that must be dry cleaned can be preshrunk by steam pressing or by a professional dry cleaner. This is especially important if you plan to use fusible interfacing, which requires more steam than normal pressing and may cause shrinkage. To make sure the fabric is on grain, begin by straightening the crosswise ends of your fabric. This may be done by pulling a crosswise thread or cutting along a woven design or crosswise rib of a knit. Next, fold the fabric

lengthwise, matching selvages and crosswise ends. If the fabric bubbles, it is off grain. Fabric that is slightly off grain can be straightened by steam pressing. Pin along selvages and both ends, matching the edges. Press from the selvages to the fold. Fabric that is very off grain must be straightened by pulling fabric in the opposite direction from the way the ends slant. Permanent-finish fabrics cannot be straightened.

How to Preshrink Fabric

Preshrink washable fabric by laundering and drying it in the same manner you will use for the finished garment.

Steam press to preshrink dry-clean fabrics. Steam evenly, moving iron horizontally or vertically (not diagonally) across the grain. After steaming, let fabric dry on smooth, flat surface for four to six hours or until thoroughly dry.

How to Straighten Crosswise Ends of Fabric

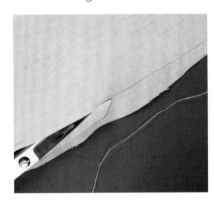

Pull threads to straighten woven fabric. Clip one selvage and gently pull one or two crosswise threads. Push fabric along threads with your other hand until you reach opposite selvage. Cut fabric along pulled thread.

Cut on a line to straighten a stripe, plaid, check, or other woven design. Simply cut along a prominent crosswise line. Do not use this method for printed designs, because they may be printed off grain.

Cut on a course (a crosswise rib) to straighten ends of a knit. It may be easier to follow along the course if you first baste mark it with contrasting thread or use a marking pencil or chalk.

Prepare a large work area and assemble all the pattern pieces for your view and press them with a warm, dry iron to remove folds and wrinkles. Find the layout for the view, fabric width, and pattern size you are using. When working with a napped or other directional fabric choose a "with-nap" layout.

Fold the fabric as indicated on the layout or as best suits your fabric width. Cottons and linens are usually folded right side out on the bolt; wools, wrong side out. The right side of the fabric may appear shinier or flatter or have a more pronounced weave. Selvages look more finished on the right side. If you cannot tell which is the right side, simply pick the side you like best and consistently use that as the right side. A slight difference in shading that is not apparent as you cut may be noticeable in the finished garment if two different sides are used.

The layout diagram indicates the placement of the selvages and fold. Most garments are cut with the fabric folded along the lengthwise grain. If the fabric is to be cut folded on the crosswise grain, the fold is labeled "crosswise fold" on the layout. The crosswise fold should not be used on napped or other directional fabrics.

Place the pattern pieces on the fabric as indicated in the layout. The symbols and markings used in layout diagrams are standardized for all major pattern companies. A white pattern piece indicates that this piece is to be cut with the printing facing up. A shaded piece should be cut with the printing facing down.

When a pattern piece is shown half white and half shaded, it should be cut from folded fabric. Cut the other pieces first and refold the fabric to cut this piece. A pattern piece shown extending beyond the fold is cut from a single layer rather than the usual double layer of fabric. After cutting the other pieces, open the fabric right side up and position this piece by aligning the grainline arrow with the straight grain of the fabric.

How to Pin Pattern Pieces in Place

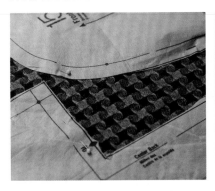

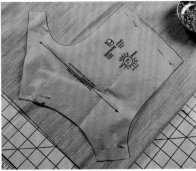

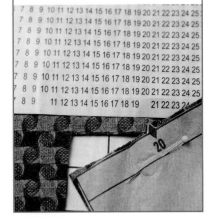

Pin in the seam allowance, placing pins parallel to the cutting line. Pin corners of pattern diagonally. Space pins about 3" (7.5 cm) apart, closer together on curves or on slippery fabrics.

Place grainline arrow of straight-grain pattern pieces parallel to the selvage of woven fabrics and parallel to a rib for knits. Measure from each end of the arrow to the selvage or rib, shifting the pattern until the distances are equal. Pin both ends of the grainline so pattern will not shift. Continue pinning as directed in previous caption.

TIP

For sewing patterns with a lot of pieces and many notches to match up, it can be helpful to transfer the numbers to the fabric using small numbered stickers

Select simple styles for plaids and stripes. Complicated fashions can detract from or distort the fabric design. Avoid diagonal bustline darts, long horizontal darts, and patterns designated "not suitable for plaids and stripes."

Always buy extra yardage to allow for matching the design at the seams. The extra amount needed depends on the size of the repeat (the four-sided area in which the pattern and color of the design are complete) and the number and lengths of major pattern pieces. Usually an extra ¼ to ½ yd. (0.25 to 0.5 m) is sufficient.

It is easier to work with even plaids and balanced stripes than uneven plaids and unbalanced stripes. Even plaids have the same arrangement of colors and stripes in both lengthwise and crosswise directions. The area of repeat is perfectly square. In uneven plaids, the color and stripes form a different arrangement in the lengthwise or crosswise direction, or both. Balanced stripes repeat in the same order in both directions; unbalanced stripes do not. To avoid having to match two layers of yardage it is recommended that each pattern piece be layed out in a single layer.

Before cutting and layout, decide the placement of plaid design lines within the garment and where they will fall on the body. Avoid placing a dominant horizontal line or block of lines at the bustline and waistline if possible. Experiment with the fabric draped from shoulder to hem. Some plaid garments look more balanced when the hemline falls at the bottom of a dominant crosswise line. If you wish to draw the eye away from the hemline, place the hemline between two dominant lines. When laying out plaids and stripes, match stitching lines, not cutting lines.

To match at the seams, lay out each piece in a single layer beginning with garment front. Place dominant vertical lines at the center front and center back, or position the pattern so the center front is halfway between two dominant vertical lines. Position the sleeve in the same way, using the shoulder dot as the guide for centering the sleeve on or between the dominant vertical lines.

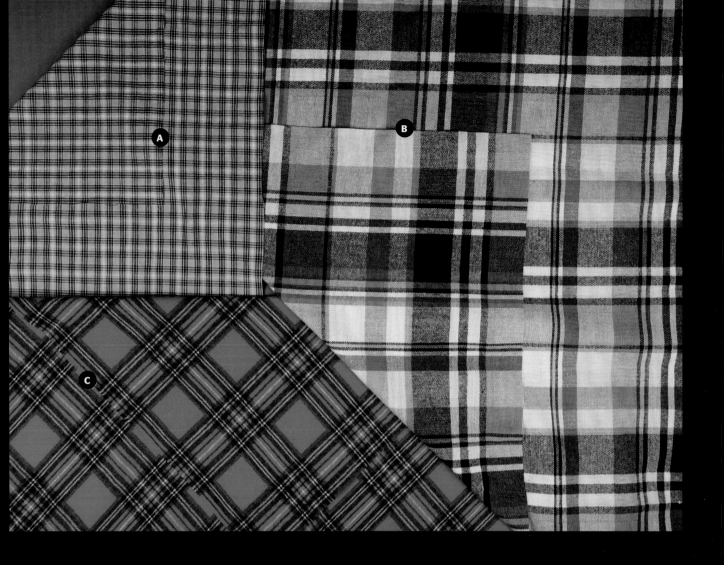

Although it is not always possible to match the design at every seam, try to match: crosswise bars at vertical seams such as center front and back, and side seams; set-in sleeves to the bodice front at armhole notches; lengthwise stripes where possible; and pockets, flaps, and other details to the area of the garment they will cover. The plaid may not match at the shoulder seams or the back notch in the armhole of a set-in sleeve.

Identifying even and uneven plaids.

A **An even plaid** has lengthwise and crosswise color bars that match when the repeat is folded diagonally through the center.

B **An uneven plaid** may have differing color bars in one or more directions.

C **An uneven plaid** may have matching color bars but not form a mirror image when folded diagonally because the repeat is not square. This type of uneven plaid is the most difficult to identify.

How to Lay Out Uneven Plaids

Lay out pattern on single layer of fabric, flipping pattern pieces over to cut right and left halves. Place most-dominant color bar at center front and center back, or position the pattern so the center front is halfway between two dominant vertical lines. Place pattern pieces in only one direction using with-nap layout. Plaid will repeat around the garment instead of forming a mirror image on each side of the center front and center back seams.

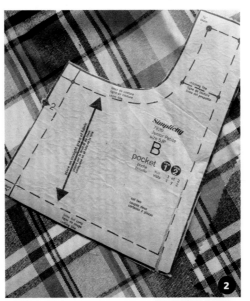
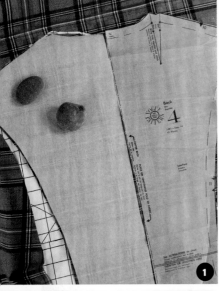

Tips for Laying Out Plaid Fabrics

1 **Cut single layers,** beginning with front pattern piece, for all pieces. For pieces cut "on fold," create a complete pattern piece by taping or placing tissue paper. Use dominant part of design for center front and center back. Match notches at side seams of front and back. Center sleeve at same dominant part of design as center front. The design should match at the notches of the sleeve front and armhole of garment front; notches at back may not match.

2 **Cut on true bias** to avoid time-consuming matching for pockets, cuffs, yokes, and separate front bands. Center a dominant design block in each pattern piece.

3 **Use cut pieces as guides** for exactly matching plaids on their details. In 3A, the jacket front with a patch pocket is aligned with the fabric from which the pocket will come, allowing its pocket guidelines to simplify positioning the pocket pattern, 3B.

4 **Use cut pieces as patterns** for mirror-image pieces cut individually. Once the first mirror-image piece is cut, flip and lay this piece on your fabric, matching plaid lines and use this piece as a pattern to cut the second piece.

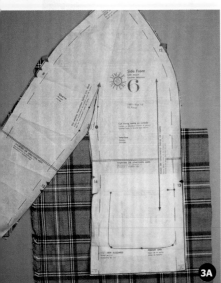
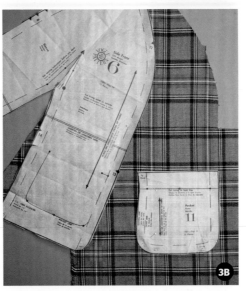
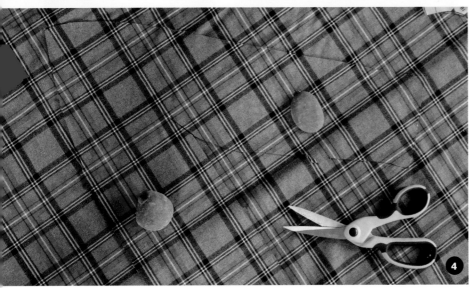

Directional fabrics include napped fabrics such as corduroy, velveteen, and flannel; plush fabrics such as fake fur; shiny fabrics such as taffeta and satin; and print fabrics with one-way designs. Other fabrics that can be directional include some twill weave fabrics such as denim and gabardine, and knits such as jersey, single, or double knits that appear lighter or darker depending on the direction of the grain.

To prevent the garment from having a two-toned look or having its design running in two different directions, all pattern pieces must be laid out on napped fabrics with their tops facing the same direction. Napped fabrics can be cut with the nap running either up or down. Nap running up gives a darker, richer look. Nap running down looks lighter and usually wears better. Plush and fur fabrics look best with the nap running down. Shiny fabrics can be cut in whichever direction you prefer. One-way designs should be cut so that the design will be right side up when the garment is completed.

How to Lay Out Directional Fabrics

Choose the direction your fabric will run, then lay out the pattern pieces according to the with-nap

> **TIP**
>
> Very often when machine stitching, the bottom fabric layer will be pulled by the feed dogs with each stitch just the tiniest fraction of an inch more than the top fabric. By the time a seam line is stitched, those tiny fractions add up and stripes, plaids, and matched fabric patterns become misaligned. A walking or even feed foot has an extra set of feeder dogs just for the top fabric and can be an invaluable tool for keeping stripes, plaids, and matched patterns aligned perfectly during sewing.

layout on the pattern direction sheet. To ensure proper placement, mark each pattern piece with an arrow pointing to the top of the piece. Sometimes, the pattern calls for a crosswise fold. In this case, fold the fabric as the layout indicates, then cut along the foldline. Turn the top layer of fabric around so the nap runs in the same direction as the nap of the lower layer of fabric, and cut both layers at the same time.

Cutting Tips

Arrange your cutting table so you can move around and reach the pattern from all angles. If your cutting surface is not this accessible, cut groups of pattern pieces apart from the rest of the fabric so you can turn these smaller pieces around.

Accuracy is important, since a mistake in cutting cannot always be corrected. Before cutting, double-check placement of pattern pieces and alterations. Before cutting plaids, one-way designs or directional fabrics, make sure the fabric is folded and laid out correctly. Basting tape (page 38) or temporary spray

adhesive may be helpful to keep fabric from shifting. Heavy or bulky fabric can be cut more accurately one layer at a time. Slippery fabric is easier to cut if you cover the table with a sheet, flannel, a blanket, paper, or other nonslip material.

Choose sharp, plain or serrated blade, bent-handled shears, 7" or 8" (18 or 20.5 cm) in length. Take long, firm strokes, cutting directly on the cutting line. Use shorter strokes for curved areas. Keep one hand on the pattern near the cutting line to prevent the pattern from shifting and to provide better control.

The rotary cutter (page 34) is especially useful for cutting leather, slippery fabrics, or several layers of fabric. Some rotary cutters are especially designed to be used by right- or left-handed sewists. A rotary cutter is used with a vinyl self-healing cutting mat. Use a smaller rotary cutter for tight curves, slashes, and notches.

Notches can be cut outward from the notch markings into the body of the fabric, or with short snips into the seam allowance. Be careful not to snip beyond the seamline. Use snips to mark the foldlines and stitching lines of darts and pleats, and the center front and center back lines at the top and bottom. Mark the top of the sleeve cap above the large dot on the pattern with a snip. On bulky or loosely woven fabric where snips cannot be easily seen, cut pattern notches out into the margin. Cut double or triple notches as one unit, not separately.

After you finish cutting, save scraps to test stitching or pressing techniques, make trial buttonholes, or cover buttons. Arrange all the pieces in their approximate finished sequence, or drape and pin to a dress form. For accurate marking and easy identification, leave each pattern piece pinned in place until you are ready to sew that piece. Often, the pattern piece contains a bit of information that is required at the sewing stage.

Your pattern may call for bias strips of fabric to enclose raw edges such as necklines or armholes. Or you may chose to enclose edges in bias tape as a design element or to finish raw edges in bias tape for professional-looking Hong Kong seams. Ideally, bias strips are cut from a piece of fabric long enough to fit the area to be enclosed. Bias strips may also be pieced together to form a strip of the correct length.

How to Cut and Join Bias Strips

Fold woven fabric diagonally so that a straight edge on the crosswise grain is parallel to the selvage or lengthwise grain. The 45-degree foldline is the true bias. Cut fabric along the foldline to mark the first bias line.

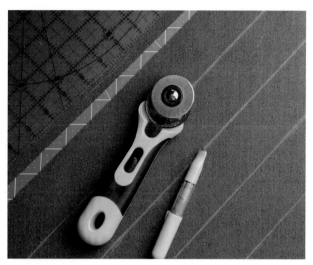

Mark successive bias lines with a marking pencil or chalk and yardstick or see-through ruler. Cut along marked lines. When a bound finish is called for in a pattern, the pattern will specify the length and width of bias strips needed. If sewing a very heavy fabric, a wide wale corduroy, for example, you will need to cut wider strips.

Join bias strips if piecing is necessary. With right sides together, pin strips together with shorter edges aligned. Allow ¼" points to peek from each side. Strips will form a V. Stitch a ¼" (6 mm) seam. Press seam open. Trim points of seams even with edge of bias strip.

Once your layout is cut, you are not quite ready to sew the pieces together. Transferring the pertinent marks from the pattern piece to your garment piece is like having roadsigns along your journey: Turn here, stop here, do not enter, and so on.

In marking, pattern symbols are transferred to the fabric after cutting and before the pattern is removed. These markings are your reference points to help you through all stages of garment construction. Pattern symbols that should be marked include construction symbols and position marks for placement of details.

Marking is usually done on the wrong side of the fabric. Some symbols, such as pocket placement and buttonholes, should be transferred from the wrong side to the right side of the fabric (not marked on the right side).

There are several ways to transfer markings, each suitable for different fabrics. Choose whichever gives you the fastest, most accurate marking.

Pins are a quick way to transfer markings. They should not be used on fine fabrics or those on which pin marks would be permanent, such as silk or synthetic leathers. Use pin marking only when you plan to sew immediately, since pins may fall out of loose weaves or knits.

Tailor's chalk or dressmaker's pencil, used with pins, are suitable for most fabrics.

Tracing wheel and dressmaker's tracing paper work best on plain, flat-surfaced fabrics. The wheel may damage some fabrics, so test on a scrap first. It is best to use this technique on a hard, smooth, flat surface. Place a piece of card stock under the fabric to protect wood surfaces. On most fabrics, both lay-ers can be marked at once. Some tracing paper has a chalky marking substance and others have a more waxy consistency. The chalky kind of dressmakers' tracing paper marks more easily on most fabrics, however, the marks have tendency to brush out with handling. The waxy kind may not transfer well to some kinds of fabrics, but when it does, remains reliably visible throughout construction. Gener-ally, you should use the color of paper, close to your fabric color while still being visible (this book may use highly contrasting tracing paper to show detail). Waxy transfer lines sometimes show up better under fluorescent light.

Liquid textile markers are felt-tip pens designed es-pecially for fabric. The marker transfers through the pattern tissue onto the fabric. The ink rinses out with water or disappears on its own, so liquid markers can be used on the right side of most fabrics.

Machine basting transfers markings from the wrong side of the fabric to the right side. It can also be used to mark intricate matching points or pivot points. After marking on the wrong side, Machine stitch through the marking. Use a long stitch length or speed-basting stitch, with contrasting color thread in the bobbin. The bobbin thread marks the right side. To mark a pivot point, stitch on the seamline with regular-length stitching and matching thread. Leave the stitching in place as a reinforcement.

Snips or clips can be used on most fabrics except loosely woven tweeds and bulky wools. With the point of scissors, snip about ⅛" to ¼" (3 to 6 mm) into the seam allowance.

Pressing can be used to mark foldlines, tucks, or pleats. It is a suitable method for any fabric that holds a crease.

How to Mark with Chalk, Pencil, or Liquid Marker

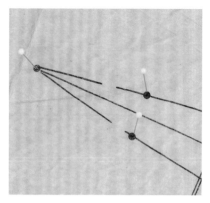

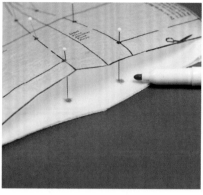

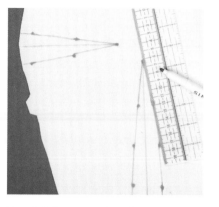

Insert pins straight down through pattern and both layers of fabric at marking symbols.

Remove pattern carefully by pulling over pinheads. Mark top layer with chalk, pencil, or marker at pinpoints on wrong side.

Turn fabric over and mark other layer at pinpoints. Remove pins and separate layers.

How to Mark with Basting or Pressing

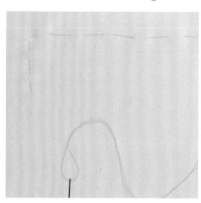

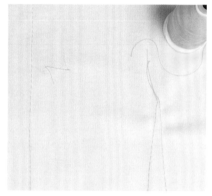

Hand baste with long and short stitches to mark one layer of fabric. Stitch through pattern and fabric along a solid line, using short stitches on the tissue side and long stitches through fabric. Carefully pull pattern tissue away.

Machine baste to transfer pencil, chalk, or tracing paper markings from the wrong side to the right side. Use contrasting thread in the bobbin, longest stitch on machine. Do not use machine basting on fabrics that mar. Do not press over machine basting.

Press to mark foldlines, tucks, and pleats. Pin pattern to a single layer of fabric. Fold pattern and fabric along marking line. Press along the fold with a dry iron.

How to Mark with Tracing Wheel and Tracing Paper

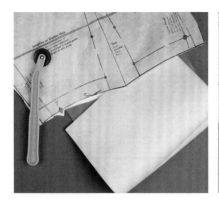

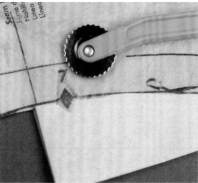

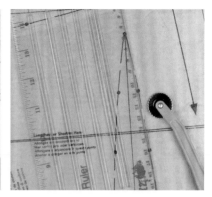

Place tracing paper under pattern with carbon sides facing the wrong side of each fabric layer.

Mark notches and other large symbols with short lines perpendicular to the stitching line or an X. Use short lines to mark the ends of darts or pleats.

Use a ruler when rolling tracing wheel over lines to be marked, including center foldlines of darts, to help draw straight lines.

Timesaving Marking Techniques

Snips can be used to mark notches, ends of darts, foldlines, or center front and back locations. Make tiny snips, 1/8" (3 mm) deep, into seam allowance. Snip through pattern and both fabric layers with point of scissors.

Pins can mark darts, dots, or foldlines without the help of marking pencil. Insert pins through pattern and fabric. Pull pattern carefully over pinheads. Mark bottom layer with second set of pins. Secure first set of pins to mark top layer.

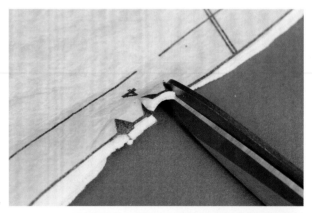

Sewing Techniques

Seams

A seam is the basic element in all garment construction. It is created by stitching two pieces of fabric together, usually ⅝" (1.5 cm) from the cut edge. Perfect seams are the most obvious sign of a well-made garment. Puckered, crooked, or uneven seams spoil the fit and the look.

In addition to holding a garment together, seams can be used as a design element. Seams placed in unusual locations or topstitched with contrasting thread add interest to a garment. Most plain seams require a seam finish to prevent raveling. A seam finish is a way of treating or enclosing the raw edges of seam allowances so they are more durable and do not ravel.

Variations of the plain seam include bound, encased, topstitched, and eased seams. Some, such as the flat-fell seam, add strength or shape. Others, such as French or bound seams, improve the appearance of the garment or make it longer wearing.

At the machine, position the bulk of the fabric to the left of the machine needle, with cut edges to the right. Support and guide fabric gently with both hands as you stitch.

Use guidelines etched on the throat plate of the machine to help you sew straight seams. For extra help, use a seam guide or strip of masking tape placed the desired distance from the needle. Use the thread cutter often located at the back of the presser bar assembly or at the side of the machine to cut threads after stitching or use a thread clipper to cut threads.

Plain Seams

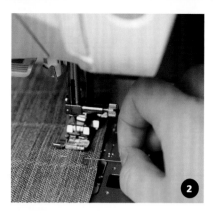

1 **Pin seam, right sides of fabric together,** at regular intervals, matching notches and other markings precisely. Place pins at right angles to seamline, usually ⅝" (1.5 cm) from edge, with points just beyond seamline and heads toward cut edge for easy removal.

2 **Secure stitching with backstitching.** Then stitch forward on seamline, removing pins as you come to them. Backstitch ½" (1.3 cm) at end to secure the stitching. Trim threads.

3 **Press over stitching line on wrong side** to press seam flat. This blends stitches into fabric. Then press seam open. Use your fingers or the blunt end of a point turner to open seams as you press. If seam is curved, such as hip area of skirt or pants, press over curved area of a tailor's ham.

Curved Seams

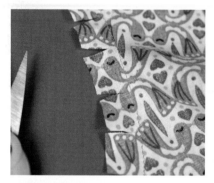

Stitch a line of reinforcement just inside the seamline of inner curve of center panel. Clip into seam allowance all the way to the stitching line at intervals along the curve.

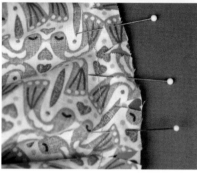

Pin inner and outer curves, right sides together with clipped edge on top, spreading clipped inner curve to match all markings and fit outer curve.

Stitch on seamline with clipped seam on top, using shorter stitch than usual for the fabric and being careful to keep the lower layer of fabric smooth.

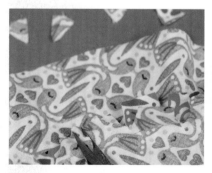

Cut out wedge-shaped notches in the seam allowance of outer curve by making small folds in seam allowance and cutting at slight angle. Be careful not to cut into stitching line.

Press seam flat to embed and smooth the stitches. Turn over and press on the other side. Press seam open over curve of tailor's ham, using tip of iron only. Do not press into body of garment. If not pressed to contour, seamlines become distorted and look pulled out of shape.

Encased seams differ from bound seams in that no additional fabric or binding is used. The cut edges of seam allowances are enclosed within the seam itself. Encased seams are best suited to lightweight fabrics, since the additional bulk created is not a problem. These seams are especially appropriate for sheer fabrics, because no raw or contrasting edges show through. Use a straight-stitch foot and needle plate (page 18) to keep sheer fabric from being pulled into the feed.

Use encased seams for blouses, unlined jackets, lingerie, or sheer curtains. They are also an excellent choice for children's clothes, because they stand up to rugged wear and repeated laundering.

Self-bound and flat-fell seams begins with a plain seam. One seam allowance is then folded over the other and stitched again. These methods produce a finished look from both sides, making them good for reversible clothing sewn from a single fabric, reversible tablecloths and room-dividing curtains.

Mock flat-fell seams look like a regular flat fell seam from the garment right side, but have an exposed edge on the garment wrong side. A mock flat-fell seam is a good choice for thicker fabrics.

French seams look like a plain seam on the right side and a narrow tuck on the wrong side. A French seam begins by stitching the wrong sides of the fabric together. This seam is difficult to sew in curved areas, so is best used on straight seams.

Mock French seams begin with a plain seam. Seam allowances are trimmed, folded to the inside and stitched along the folds. The self-bound and mock French seams can be used in curved or straight areas.

How to Sew a Self-Bound Seam

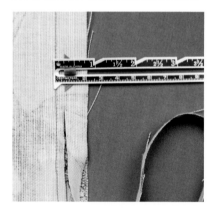

Trim one seam allowance to ⅛" (3 mm) after stitching a plain seam (contrasting thread used to show detail). Do not press open.

Fold the untrimmed seam allowance over the trimmed seam allowance, enclosing the narrow trimmed edge. Bring the raw edge of the untrimmed seam allowance to the seamline, press flat to that side, and pin.

Stitch on the folded edge, as close as possible to first line of stitching. Press seam to one side.

How to Sew a French Seam

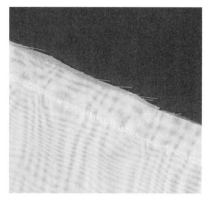

Pin wrong sides of fabric together.
Stitch ⅜" (1 cm) from edges on right side
of fabric (contrasting thread used to
show detail).

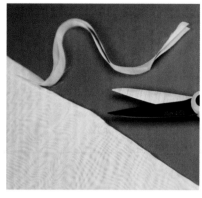

Trim seam allowance to ⅛" (3 mm).

Fold right sides together, with stitching line on fold. Press flat.

Stitch ¼" (6 mm) from fold. This step
encases cut edges.

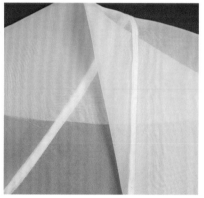

Check right side to be sure no raveled
threads are showing. Press seam to
one side.

How to Sew a Mock French Seam

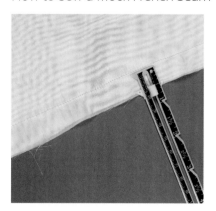

Stitch a plain seam, fabric right sides together (contrasting pink thread used to
show detail). Trim both seam allowances
to ½" (1.3 cm). Press open.

Press ¼" (6 mm) on each seam allowance toward inside of seam, so cut
edges meet at stitching line.

Stitch pressed edges together, stitching as close to folds as possible. Press
seam to one side.

How to Sew a Mock Flat-fell Seam

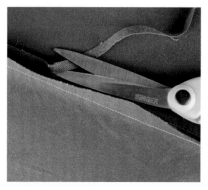

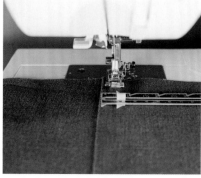

Stitch a plain seam. Trim lower seam allowance to ¼" (6 mm). Press seam allowances to one side.

Topstitch on right side of garment, ¼" to ½" (6 mm to 1.3 cm) from the seamline. Edgestitch close to the seamline.

Finished seam looks like the flat-fell seam on the right side but has one exposed seam allowance on wrong side.

How to Sew a Flat-Fell Seam

Pin fabric wrong sides together at seamline. Stitch, taking the usual ⅝" (1.5 cm) seam allowance. Press seam allowances open. Trim one seam allowance to ⅛" (3 mm).

Turn under ¼" (6 mm) on the wider seam allowance and pin folded seam allowance to garment, concealing trimmed lower edge. Press.

Edgestitch on fold, removing pins as you come to them. Finished seam is a reversible flat seam with two visible rows of stitching on one side.

Stretch Seams

A serger stitch is considered the preferred way to sew stretch fabrics, but most conventional machines offer a variety of very good stretch-stitch options. Stretch knit fabrics include jersey, stretch terry, stretch velour, high-performance activewear knits, as well as many other knits. Stretch woven fabrics include a percentage of Lycra/elastan with their cotton content. Examples include stretch denim, corduroy, and poplin. Unless the item is very loose fitting, sewing these fabrics will require stretch stitches, so the seams do not pop open with

movement. In addition to classic zigzag, most sewing machines offer a number of different stitches, which will give with a stretch fabric.

Test the stitch on a scrap of your stretch fabric to determine whether it is appropriate for the fabric's weight and elasticity. Since many of the special stretch stitches comprise complex combinations of tiny straight stitches and zigzag stitches, they are cumbersome and time consuming to remove: double-check your garment before stitching.

1. **Straight and zigzag** seam combines a straight seam with the stretchiness of zigzag. This is a suitable finish for knits that tend to curl along the raw edges.

2. **Three-step zigzag** stitch is a great all-rounder for sewing stretch fabrics. A narrow three-step zigzag works well to close seams, while a wider one is a functional and attractive topstitching option. The three-step zigzag also works especially well for adding elasticized edges to activewear.

3. **Zigzag** is the default stitch or sewing knits on a conventional machine. Vary the stitch width according to the elasticity of your fabric. Use zigzag for any overedge stitching. Compared to many other stretch stitches, zigzag stitches are easy to remove.

4. **Slant overedge** stitch is formed by a forward/backward/sideways motion on reverse-action machines. Most newer electronic machines will have stitch options similar to this, which make strong, stretchy seams. This family of stitches is a good choice for seams that are subject to a lot of stress, such as armholes.

5. **Twin-needle straight** stitch forms two even rows of straight stitches on the garment right side. Because the bobbin thread must hook around two threads at once, the underside automatically forms a zigzag and that makes twin and triplet needles appropriate for stretch applications.

Taped seams are used in areas where you do not want your fabric to stretch, such as shoulder seams.

How to Sew a Taped Seam

1 **Pin twill tape,** thin polyester ribbon, or strips of nonstretch tricot interfacing over garment pieces pinned right sides together. Position seam tape, so it laps ⅜" (1 cm) into the seam allowance.

2 **Stitch,** using double stitched, straight and zigzag, overedge, or narrow zigzag seam. Press seam open or to one side, depending on selected seam.

3 **Trim seam allowance** close to stitching, taking care not to cut into seam binding.

Seam Finishes

A seam finish elevates your work to couture sewing and improves the appearance and function of any garment. Seams are finished to prevent woven fabrics from raveling and knit seams from curling. Some seam finishes also strengthen seams and act as a second line of defense for the primary seam, preventing tears.

It's a good sewing habit to finish a seam immediately after it is sewn, before it is crossed by another seam. Select a finish for your seams that does not add bulk or show an obvious imprint on the right side of the garment when pressed. Try several different seam finishes on fabric scraps and see which works best.

The seam finishes shown here all begin with a plain seam. They can also be used as edge finishes for facings and hems.

A **Selvage** finish requires no extra stitching. Good for long, straight seams of woven fabrics, it requires adjusting the pattern layout so that the seam is cut on the selvage.

B **Stitched and pinked** seam finish is suitable for firmly woven fabrics. It is a quick and easy finish that prevents raveling and curling.

C **Turned and stitched** finish (also called clean-finished) is suitable for light- to medium-weight woven fabrics. Short of hand stitching, this method is the most time consuming, but it produces the most elegant results.

D **Zigzag** seam finishes prevent raveling and are good for knits, because they have more give than straight-stitched finishes.

BASIC SEAM FINISHES

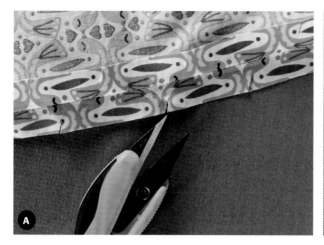

Selvage finish. Adjust pattern layout so that edges of a straight seam are cut on selvage. To prevent uneven shrinking and puckering, clip diagonally into both selvages at 3" to 4" (7.5 to 10 cm) intervals after seam is stitched.

Stitched and pinked finish. Stitch ¼" (6 mm) from edge of each seam allowance. Press seam open. Trim close to stitching with pinking or scalloping shears.

TURNED AND STITCHED FINISH

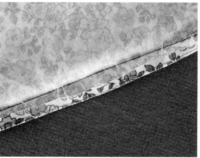

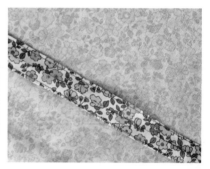

Stitch ⅛" to ¼" (3 to 6 mm) from edge of each seam allowance. The stitching makes turning easier, especially along curves. On straight edges, this stitching may not be necessary.

Turn under seam allowance on stitching line.

Stitch close to edge of fold, through seam allowance only. Press seam open.

ZIGZAG FINISHES

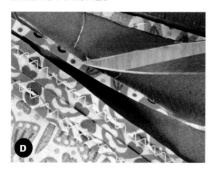

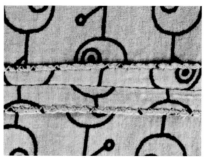

Set zigzag stitch for maximum width. Stitch near, but not over, edge of each seam allowance. Trim close to stitching, being careful not to cut into stitching.

Set zigzag stitch narrower and stitch so one side of stitch goes over the edge. Press edges under first for an even cleaner look.

Choose a three-step zigzag stitch to reduce tunneling. Stitch near, but not over, edge of each seam allowance. Trim close to stitching, being careful not to cut into stitching.

These finishes totally enclose the cut edge of seam allowances with a much lighter-weight fabric to prevent raveling and enhance the appearance of the inside of the garment. Bound seam finishes are a good choice for unlined jackets, especially those made of heavy fabrics or those that ravel easily.

The most commonly used bound finishes are the bias bound, tricot bound, and Hong Kong finishes. Medium-weight fabrics such as chino, denim, linen, gabardine, and flannel, and heavyweight fabrics such as wool, velvet, velveteen, and corduroy are good candidates for the three. Begin each finish by sewing a plain seam. Bound finishes can also be used on hem or facing edges.

Bias bound is the easiest bound finish. Use purchased double-fold bias tape, available in cotton, rayon, or polyester, to match the fashion fabric.

Tricot bound is an inconspicuous finish for most fabrics. Precut sheer nylon strips are available in $5/8$" (1.5 cm) or $1/4$" (3.2 cm) width. Use the narrower width for binding seams.

Hong Kong finish is a couture technique used on designer clothing, but because it is so easy and gives such a fine finish to the inside of a garment, it has become a favorite of many home sewers.

How to Sew a Hong Kong Finish

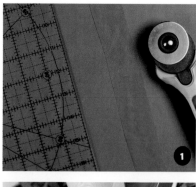

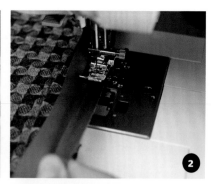

1 **Cut bias strips of lining fabric** 1¼" (3.2 cm) wide. Join strips as necessary (page 82) to form strips twice the length of the seams to be finished.

2 **Align bias strip on right side** of seam allowance. Stitch ¼" (6 mm) from cut edge, stretching bias slightly as you stitch. Use edge of presser foot as stitching guide. Trim seam allowance of heavy fabric to ⅛" (3 mm) to reduce bulk. Lightweight fabric does not need to be trimmed.

3 **Press bias strip back** over cut edge of seam allowance. Fold bias strip to the underside, enclosing the cut edge. Pin bias strip in place through all layers. The cut edge of bias strip needs no finishing, since a bias cut does not ravel.

4 **Stitch in the ditch** (the groove where the bias strip and fabric were stitched together). This stitching is hidden on the right side and catches cut edge of bias strip underneath. Press lightly.

Serger Seams and Seam Finishes

Serged seams can be used on many garments. Your instruction manual may include suggestions for where stitches are used. Garment style, fabric selection, and personal preference will help you decide which seams to use. The serged seam, alone, is not always suitable for garment construction. Many seams are sewn using both the serger and the conventional machine. For example, pants, jackets, or garments requiring adjustable fit, or seams that will be subjected to a great amount of stress, should be sewn with a pressed-open conventional seam and overedged seam allowances.

Types of Seams and Seam Finishes

Overlock seams (page 22) are appropriate for wovens and knits. Choose the 3-thread overlock for loosely fitted or nonstressed seams. The more secure 4-thread and 5-thread safety stitches are used primarily for wovens because the chainstitch may pop when stretched. The 3-thread and 4-thread mock safety stitches, designed for durable stretch seams, may also be used on wovens.

Overedge seam finish for conventional seams is used when it is desirable to keep the entire $5/8$" (1.5 cm) seam allowance. It is the best choice for tailored garments sewn from wool, linen, and silk suitings. It is also recommended whenever fit is uncertain to allow for letting out seams.

Reinforced seam is recommended for seams that will be stressed.

French seam is used for sheers and loosely woven fabrics. The seam will add bulk, so it is best used on full, gathered items such as skirts and curtains.

Rolled seam may be used instead of French seams for laces and for sheers that are firmly woven.

Mock flat-fell seam is used for denim and other heavyweight woven fabrics.

Gathered seam is finished in one easy step, using differential feed and a shirring foot. An alternate method uses the conventional machine with the serger.

Mock flatlock seam is used for a decorative effect, with decorative thread used in the upper looper.

Flatlock on a fold is used to create a decorative faux seam by folding the fabric, then stitching the fold on a serger.

Overedge seam finish for conventional seam. Stitch ⅝" (1.5 cm) seam, right sides together, using conventional machine. Stitch seam allowances, slightly trimming raw edge, using overedge or overlock stitch.

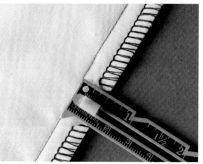

Reinforced seam. Stitch ⅝" (1.5 cm) seam, right sides together, using conventional machine; use narrow zigzag on moderate-stretch knits. Serge seam allowances together ⅛" (3 mm) from seamline.

French seam. Overedge seam, wrong sides together, with left needle positioned ¼" (6 mm) inside seam allowance. Fold fabric, right sides together, enclosing overedged fabric; press. Straight stitch close to enclosed stitches, using zipper foot on the conventional machine.

Rolled seam. Place fabric right sides together. Stitch seam, using a rolled hem stitch, with needle positioned on seamline; trim excess seam allowance. Press. Add tricot bias binding to stabilize a rolled lace edge, if needed.

How to Sew a Mock Flat-Fell Seam

Fabric right sides together. Stitch, using a conventional machine. Serge seam allowances together, trimming slightly.

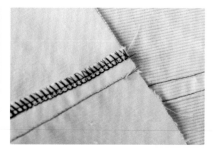

Press seam allowance to one side; topstitch from right side next to seamline using a conventional machine. Topstitch again, ¼" (6 mm) away, through all layers.

How to Sew a Reversible Lapped Seam

1 Stitch each single-layer seam allowance, using overedge or overlock stitch and aligning needle to seamline.

2 Lap garment sections so seamlines meet; glue baste.

3 Straight stitch through all layers ⅛" (3 mm) from serged stitches, from both sides of garment, using conventional machine.

How to Sew a Gathered Seam

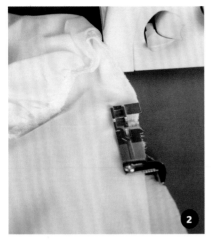

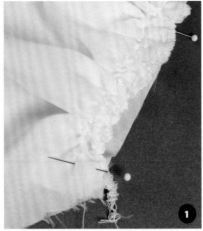

1 **Replace regular presser foot** with shirring foot and set differential feed to a larger number.

2 **Align edges** of two fabric layers together; position layers so fabric to be gathered is on the bottom.

3 **Overlock the seam** with needle positioned on the seamline

ALTERNATE METHOD

1 **Baste in seam allowance** near seamline, using conventional machine. Overedge seam allowance, slightly trimming raw edge. Align overedged fabric to corresponding section, right sides together, matching as necessary; pin. Pull bobbin thread and serger needle thread, gathering fabric to fit.

2 **Stitch seam with conventional machine.** Overedge seam allowances, using serger. Or, overlock seam, with left needle positioned on seamline, trimming away excess seam allowance; remove pins as they approach knives.

How to Sew a Mock Flatlock Seam

1 **Use decorative thread** in upper looper. Serge fabric, wrong sides together; press seam to one side with decorative thread on top.

2 **Topstitch decorative serged seam** through all layers, using conventional machine.

How to Flatlock on a Fold of Fabric

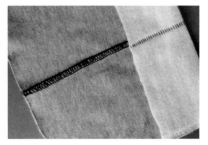

Mark stitch placement line on right side of fabric. Fold, wrong sides together, on marked line. Adjust serger for flatlock stitch. Place fabric slightly to the left of knives.

Serge seam without trimming fold of fabric. Position stitches half on and half off fabric.

Open the fabric and pull the stitches flat.

Fusible stabilized seam uses fusible interfacing strips to stabilize seams. Interfacing can also be used as a stable base for decorative edge finishes on stretchy knit or bias-cut fabrics.

Elastic stabilized seam uses transparent elastic to allow full stretch and recovery in a serged seam, but it prevents fabric from stretching out of shape.

Nonstretch stabilized seam uses twill tape, seam tape, or ribbon to prevent stretching of the fabric at the seamline.

Slight-stretch stabilized seam uses tricot bias binding to reinforce and stabilize a seam where slight stretch is desired. Use this method for stabilizing seams in sweater knits and T-shirt knits, which need support without completely restricting the stretch of the fabric.

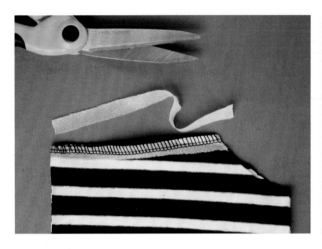

Fusible stabilized seam. Cut ¾" (2 cm) strip of fusible knit interfacing the length of the seam. Fuse to wrong side of garment. Stitch seam.

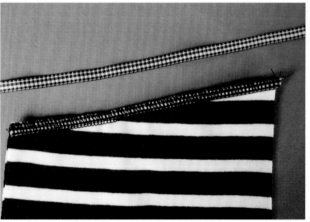

Nonstretch stabilized seam. Serge as in elastic stabilized seam; use twill tape, seam tape, or ribbon, and adjust foot tension so it does not drag on stabilizer. Decrease differential feed slightly, if required, to prevent seam puckering.

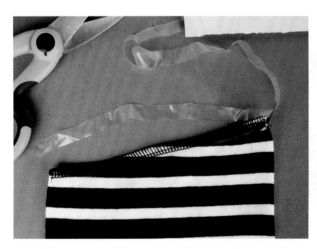

Elastic stabilized seam. Use elastic tape foot, if available, or use regular presser foot; adjust foot tension to drag slightly against elastic or increase differential. Serge seam without trimming elastic.

Slight-stretch stabilized seam. Cut a strip of tricot bias binding the length of the seam. Increase differential feed slightly to ease fabric and prevent overstretching seam. Serge through relaxed strip; trim excess binding close to stitches.

Darts

A dart is used to shape a flat piece of fabric to fit bust, waist, hip, or elbow curves. There are two types of darts. A single-pointed dart is wide at one end and pointed at the other. A shaped dart has points at both ends. It is usually used at the waistline, with the points extending to the bust and hips. Besides providing a closer fit, darts are also used to create special designer touches and unique styles. Perfect darts are straight and smooth, not puckered at the ends. The darts on the right and left sides of the garment should have the same placement and length.

Dart Techniques

Wide darts and darts in bulky fabrics should be slashed open on the foldline and trimmed to ⅝" (1.5 cm) or less. Slash to within ½" (1.3 cm) of point. Press dart open and press point flat.

Press darts over the curve of a tailor's ham to maintain the built-in curve. Vertical darts are usually pressed toward the center front or center back. Horizontal darts are usually pressed downward.

How to Sew a Single-Pointed Dart

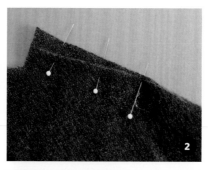

1 **Mark dart** using appropriate marking method for fabric.

2 **Fold dart on centerline,** matching stitching lines and markings at the wide end, the point, and in between.

3 **Stitch from wide end** to point of dart. Backstitch at beginning of stitching line.

4 **Shorten stitch length** to 12 to 16 stitches per inch (2.5 cm) when ½" (1.3 cm) from point. Take last two or three stitches directly on fold. Do not backstitch at the point, because this may cause puckering. Continue stitching off edge of fabric.

5 **Raise presser foot and pull dart** toward front. About 1" (2.5 cm) back from point of dart, lower presser foot and secure thread by stitching several times in fold of the dart with stitch length set at 0. Clip threads.

6 **Press folded edge of dart flat,** being careful not to crease fabric beyond the point. Then slash and press dart open over curve of tailor's ham. For a neat, flat finish, press darts before they are stitched into a seam.

Shaped or fisheye darts have points at either end and are used, for example, to take in volume around the waist. They are stitched in two steps, beginning at the waistline and stitching toward each point. Overlap stitching at waist about 1" (2.5 cm). Clip dart fold at waistline and midway along points, to within ⅛" to ¼" (3 to 6 mm) of stitching to relieve strain and allow dart to curve smoothly.

How to Sew a Shaped Dart

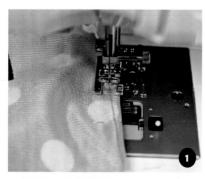

1 **Start stitching in the center** of the dart. Taper to point of dart. When ½" (1.3 cm) remains, shorten stitch length to 12 to 16 stitches per inch (2.5 cm).

2 **Take last two or three stitches** directly on fold. Do not backstitch at the point, because this may cause puckering. Continue stitching off edge of fabric.

3 **Raise presser foot** and pull dart toward front. About 1" (2.5 cm) back from point of dart, lower presser foot and secure thread by stitching several times in fold of the dart with stitch length set at 0. Clip threads close to knot.

4 **Turn your work around** and repeat the above steps for the other half of the fisheye dart.

Gathers

A soft, feminine garment line is often shaped with gathers, which define waistlines, cuffs, yokes, necklines, or sleeve caps. Soft and sheer fabrics produce a draped look when gathered; crisp fabrics create a billowy effect.

Gathers start with two stitching lines on a long piece of fabric. The stitching lines are then pulled at each end to draw up the fabric. Finally, the gathered piece is sewn to a shorter length of fabric.

The stitch length for gathering is longer than for ordinary sewing. Use a stitch length of 6 to 8 stitches per inch (2.5 cm) for medium-weight fabrics. For soft or sheer fabrics, use 8 to 10 stitches per inch (2.5 cm). Experiment with the fabric to see which stitch length gathers best. A longer stitch helps to draw up the fabric, but a shorter stitch gives more control when adjusting gathers.

Before you stitch, loosen the upper-thread tension. The bobbin stitching is pulled to draw up the gathers, and a looser tension makes this easier.

If the fabric is heavy or stiff, use heavy-duty thread in the bobbin. A contrasting color in the bobbin also helps distinguish it from the upper thread.

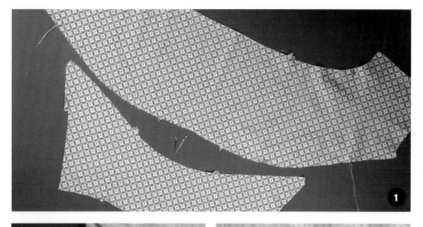

1 **Stitch ½" (1.3 cm) from raw edge** on right side of fabric along gathered edge. Loosen upper tension and lengthen stitches. Stitch a second row in seam allowance, ¼" (6 mm) away from first row.

2 **Pin stitched edge** to corresponding garment section, right sides together, at ends and all markings. If there are no markings, divide both edges into quarters and match.

3 **Pull both bobbin threads** from one end, sliding fabric along thread to gather. When half the gathered section fits the straight edge, twist bobbin threads around pin in a figure eight. Pull bobbin threads from other end to gather remaining half.

4 **Distribute gathers evenly** between frequent pins. Reset stitch length and tension for regular sewing.

5 **Stitch, gathered side up,** just outside gathering lines. Adjust gathers between pins as you stitch. Hold gathers taut with fingers on both sides of needle to keep gathers even.

6 **Trim seam allowances** and press allowance on wrong side, using tip of iron. Open and press seam in the desired direction: toward gathers for puffy look, toward garment for smoother look.

7 **Press into gathers with point** of iron on right side of garment, lifting iron as you reach seam. Do not press across gathers.

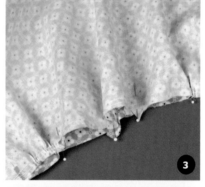

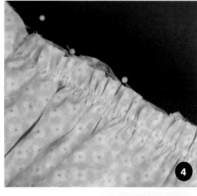

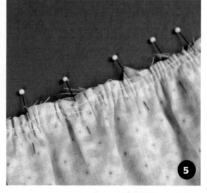

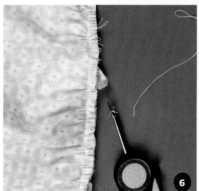

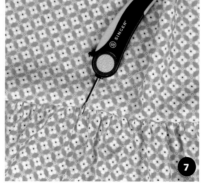

Gathers formed with elastic offer comfortable and easy fit. This technique ensures uniform gathers and creates shape that is more relaxed and flexible than other shape builders.

Elastic can be stitched directly to the garment or inserted in a casing. A casing is a tunnel for elastic, created with a turned-under edge or with bias tape stitched to the fabric. Choose an elastic that is suitable to the sewing technique and area of the garment where it is used (see page 40).

Elastic in a casing can be any width. Use a firm, braided, or nonroll elastic. Braided elastic has lengthwise ribs, and narrows when stretched.

Stitched elastic calls for woven or knitted elastics that are soft, strong, and comfortable to wear next to the skin. On short areas such as sleeve or leg edges, it is easiest to apply the elastic while the garment section is flat. At a waistline, overlap the ends of the elastic and stitch to form a circle before pinning to the garment.

Cut elastic the length recommended by the pattern. This length includes a seam allowance. To add elastic when the pattern does not call for it, cut the elastic slightly shorter than the body measurement plus seam allowance. Allow 1" (2.5 cm) extra for a stitched elastic seam, ½" (1.3 cm) extra for overlapping elastic in a casing.

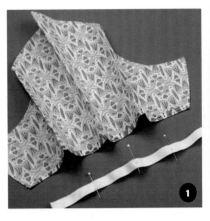

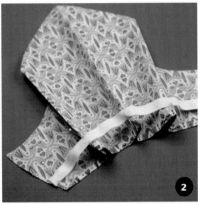

How to Sew Stitched Elastic

1. **Fold elastic and fabric into fourths.** Mark foldlines of elastic and garment with pins.

2. **Pin elastic to wrong side** of garment, matching marking pins. Leave ½" (1.3 cm) seam allowance at each end of elastic.

3. **Stitch elastic to fabric,** stretching elastic between pins, with one hand behind needle and other hand at next pin. Apply with a zigzag, multistitch zigzag, or two rows of straight stitching, one along each edge.

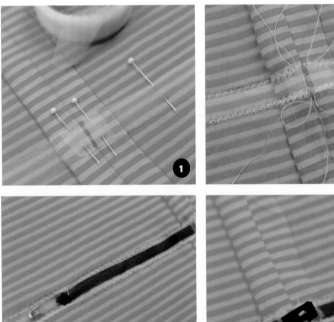

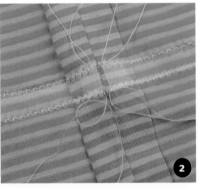

How to Sew Elastic in Casing (Waistline Seam)

1. **Pin sheer bias tricot strip** or bias tape that is ¼" (6 mm) wider than the elastic to inside of garment along marked casing lines, beginning and ending at one side seam. Turn under ¼" (6 mm) at each end of bias tape and pin to seamline. For easy application, work on ironing board with garment wrong side out.

2. **Stitch tape close to edges,** leaving opening at seam to insert elastic. A small zigzag stitch works well with tricot tape. Do not backstitch at ends of stitching, because this stitching shows on the right side of the garment. Instead, pull all four ends to inside and knot.

3. **Insert elastic through casing** using a bodkin or safety pin, taking care not to twist elastic. Place a large safety pin across free end of elastic to prevent it from pulling through.

4. **Lap ends of elastic** ½" (1.3 cm) and sew together with straight or zigzag stitches, stitching forward, backstitching, and forward again. Clip thread ends. Ease elastic back into casing.

5. **Slipstitch ends of casing together.** Distribute gathers evenly along the elastic.

Sleeves

Whether short or long, all sleeves are one of three basic styles: set-in, kimono, or raglan. Set-in sleeves have a rounded cap that is larger than the corresponding part of the armhole. The cap must be eased to fit smoothly into place. As a softer fashion detail, set-in sleeves may also have gathers or pleats in the sleeve cap. The traditional method of setting in sleeves uses two rows of easestitching on the sleeve to fit the cap into place. The flat method, opposite, is used for a man-tailored shirt sleeve, which has less ease than classic set-in styles. The sleeve is inserted along the armscye before the sleeve and garment side seams are stitched.

Kimono sleeves extend without seams from garment front and back sections. Shoulder shaping is rounded, as in raglan sleeves. Kimono sleeves are often loosely fitted and drape softly under the arms. Even loose-fitting kimono sleeves are subject to stress in the underarm area. Reinforce this curved seam with tape, two rows of stitching, shortened stitches, or a reinforcing stretch stitch.

Raglan sleeves have a slanted seam in the front and the back. Most raglan sleeves have a seam that curves over the shoulder and extends the length of the sleeve. This seam shapes the shoulder in a rounded way. In some patterns darts, instead of seams, shape the shoulders. For more comfort and better fit, stitch the sleeve and side seam before setting in the sleeve.

Shaping aids, such as sleeve puffs and shoulder pads, are needed to complete some sleeve treatments. Sleeve puffs are small pads that support gathered sleeve caps. Puffs lift gathers so the sleeve hangs straight and smooth.

Tips for Sewing Sleeves

Pattern markings such as notches, dots, and shoulder seam marks help to position set-in sleeves. More fabric must be eased at the back of the sleeve than at the front. No fabric should be eased into the armhole at the top of the sleeve cap for 1" (2.5 cm) at center dot.

Notches on pattern pieces tell which way sleeve and armhole edges should face. Double notches indicate the back of the sleeve and armhole. A single notch indicates the front. Mark notches with ¼" (6 mm) snips into the seam allowance.

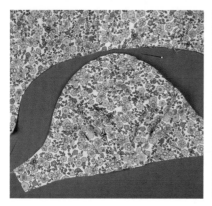

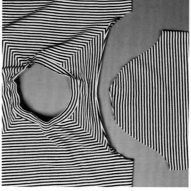

The flat method of construction is quick and easy for sewing knit and woven shirts and tops with simple sleeves. The body side seams and sleeve underarm seams are then sewn in one pass, so these must be designed to be continuous, not offset.

How to Sew a Flat Sleeve

Pin sleeve to armhole, right sides together, matching notches and small dots.

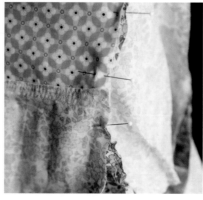

Pin on garment sidee, easing sleeve cap to fit.

Stitch sleeve to armhole with garment side up.

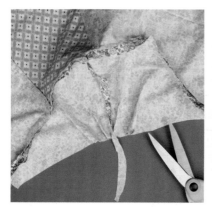

Press seam away from sleeve and finish seam allowances as desired. Trim garment seam allowance to ¼" (6 mm) for flat fell seam.

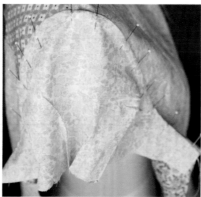

Fold and pin sleeve seam allowance over trimmed seam for flat felling. Top-stitch sleeve seam on the right side of garment ¼" (6 mm) from the seamline. (Topstitching is optional when sewing shirts and tops.)

Pin side seam of garment and sleeve together. Stitch in one continuous seam. Reinforce underarm area with short stitches or flat fell seam.

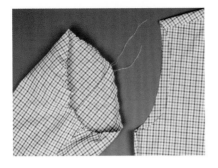

Sleeves with more complex sleeve caps and without underarm seams that are continuous with the garment's side seam must be set in after the sleeve and the garment's side seam are both closed. With any sort of sleeve, setting in gives maximum control over sleeve position in the armhole.

How to Sew a Set-In Sleeve

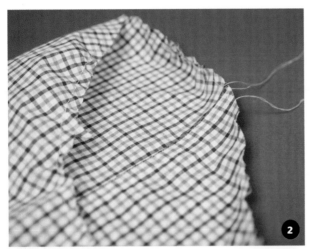

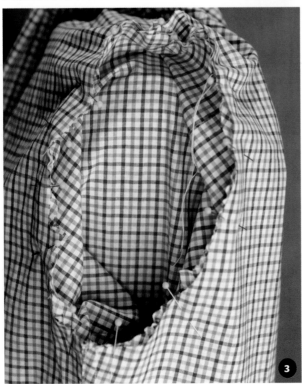

1 **Stitch underarm sleeve seam,** right sides together. Press seam flat, then press seam open. Use sleeve board or seam roll to prevent impression of seam on top of sleeve. Close garment side seam.

2 **Easestitch cap** of sleeve (the area between front and back notches) on right side, slightly inside seamline. Easestitch sleeve cap again, ⅜" (1 cm) from edge.

3 **Turn sleeve right side out. Turn garment inside out.** Insert sleeve into armhole, right sides together, matching notches, small dot markings, underarm seam, and shoulder line. Insert pins on seamline for best control of ease.

4 **Draw up bobbin threads** of easestitching lines until cap fits armhole. Distribute fullness evenly, leaving 1" (2.5 cm) flat (uneased) at shoulder seam at top of sleeve cap.

5 **Add pins at close intervals,** using more pins in front and back where the bulk of the ease is located.

6 **Check sleeve from right side** for smooth fit and correct drape. Adjust if necessary. There can be tiny pleats or puckers in seam allowance but not in seamline.

7 **Secure ends of easestitching thread** by making a figure eight over each pin at front and back notches.

8 **Stitch just outside easestitching line,** sleeve side up, starting at one notch. Stitch around sleeve, past starting point, to other notch, reinforcing underarm with two rows of stitching. Remove pins as you come to them.

9 **Trim seam allowance to ¼"** (6 mm) between notches at underarm only. Do not trim seam allowance of sleeve cap. Zigzag seam allowances together.

10 **Press seam allowance of sleeve cap only,** using press mitt or end of sleeve board. Do not press into the sleeve.

Sleeve Details

Long sleeves on shirts, blouses, and lightweight jackets often have cuffs with buttoned closings. In many ways, sewing cuffs is similar to sewing collars. The tips on page 144 for trimming, interfacing, and pressing collars apply to cuffs, too.

Apply interfacing to half of a one-piece cuff. The interfaced half of the cuff shows on the outside of the finished sleeve. The half without interfacing is folded to the inside to form a self facing. Interface one section of a two-piece cuff; this section belongs on the outside of the sleeve. The other cuff section forms the facing on the inside.

Apply cuffs, using either topstitching or hand finishing. Topstitching is usually faster, because it is done by machine. Cuffs without topstitching require hand finishing, but no stitches show on the outside.

Continuous bound placket is a slit bound with a strip of self fabric. The binding strip is cut on the lengthwise fabric grain for stability. When the cuff is closed, this placket is hidden from view.

Shirt-style placket is a box-shaped sleeve opening finished with a shaped outer binding. The binding is folded and stitched so the edges of the placket overlap neatly. Adapted from menswear tailoring, this type of placket is found on patterns with traditional details. When the cuff is closed, the pointed portion of the binding shows on a shirt-style placket.

Staystitch along placket mark with a short straight stitch. Make one stitch across the top. Slash up to, but not through, staystitching.

Press binding edges under ¼" (6 mm). Pin one edge of binding to slash right sides together just covering stay stitches. Stitch along fold.

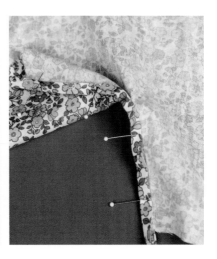

Fold binding over edge and pin. Stitch in ditch from garment right side to secure binding.

Line up edges of binding on wrong side of sleeve; stitch diagonal tacks at top fold of binding to keep binding inside sleeve when cuff is finished.

Press binding flat on underlapping back placket edge. Press binding under on overlapping front placket edge. Attach cuff (page 142).

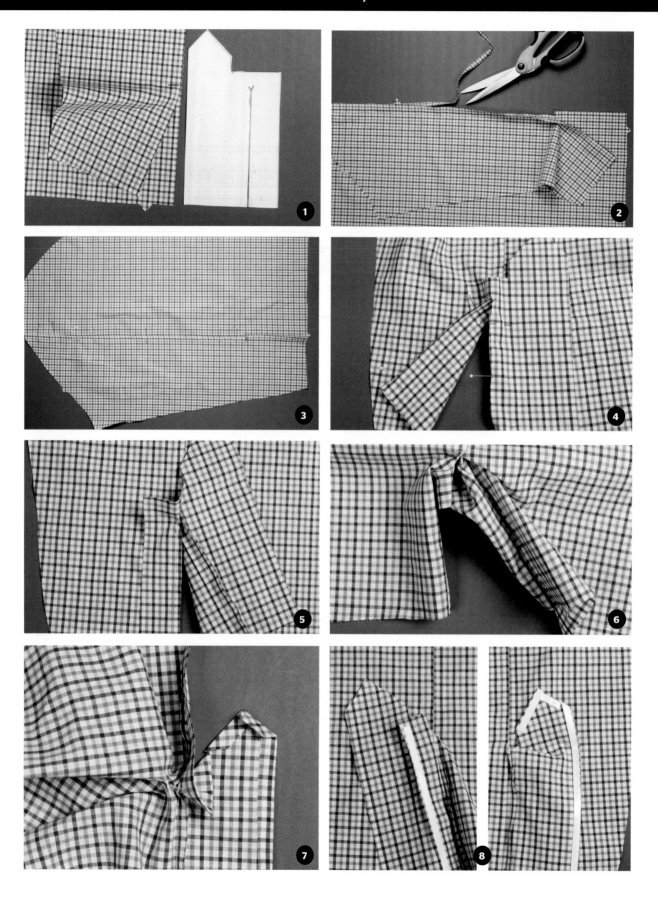

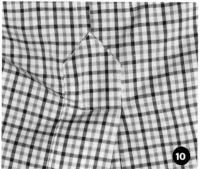

1 **Stitch two-piece dress shirt sleeve** seam up to mark indicating top of placket slash.

2 **Clip larger-side seam allowance** at mark and trim above mark to ¼" (6 mm).

3 **Turn opposite seam allowance over** trimmed seam allowance, pin, press and stitch for flat fell seam.

4 **Align placket piece, right side down,** to edge of cuff and placket slash over unstitched portion of sleeve seam and pin.

5 **Stitch placket to sleeve around the slash** ¼" (6 mm) from edge. Press the notch at slash top up.

6 **Turn placket through slash** to sleeve right side. Press the encased slash seams.

7 **Press edges of placket under** ¼" (6 mm).

8 **Double-sided water soluble tape** can help hold crisp folds exactly in place.

9 **Arrange placket layers** into final positions. Press, then lift overlap to edgestitch the underlap edge of the placket to the shirt sleeve slash.

10 **Beginning at top of the slash below,** edgestitch straight across and then up the side and over the top of the placket in the shape of a house. Stitch through all layers. Continue stitching down the length of the placket until you reach the cuff edge. Edgestitch as close to the placket edge as possible for a tailored look. Edgestitch outer fold of overlap to top of opening, if desired. Pull threads to underside and tie.

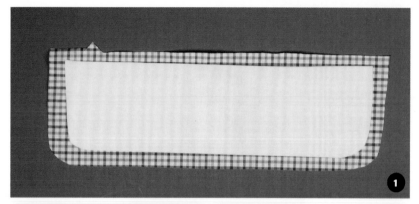

1. **Fuse interfacing to outer cuff;** if cuff pattern is constructed of two mirror-image pieces, cut interfacing to match one piece, without seam allowances. If cuff is constructed from one piece, fold cuff pattern in half and cut fusible interfacing from folded pattern, eliminating seam allowances.

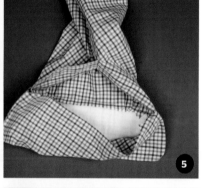

2. **Stitch two cuff halves,** right fabric sides together, along the bottom edge if two pieces and sides up to the end of the interfacing. Trim and grade seam allowances.

3. **Turn cuff right side out** and press encased seams.

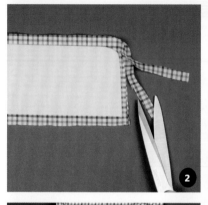
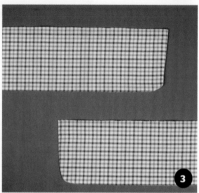

4. **Pin and stitch right side of sleeve** to interfaced side of cuff, matching markings. Be sure ends of cuff are even with finished placket edges. Do not trim seam allowances.

5. **Tuck step-4 seam allowances inside** cuff, then fold seam allowances of free inner-cuff edge inside so the folded edge just covers the step-4 seam line.

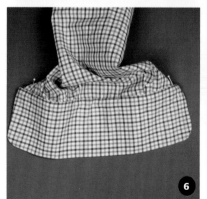
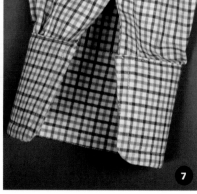

6. **Pin free edge from right side** all along cuff length, keeping placket edges free at each end.

7. **Catch and close free inner edge** by edgestitching along outer cuff edge. Continue edgestitching around entire cuff perimeter, then topstitch, if desired.

How to Sew a Shoulder Pad for Dress or Blouse

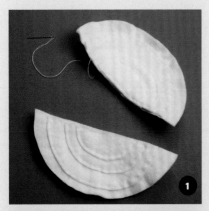

1 **Cut four circles of ¹⁄₁₆" (3 mm) batting,** the largest circle having a diameter of 7½" (19 cm) and each consecutive circle being about ½" (1.3 cm) smaller. Cut these circles in half to make 8 semicircles. Align the straight edges and stitch the smallest semicircle to the one next up in size with running stitches. Stack and stitch the remaining two semicircles in the same manner. Makes a ½" (1.3 cm)-thick shoulder pad.

2 **Cut two circles of fabric,** each having a diameter of 8½" (21.5 cm). Mark and stitch three parallel fisheye darts on one half of the fabric circle. This will form the fabric into a slight cup shape.

3 **Stitch a line of basting stitches** ⅜" (1 cm) around the circle of fabric. Gently ease the basting stitches so that the edge of the fabric circle begins to curl toward the wrong side. Lay the shoulder pad inner into the fabric cover, aligning the top of the insert with the shoulder pad cover without the fisheye darts.

4 **Continue to ease the basting stitches** until the edge of the shoulder pad inner is covered by the fabric and the half without the insert curls in against the wrong side of the fabric. Fold the fabric outer in half beneath the under side of the shoulder pad inner and pin around the open edge. Edgestitch the open edge closed through all layers.

YOU WILL NEED

- ¹⁄₁₆" (3 mm) batting
- Self fabric as main garment

Collars

Collars are important details worthy of careful sewing. A well-made collar encircles your neck without rippling or pulling and keeps its neat appearance while worn. Pointed tips should match. Edges should be smooth and flat.

Interfacing, usually cut from the collar pattern piece, adds shape, support, and stability. Most collar styles benefit from the slightly firm finish provided by fusible interfacings. Select the special crisp type of fusible interfacing suitable for men's shirts if you are working with classic shirting fabrics. If your fabric is soft or delicate, like challis or crepe de chine, choose a lightweight fusible that bonds at low iron temperatures.

Convertible collar looks similar to the notched collar and lapels on a tailored blazer. The front facings fold back to form the lapels. This collar can be worn open or closed. The top button is usually omitted on casual wear.

Shirt collar with a stand comes from menswear traditions. There are two separate sections: the collar and the stand between collar and neckline. In some patterns, the stand is an extension of the collar section. This eliminates one seam and is faster to sew, but the sewing methods for both versions are similar. For a professional look, topstitch collar edges and stand seams close to the edge.

Standing collar may be shaped or cut double depth and folded along its length to form a self facing.

Tips for Sewing Collars

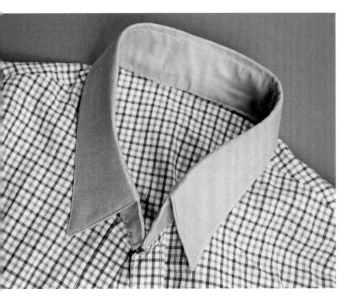

Trim outer edges of undercollar a scant ⅛" (3 mm) so the seam rolls toward the underside of the collar when stitched and turned. Pin right sides of collar and undercollar together with outer edges even.

Press collar seam open on a point presser; turn collar right side out. Gently push collar points out with a point turner. Press collar flat, allowing the seam to roll slightly toward the undercollar.

Roll collar into its finished position and pin. If necessary, trim raw edge of undercollar so it is even with upper collar edge. This makes the collar roll properly when it is sewn in place.

How to Sew a Round Collar (fusible interfacing)

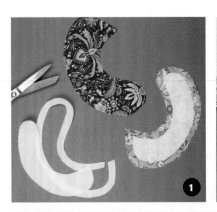

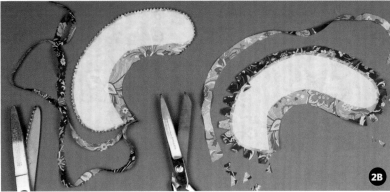

1 **Trim seam allowances from fusible interfacing** and fuse to wrong side of upper collar, following manufacturer's directions.

2 **Stitch right sides of collar and facing together** with slightly shortened stitches.

3 **Press outer seam open,** even though seam is enclosed. This flattens stitching line and makes collar easier to turn. Trim seam allowances close to stitching line, using pinking shears. Another option is to clip and grade seam allowances. Turn and press.

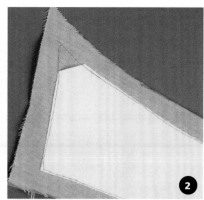

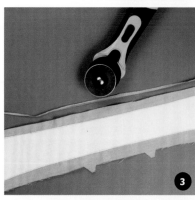

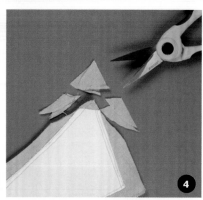

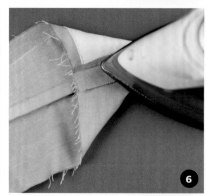

1 **Cut one interfacing piece** from the upper-collar pattern. Trim seam allowances to ⅛" (3mm) and take points off diagonally, just inside seamline.

2 **Machine-baste interfacing** to wrong side of upper collar, ¹⁄₁₆" (1.5 mm) from edge.

3 **Trim a scant ⅛"** (3 mm) from outer edges of undercollar. This keeps undercollar from rolling to right side after collar is stitched to the neckline. Pin right sides of collar and undercollar together with outer edges even.

4 **Stitch on seamline,** taking one or two short stitches diagonally across each point instead of making a sharp pivot. This makes a neater point when the collar is turned. Trim points, first across the point, close to stitching, then at an angle to the seam on each side of the point.

5 **Grade seam allowances** by trimming undercollar seam allowance to ⅛" (3 mm) and collar to ¼" (6 mm).

6 **Press seam open on a point presser.** Turn collar right side out.

7 **Push points out gently** with a point turner. Press collar flat, rolling seam slightly to the underside so it will not show on finished collar. Topstitch outer edge of the collar as desired.

How to Prepare Collar

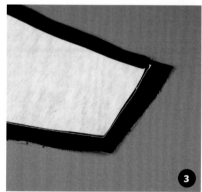

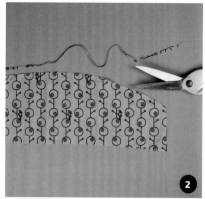

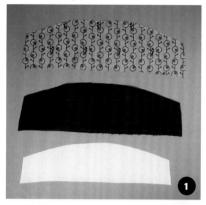

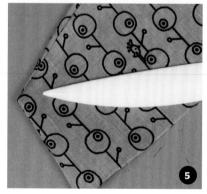

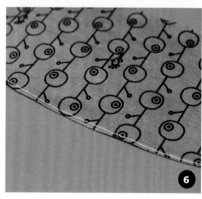

1 **Cut interfacing to match outer collar** (which in this case already has another interfacing layer fused overall), without seam allowances.

2 **Trim a scant ⅛"** (3 mm) from edge of undercollar piece.

3 **Fuse interfacing to outer collar** piece. inside seam lines. Pin undercollar to collar outer along the outer edge and stitch.

4 **Collar pieces will bow** slightly because of the the smaller undercollar.

5 **Turn collar and use a point turner** in the corners, after grading allowances and trimming points as shown on page 146. The collar outer will roll over the edge of the undercollar piece.

6 **Press and edge stitch** very close to the edge.

How to Join Collar to Yoke and Facings

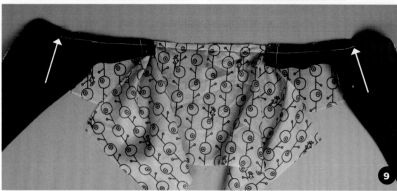

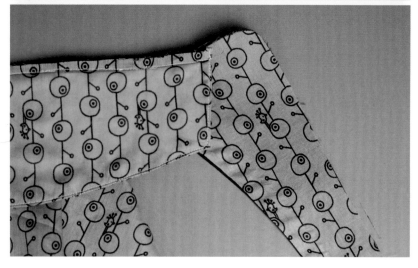

7 **Interface front facings** and finish facing edges with method appropriate to fabric. In this case, the fusible is pinned, adhesive, side up to the right side of the facing's inner edge and stitched but not pressed. Seam allowances trimmed, then the interfacing is turned to the wrong side and fused, finishing the edge neatly.

8 **Stitch short ends of facing** pieces to yoke lining with fabric right sides together.

9 **Match collar and yoke** right sides together at center backs and pin. Stitch completed upper collar along neckline. Clip seam allowance at each end of collar (arrows).

How to Join Collar and Facings to Fronts

10 Stitch shoulder seams of shirt fronts to yoke. Press seam allowances toward shirt back.

11 Pin shirt front openings along facings and neckline. Stitch from hem to hem across neckline.

12 Turn facings and collar right side out and press. On inside, turn under yoke lining shoulder seam allowances and press to cover yoke/front seams. Topstitch to close shoulder seam from garment right side.

13 Edge stitch across neckline and along both facing edges (contrasting thread used to show detail).

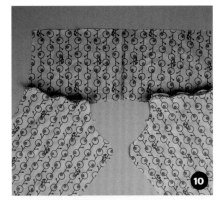

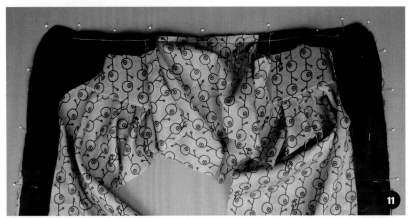

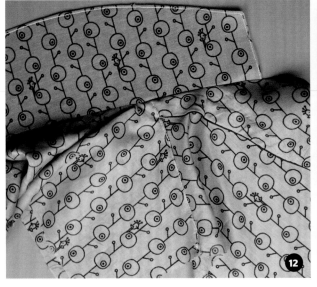

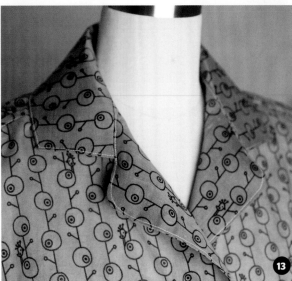

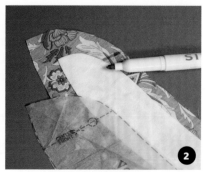

1. **Trim seam allowances** from stand interfacing. Interface one or both stand sections.

2. **Transfer collar placement marks** clearly from pattern.

3. **Sandwich shirt neckline** between the stand sections, right sides together.

4. **Stitch stand to neck seam.** Stop ⅝" (1.5 cm) from stand edges (arrow).

5. **Trim** and grade seam.

6. **Roll shirt fronts out of the way,** then stitch curve from neck seam to collar placement mark (arrows). Clip to seamline at marking and along curve; trim.

7. **Turn stand** right side out.

8. **Stitch collar** to right side of outside stand, with undercollar next to stand. Trim and grade seam; press seam toward stand.

9. **Press under inside stand** seam allowance and trim to ¼" (6 mm). Pin pressed edge of stand to cover stitching line.

10. **Edgestitch** around stand through all fabric layers.

Waistbands

Because a waistband supports the entire garment, it must have a strong and sturdy outer edge finish and, therefore, be cut on the lengthwise grain of the fabric.

Waistbanding is a long strip of fusible interfacing with elongated perforations down the center for easy folding. Preferences and sewing methods have changed and waistbanding is no longer commonly available. Alternatively, ¾" (2 cm) or 1" (2.5 cm) waistband elastic can be used as traditional waistbanding. Waistband elastic will provide support and shape, however, without the stiffness of waistbanding. When using waistband elastic the elastic, will not be stretched at all but will, instead, function to hold the waistband's form. Because elastic is not particularly suited to take buttonholes, this method uses small pieces of interfacing attached to the ends of the elastic.

Cut a waistband long enough for adequate ease and overlap allowance. The length should equal your waist measurement plus 2 ¾" (7 cm). The extra amount includes ½" (1.3 cm) for ease, 1¼" (3.2 cm) for seam allowances, and 1" (2.5 cm) for overlap. You may cut the waistband longer for more overlap as a design element. The width should be twice the desired finished width plus 1¼" (3.2 cm) for seam allowances.

How to Sew a Waistband (Method 1)

1 Cut waistband on the lengthwise grain, ideally along the selvedge. Cut waistband elastic equal to the length of your waistband piece minus 4" (10 cm). Cut two pieces of woven interfacing the width of the elastic to add to the ends of the waistband elastic, one piece 5" (12.5 cm) and the other 3" (7.5 cm).

2 Fold interfacings in half and overlap the ends of the elastic by ½" (1.25 cm) then fuse the two halves together and to the ends of the elastic. Secure the interfacing further to the elastic with stitches. This finished piece of elastic plus interfacing pieces should measure exactly as long as the waistband piece, less 1" (2.5 cm) for seam allowances.

3 Finish the inside edge, if you have not cut it along the selvedge, for example, by encasing the inside edge with double-fold bias tape.

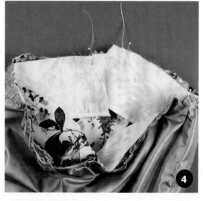

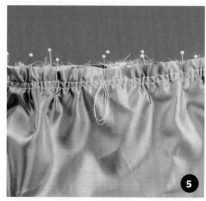

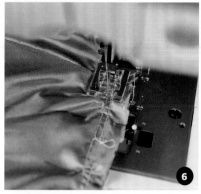

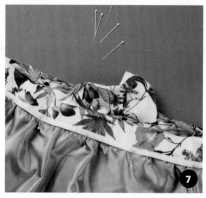

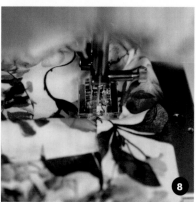

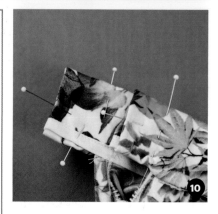

4 **Pin unfinished edge of waistband** to garment right sides together, matching notches. Stitch a ⅝" (1.5 cm) seam.

5 **Ease garment to fit waistband** as required or if the skirt design calls for gathering.

6 **Stitch waistband to garment.** Stitch along lower basting stitch line, if present.

7 **Turn waistband up.** Press seam allowance toward waistband. Grade the seam allowances to ¼" (6 mm) on the waistband and ⅛" (3 mm) on the garment to eliminate bulk. Turn waistband over top edge and pin.

8 **Stitch in ditch** from garment right side to secure waistband. Edge stitch around tucked ends. Remove pins as you go.

9 **Insert waistband elastic** piece into casing with a bodkin. Make sure the longer interfacing piece is inserted into the waistband overlap.

10 **Tuck in waistband ends** and pin. Edge stitch around tucked ends.

TIP

Most waistbands call for a turned-under edge as a finish on the inside. A faster, less bulky method requires changing the pattern layout so the waistband pattern is cut with one long edge on the selvage. Because the selvage does not ravel, a turned-under edge is not necessary.

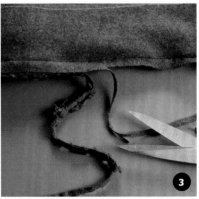

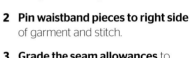

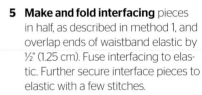

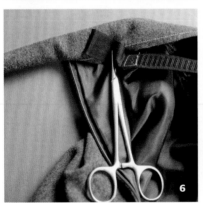

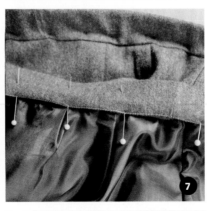

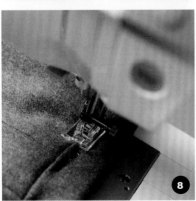

1. **Stitch a line of staystitches** ¼" (6 mm) from the waistband piece edge if you have not cut one edge, along the selvedge.

2. **Pin waistband pieces to right side** of garment and stitch.

3. **Grade the seam allowances** to ¼" (6 mm) on the waistband and ⅛" (3 mm) on the garment to eliminate bulk.

4. **Turn waistband** to garment right side, so that waistband wrong side is facing out. Stitch around waistband ends to edge of garment. Trim corners for a smooth turn.

5. **Make and fold interfacing** pieces in half, as described in method 1, and overlap ends of waistband elastic by ½" (1.25 cm). Fuse interfacing to elastic. Further secure interface pieces to elastic with a few stitches.

6. **Turn the waistband right side out.** With the aid of a knitting needle or something similar, shape the corners of the waistband ends. Insert the elastic piece into the waistband. Make sure the longer interfacing piece is placed into the waistband extension.

7. **Tuck under bottom edge,** folding along staystitching and pin.

8. **Stitch in ditch** from garment right side. Remove pins as you go.

Hems

Unless it is decorative, the hem for most garments should be virtually invisible from the right side. Use thread the same shade as, or slightly darker than, your fabric.

When hemming by hand, pick up only one or two threads from the outer fabric in each stitch. Do not pull the thread too tight during stitching. This causes the hem to look puckered or lumpy. Press carefully, as overpressing creates a ridge along the edge of the hem.

The width of the hem is determined by the fabric and garment style. A hem allowance of up to 3" (7.5 cm) may be given for a straight garment; 1½" to 2" (3.8 to 5 cm) for a flared one. Sheer fabrics, no matter what the style, are usually finished with a narrow, rolled hem. A narrow hem on soft knits helps keep them from sagging. Machine stitched and topstitched hems are fast and permanent.

Before hemming, let the garment hang for 24 hours, especially if it has a bias or circular hem. Try the garment on over the undergarments you will wear with it. Check to be sure it fits and hangs correctly. Wear shoes and a belt if the garment is to be belted.

Hemlines are usually marked with the help of a second person using a pin marker or yardstick. Mark the hemline with pins or chalk all around the garment, making sure the distance from the floor to the hemline remains equal. Stand in a normal position and have the helper move around the hem. Pin hem up, and try on the garment in front of a full-length mirror to double-check that it is parallel to the floor.

Pant-leg hems cannot be marked from the floor up, as skirts and dresses are. For standard-length pants, the bottom of the pant legs should rest on the shoe in front and slope down slightly toward the back. Pin up the hem on both legs, and try on in front of a mirror to check the length.

Before stitching, finish the raw edges of the hem to keep the fabric from raveling and to provide an anchor for the hemming stitch. Select the hem finish (opposite) and stitch that is appropriate to the fabric and the garment.

Blindstitching by machine makes a fast, sturdy hem on woven and knit fabrics. Most sewing machines have this built-in stitch. A special foot is needed to blindstitch, one that has a bar through the center over which enough slack in the thread is created for a smooth turn. The stitching guides on a blindstitch hem foot makes blindstitching easy, keeping the body of the garment clear of the turned up edge.

Seam binding or lace provides a finish suitable for fabrics that ravel, such as wool, tweed, or linen. Lap seam binding ¼" (6 mm) over the hem edge on the right side of the fabric. Edgestitch the binding in place, overlapping ends at a seamline. Use woven seam binding for straight hems, stretch lace for curved hems and knits. Hem light- to medium-weight fabrics with the catchstitch, bulky fabrics with the blindstitch.

Hem Finishes and Stitches

Topstitched hem finishes the raw edge and hems the garment all in one step. Turn up hem 1½" (3.8 cm) and pin in place. For ravelly fabrics, pink or turn under raw edge. On right side, topstitch 1" (2.5 cm) from folded edge. Above, a second row of topstitching is applied as a design detail.

Twin-needle stitched hem is suitable for knits and casual styles. The twin needle produces two closely spaced parallel lines of stitching on the right side and a zigzag-type stitch on the wrong side. Turn hem up desired amount and stitch through both layers from right side, using seam guide. Trim excess hem allowance after stitching.

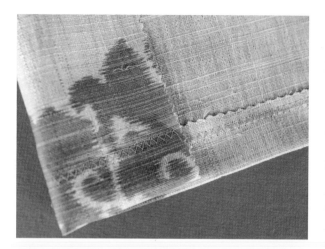

Zigzag finish is appropriate for knits and fabrics that ravel, because the stitch gives with the fabric. Stitch close to raw edge with zigzag stitch of medium width and length. Trim close to stitching. Then hem with a blindstitch, blind catchstitch, or machine blindstitch.

Pinked and fused hem is a fast and easy finish for lightweight woven fabrics. Apply a fusible web strip between the hem and the garment. Steam press, following manufacturer's instructions.

Bound hem finish is appropriate for heavy woolens and fabrics that ravel easily. Finish raw edge of hem in double-fold bias tape or Hong Kong finish (page 124). Hem with blindstitch or blind catchstitch. Be careful not to pull hemming thread too tight or fabric will pucker.

Mark garment an even distance from the floor using pins or chalk and a yardstick or skirt marker. Have a helper move around you so you do not need to shift position or posture. Place marks every 2" (5 cm).

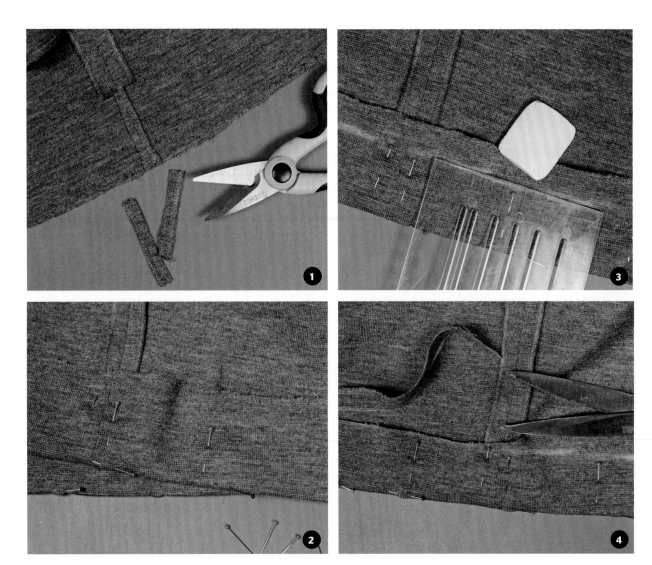

1 **Trim seam allowances in hem** by half to reduce bulk. Trim seams from bottom of garment to hem stitching line only.

2 **Fold hem up along marked line** (here, pin marked), inserting pins at right angles to the fold at regular intervals. Fit garment to check length. Hand baste ¼" (6 mm) from folded edge. Press edge lightly, easing hem to fit garment.

3 **Measure and mark** the desired hem depth, adding ¼" (6 mm) for edge finish. Work on ironing board or table, using a seam gauge to ensure even marking.

4 **Trim excess hem allowance** along markings. Finish raw edge according to fabric type (page 58). Pin finished edge to garment, matching seams and centerlines.

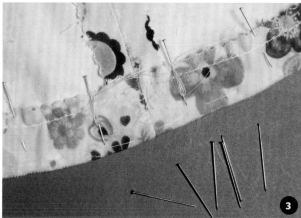

Curved hems have extra fullness that must be eased to fit garment as shown. Finish raw edge using zigzag stitching, bias tape, seam binding, or pinking. Pin hem edge to garment, matching seams and centerlines. Hem using machine blindstitch or appropriate hand-hemming stitch.

1 **Loosen machine tension** and ease stitch ¼" (6 mm) from edge, stopping and starting at a seamline. Leave thread tails for easing. Baste at marked hemline.

2 **Draw up bobbin thread** by pulling up a loop with a pin at intervals, easing fullness to smoothly fit garment shape. Do not draw hem in too much or it will pull against garment when finished. Press hem over a press mitt to smooth out some fullness.

How to Machine Blindstitch

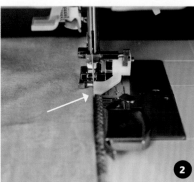

1 **Hand-baste hem** to garment ¼" (6 mm) from raw edge. Adjust machine to blindstitch setting and attach blindstitch foot. Select zigzag width and stitch length, following guidelines in your machine manual.

2 **Place hem allowance face down** over feed of machine. Fold bulk of garment back to basting line. The soft fold should rest against the left edge of the foot's guide (arrow). Stitch along hem close to the fold, catching garment only in zigzag stitch. Press hem flat.

Easy Edges

Any rounded woven edge—for example, a blouse neckline—can be edge finished quickly by machine with a bias-cut strip. A bias neckline facing with overlapped ends makes a neat neckline finish, and narrow Machine stitched hems finish the sleeves and lower edges of the blouse. To make the bias facing, cut a 1¼" (3.2 cm) bias strip about 2" (5 cm) longer than the neck opening, to allow for overlap.

A narrow Machine stitched hem is nonbulky, making it suitable for lightweight or silky fabrics. It can also be used for hems on garments made from satin, taffeta, or organza. Horsehair braid can be added to this narrow hem for extra body. Before stitching the hem, trim hem allowance to ⅛" (3 mm).

How to Sew a Narrow Hem

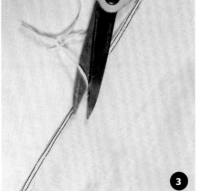

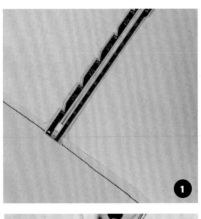

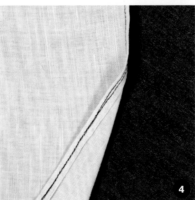

1 **Machine stitch ¼"** (6 mm) from hem edge.

2 **Turn edge to wrong side** on stitching line; press fold.

3 **Stitch close to fold,** using short stitch length. Trim excess fabric close to stitching, using appliqué scissors. Press to remove fullness, if fabric has stretched.

4 **Turn hem edge to wrong side,** enclosing raw edge. Stitch an even distance from edge.

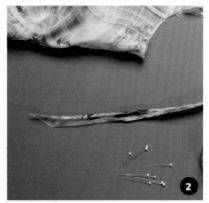

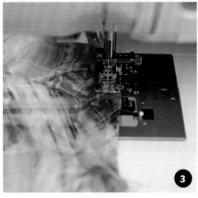

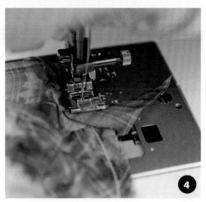

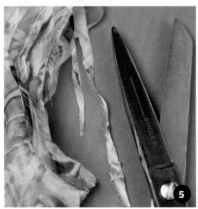

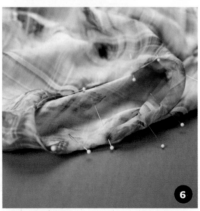

1. **Cut bias-strip facing 1"** (2.5 cm) wide.

2. **Fold strip edges to middle,** wrong sides together; press. Strip-folding notions are available for this step. Trim garment seam allowance to ¼" (6 mm).

3. **Place strip on right side** of garment, raw edges even, with end of strip 1" (2.5 cm) from center back (for neckline) or side seam (for armscye).

4. **Fold end of strip** into seam allowance; stitch around neckline along outermost fold in bias strip. Overlap ends, folding other end into seam allowance.

5. **Trim** seam allowances.

6. **Press strip** away from garment; then press it to inside of garment.

7. **Edgestitch** around neckline or armscye from right side.

Pockets

Pockets may be decorative, but many garments would seem incomplete without this functional detail. Today, even some wedding dresses and evening gowns are made with pockets in the seams to keep life's essentials, like cell phones and house keys, even important medications, always close at hand. To be useful, pockets should fall comfortably within hand's reach, which may require adjusting the pattern for the individual.

Choose a sturdy, firmly woven fabric for hidden pocket sections of in-seam and slanted pocket styles. The pocket is less likely to wear out if cut from fabric such as cotton twill or drill cloth. Tailors use a material called pocketing, a special lightweight twill, for pockets on pants and jackets. A durable lining fabric is also a good choice.

Patch pockets are sewn to the outside of a garment. Pocket edges should be neat, smooth, and securely applied. They may be interfaced for stability, lined, or self lined on tailored-lined garments.

In-seam pockets are hidden. From the outside of a garment they look like an opening in a seam.

Slanted pockets open diagonally from the waist to the sides of pants and skirts.

Welt pockets are hidden pockets with a visible slit. They may have a single or double welt and are sometimes covered with a flap.

Patch Pockets

A patch pocket is a detail to which the eye is easily drawn, so position patch pockets where they look best on your figure. Try placing the pockets above, below, or beside the placement line on the pattern to find the most flattering position that avoids accentuating the bustline or hipline.

Once you've determined the position for the pockets, double-check the placement before attaching them. Measure carefully so pockets are precisely aligned. This step is especially important when pockets are symmetrical.

Patch pockets may be applied by hand or machine. Sew the pockets on by machine for casual garments. This technique not only saves time, it also offers the most secure application. If you prefer a fine, invisible finish, sew the pockets in place by hand.

Interface patch pockets with a lightweight fusible interfacing for smooth shape and longer wear. Cut the interfacing to the hem fold at the pocket top and to the seamline at the sides and bottom of the pocket. Avoid an overly stiff pocket by cutting woven interfacings on the true bias grain.

Reinforce patch pockets at the upper corners. Stitch small triangle tacks on man-tailored shirts and sportswear. Use fine zigzag stitched bar tacks on children's clothing and rugged outdoor wear. Top-stitching may be added for further reinforcement.

How to Sew a Patch Pocket with Square Corners

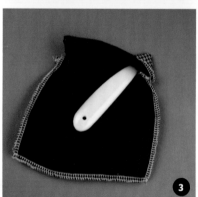

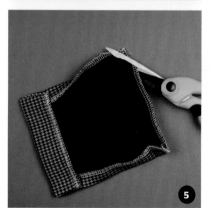

1 **Finish upper edge** of pocket. Finish the sides of the pocket against raveling, as required. Fold hem over to the fabric right side. Pull the right and left hem edges ⅛" (3 mm) beyond pocket so seams will roll toward inside. Stitch on seamline.

2 **Trim seam allowances** closely at corners.

3 **Turn finish right side out,** using point turner to push out corners.

4 **Press seam allowances** under on sides.

5 **Fold bottom seam allowance** up across lower corners so pressed fold-lines match. Press folds, then open and trim diagonally ¼" (6 mm) from corners.

6 **Press seam allowances again** to inside, forming unfinished miters at corners. Trim remaining seam allowances to reduce bulk, if not already finished. Press from right side and edgestitch or topstitch, if desired.

How to Sew a Patch Pocket with Rounded Corners

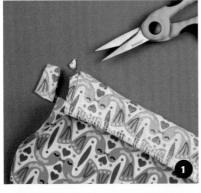

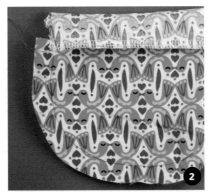

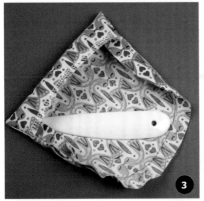

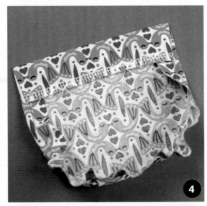

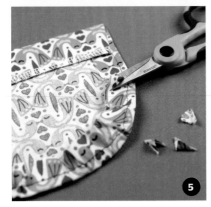

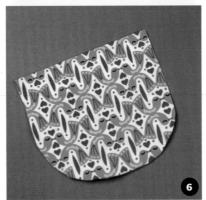

1 **Finish upper edge** of pocket exactly as for square-cornered patch. Finish the sides of the pocket against raveling, as required.

2 **Stitch on seamline** just along hem. Increase stitch length and easestitch around curves, just inside seamline (easestitching shown in contrasting thread for visibility).

3 **Turn finish right side out** and use point turner in corners.

4 **Press seam allowance** to inside of pocket. Pull thread along curve stitches to ease in extra seam allowance evenly.

5 **If necessary, notch out fullness** at corner curves to make seam allowance lie flat. Trim entire seam allowance to ¼" (6 mm).

6 **Press from right side** and edge-stitch or topstitch, if desired.

How to Sew a Self-lined Patch Pocket

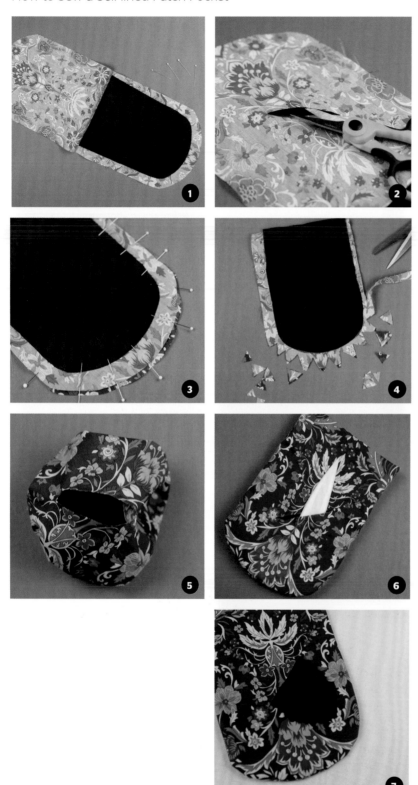

1. **Fold pocket pattern on hemline.** Place pattern fold on fabric fold and cut double pocket. Fuse interfacing on one half of pocket.

2. **Cut a 1" (2.5 cm) bias slit** on non-interfaced inner side of pocket.

3. **Pin right sides together,** pulling non-interfaced side ⅛" (3 mm) beyond edge.

4. **Stitch seam;** trim and notch.

5. **Turn pocket to right side** through slit. Press edges, rolling seam to side with slit in it.

6. **Use a point turner** in corners and along curved edges.

7. **Close slit with fusible interfacing** inserted adhesive side up.

How to Sew a Lined Patch Pocket

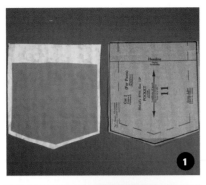

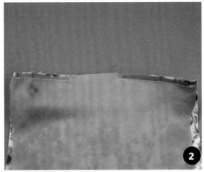

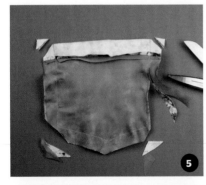

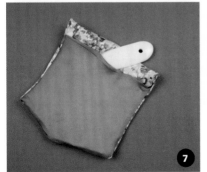

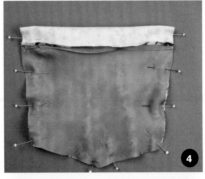

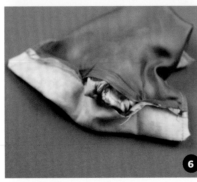

1 **Fold hem down on pocket pattern.** Mark lining cutting line ½" (1.3 cm) from upper edge of pattern. Cut lining edges a scant ⅛" (3 mm) shorter on sides and bottom.

2 **Stitch top of lining to top of pocket,** right sides together, with a ¼" (6 mm) seam, first from the left edge, then from the right edge. Leave opening for turning at center of seam.

3 **Press seam** allowance open.

4 **Bring lower edge of lining** and pocket right sides together. Stitch side and lower edges.

5 **Trim seams and corners;** notch fullness from curves of rounded pockets or trim pointed corners.

6 **Turn pocket right side out** through opening in seam.

7 **Use a point turner** to fully turn pocket edges and corners. Press pocket from lining side, rolling seam toward back of pocket.

8 **Slipstitch seam** opening closed.

How to Apply a Patch Pocket by Machine

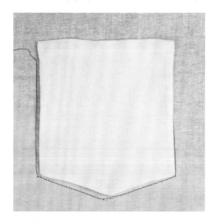

Transfer pocket placement line to right side of garment with machine basting.

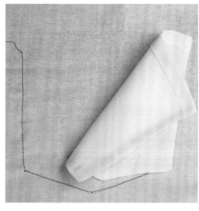

Baste pocket in place with tape, pins, or basting spray to hold pocket over the baste-marked line.

Edgestitch pocket to garment. Reinforce upper corners with stitched triangles or bar tacks.

How to Apply a Patch Pocket by Hand

Baste-mark pocket placement. Edge or topstitch pocket before applying pocket to garment.

Hand-baste pocket in position, stitching along pocket edge to use as guideline on garment wrong side.

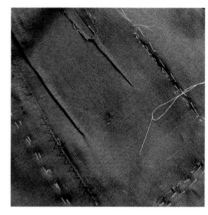

Catch stitch pocket in place working from inside of garment. Stitching should not show on garment right side.

There are three ways of cutting in-seam pockets: cutting the pocket as part of the garment, cutting a separate pocket, and cutting a garment extension plus a separate pocket.

Sewing an in-seam pocket that is part of the garment eliminates one seam but can create unwanted bulk unless the garment fabric is lightweight. Cutting a separate pocket reduces bulk, because you can use a lining fabric. The third method, us-ing an extension, reduces bulk and prevents the pocket lining from showing on the curve of the hip. To prevent the pocket opening from stretching when pockets are cut separately, stitch narrow twill or seam tape in the seam allowance of the front pocket.

Topstitching helps hold the pocket in place and flattens any bulk at the seam, giving a slimmer line in the hip area.

How to Sew an In-Seam Pocket with a Garment Extension

Edgestitch twill tape on wrong side in seam allowance of front pocket extension. Stitch pockets to front and back extensions. Trim seam to ¼" (6 mm). Press toward pocket.

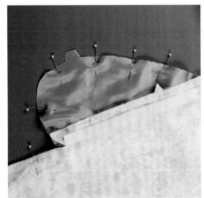

Pin garment front to garment back; machine-baste pocket opening closed. Stitch pocket and garment seam above and below pocket opening. Use short reinforcement stitches, and backstitch at opening.

Stitch around pocket, ending at side seam. Clip seam above and below extension on back garment section only, so seam can be pressed open. Press garment seam open above and below clips. Press pocket toward garment front. Finish raw edges of pocket together. Remove basting stitches.

Slanted pockets are formed from two pattern pieces: the pocket and the garment side front. The side front fills in the hip area of the garment above the pocket opening and completes the inside of the pocket. The pocket pattern can be cut from lining fabric to minimize bulk because the pocket is hidden on the inside.

How to Sew a Slanted Pocket

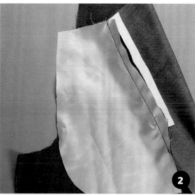

1 **Cut 2" (5 cm) strip** of sew-in interfacing or seam tape to match shape of the pocket edges. Stitch ½" (1.3cm) from edge on wrong side. Trim interfacing.

2 **Stitch pocket to garment front,** right sides together.

3 **Trim seam,** grading so pocket seam allowance is narrower. Clip curves, press seam toward pocket.

4 **Understitch seam** on pocket side, if pocket will not be topstitched, to prevent pocket from rolling to right side.

5 **Fold pocket to inside.** Press pocket edge, rolling seam toward pocket. Topstitch or edgestitch edge of pocket if it has not been understitched.

6 **Stitch pocket to garment side front.** Finish raw edges with zigzag stitches or another edge finish. Baste pocket to garment at side seam and at waist seam. Use pattern markings to line up fabric layers. Pocket should lie flat without ripples.

Double-welt pockets look like large, bound buttonholes. A welt, which is a narrow, folded strip of garment fabric, finishes each edge of the pocket opening. The pocket, cut from a lining fabric, extends from the welts on the inside of the garment.

Making welt pockets is an expert tailoring technique that requires precise marking, cutting, and stitching. Before starting, carefully check the pocket position. Once you have started making the pocket, recheck the pocket position before slashing the welt. In the photos, the wrong side of the garment has been backed with fusible interfacing.

How to Cut and Prepare a Pocket Lining

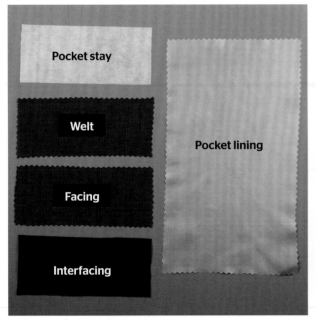

For a 5" (12.5 cm) finished welt, cut the following pocket parts 7" × 3" (18 × 7.5 cm): A pocket stay from nonwoven sew-in interfacing; a welt and a pocket facing from fashion fabric; interfacing from weft insertion fusible. Cut lining 7" × 12" to 15" (18 × 30.5 to 38 cm) or longer depending on how deep a pocket you want. Pocket depth equals half lining length minus 1.5" (3.8 cm).

1. **Fuse interfacing to wrong side of welt.** Place welt right side up, on one edge of pocket lining. Zigzag inner edge of welt to lining. Machine baste outer edge of welt to lining.

2. **Stitch pocket facing to other edge** of lining as for welt. (Contrasting thread used to show detail; use thread to match your fabric).

How to Sew a Welt Pocket

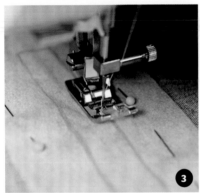

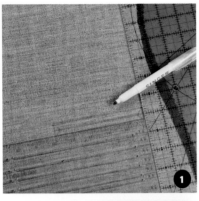

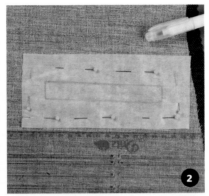

1 **Mark pocket placement** line on wrong side of garment. Draw pocket stitching box with lines ¼" (6 mm) from center line. Mark ends with short vertical lines 5" (12.5 cm) apart, 1" (2.5 cm) from ends of stay.

2 **Draw a matching center line on stay** and draw the same box around it as for the pocket placement.

3 **Position stay on wrong side** at pocket placement marking. Sew around entire box, using small stitches and beginning on one long side. This transfers pocket stitching box to right side. Do not backstitch.

4 **Pin right side of welt/pocket** section to right side of garment, centering welt over baste-marked pocket stitching box. (Welt is folded back to show placement over stitched line; Contrasting thread used to show detail.)

5 **Stitch long sides** of pocket stitching box only, working from wrong side of garment. Stop right at end marks on box, backstitching to secure threads. (Presser foot has been removed to show where stitching ends.)

6 **Machine baste exactly ¼"** (6 mm) from each long side of pocket stitching box, working from wrong side of garment. Use width of presser foot as stitching guide.

7 **Press welt/pocket section up,** working from right side of garment. Press firmly to create neat, flat fold. Pin. Lower line of machine basting is inside this fold.

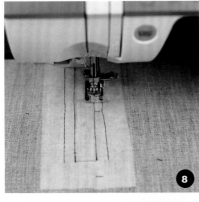

8 Stitch on lower long line of pocket stitching box from wrong side of garment. Stop exactly at end marks; backstitch to secure threads. This forms lower welt.

9 Press welt/pocket section down. Upper line of machine basting is inside fold.

10 Stitch on upper long line of pocket stitching box from wrong side of garment; backstitch to secure threads. This forms upper welt.

11 Slash welt by cutting through center of welt between stitching rows. Do not cut into garment. Remove baste stitching from upper and lower welt.

12 Place dots ⅝" (1.5 cm) from each end of the stitching box.

13 Cut through center of pocket stitching box from wrong side of garment, starting and stopping at the dots. Cut diagonally to each corner, forming triangles. Be careful to cut garment fabric only.

14 Turn welts and pocket to wrong side by pulling them through pocket opening. Make sure triangles are pulled through and folded flat between welts and pocket stay.

15 Press welts once fully turned.

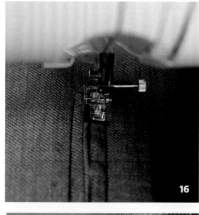

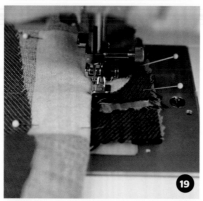

16 **Stitch in the ditch of upper welt** from right side of garment, using zipper foot. Stitch through all layers.

17 **Fold up pocket** so pocket facing covers welts. Pin facing to top of welt.

18 **Fold garment back** out of the way to prepare for stitching pocket side seams.

19 **Stitch pocket side seams,** using zipper foot; stitch close to fold of triangles at ends of pocket opening.

20 **Press pocket lining** so it lies flat.

21 **Whipstitch** edges of upper and lower welts together to hold pocket opening in place while you sew the remainder of garment.

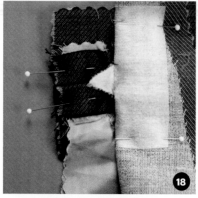

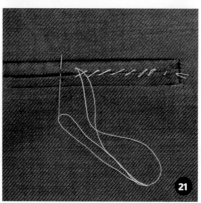

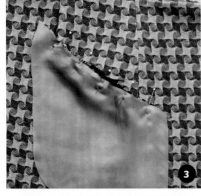

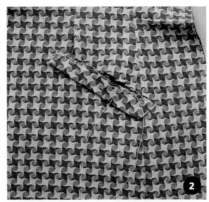

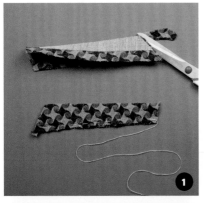

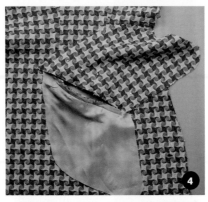

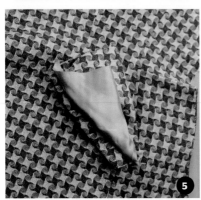

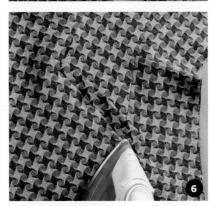

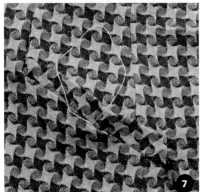

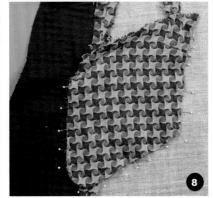

1 **Fuse interfacing to welt** wrong side. If using hair canvas or other stiff interfacing, cut interfacing in half and fuse on either side of the foldline. Fold right sides together and stitch outside edge of welt. Trim seam allowance. Turn welt right side out, press and baste lower edge.

2 **Baste open edge of welt** to lower edge of pocket slit on the garment right side.

3 **Stitch front pocket piece** (lining material) to the lower edge of pocket slit, right fabric sides together, catching the welt sandwiched between.

4 **Stitch the back pocket piece** (outer material) to the upper edge of pocket slit, right fabric sides together.

5 **Turn the front and back pocket pieces** to the garment wrong side through the pocket slit. Tuck unfinished welt edge into jacket front seam.

6 **Press** the welt seam.

7 **Move the pocket pieces** out of the way, and stitch in the ditch of the welt seam by hand with catch stitches to secure seam allowance in place. Hand tack the welt in place.

8 **On the garment wrong side,** stitch the front and back pocket pieces together along the bottom and sides.

Closures

Closures are all the elements that open and close to allow for ease of dressing. Zippers, buttons, snaps, and hooks and eyes can be incorporated inconspicuously, but they can also be used as decorative details. A stylish button, a contrasting zipper with a fashion pull tab, bold gripper snaps, or shiny grommets can be used to dress up a garment.

Select the closure best suited to the style of garment, fabric qualities, and amount of strain that will be put on the opening. For example, a heavy-duty hook-and-eye closure (opposite) can better withstand the strain on the waistband on a pair of pants than an ordinary hook and eye. For the specific type and size of closures you will need, read the Notions section on the back of the pattern envelope.

Because closures are under strain, it is important to reinforce the garment area where they are placed. Seam allowances or facings provide light reinforcement. Other closure areas should be reinforced with interfacing.

For sewing on buttons, snaps, and hooks and eyes, use an All purpose thread, and sharps or crewel needles. For heavyweight fabrics or for closures that are under considerable strain, use heavy-duty, or topstitching and buttonhole, twist thread.

Hooks and eyes are strong closures that come in several types. Regular, general-purpose hooks and eyes are available in sizes 0 (fine) to 3 (heavy), in black or nickel finishes. They have either straight or round eyes. Straight eyes are used where garment edges overlap, such as on a waistband. Round eyes are used where two edges meet, such as at the neckline above a centered zipper. Thread loops can be used in place of round metal eyes on delicate fabrics or in locations where metal eyes would be too conspicuous. Button loops, French tacks, and belt carriers are made using the same technique, starting with longer foundation stitches.

Heavy-duty hooks and eyes are stronger than regular hooks and eyes, to withstand greater strain. Available in black or nickel finishes, they are used only for lapped areas. Large, plain, or covered hooks and eyes are available for coats and jackets. These are attractive enough to be visible and strong enough to hold heavy fabric.

How to Make Thread Eyes

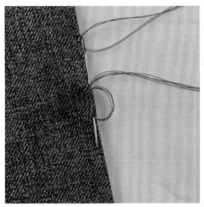 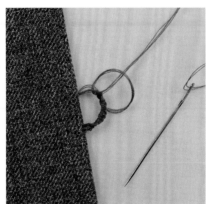 

Insert double threaded needle at edge of fabric. Take two foundation stitches the desired length of the eye. These stitches will act as the anchor on which the blanket stitch is worked. Use your pinkie, a pen, or something of a similar diameter as a form around which to make the foundation stitches.

Make blanket stitch by passing eye of needle under foundation stitches and through the loop created. Bring needle through loop, pulling loop tight against foundation stitches.

Work blanket stitch along entire length of foundation stitches. Secure stitching by taking two small backstitches. Trim threads.

How to Attach Waistband Hook and Eye

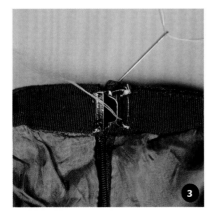

1 **Position heavy-duty hook** on underside of waistband overlap, about ⅛`" (3 mm) from inside edge. Tack hook in place with three or four stitches through each hole. Do not stitch through to right side of garment.

2 **Lap hook side over underlap** to mark position of eye. Insert straight pins through holes to mark position. Tack in place with four stitches in each hole.

Round hook (not shown) and eye is used for waistbands that do not overlap. Position hook as for heavy-duty hook. Tack through both holes and at end of hook. Position eye so it extends slightly over inside edge of fabric (garment's edges should butt together). Tack in place.

The standards of a well-made buttonhole are

- Width is appropriate to the weight of the fabric and size of the buttonhole.
- Ends are bar tacked to prevent buttonhole from tearing under stress.
- Stitches are evenly spaced on each side of the buttonhole.
- Buttonhole is ⅛" (3 mm) longer than the button.
- Stitches on each side are far enough apart so that the buttonhole can be cut open without cutting the stitches.
- Ends have not been cut open accidentally.
- Interfacing supporting the buttonhole matches the fashion fabric and is not obvious on the cut edges.
- Buttonhole is on grain; vertical buttonholes are perfectly parallel to the garment edge, horizontal buttonholes are at perfect right angles to the edge.

Horizontal buttonholes are the most secure, because they are not as apt to allow buttons to slip out. These buttonholes also absorb any pull against the closure with little, if any, distortion. Horizontal buttonholes should extend ⅛" (3 mm) beyond the button placement line, toward the edge of the garment. Be sure that the space from the centerline to the finished edge of the garment is at least three-fourths the diameter of the button. With this spacing, the button will not extend beyond the edge when the garment is buttoned.

Vertical buttonholes are used on plackets and shirt bands, usually with more buttons of a smaller size to help keep the closure secure. Vertical buttonholes are placed directly on the center front or center back line.

When a garment is buttoned, the button placement lines and centerlines of both sides must match perfectly. If the overlap is more or less than the pattern indicates, the garment may not fit properly.

Spaces between buttonholes are generally equal. You may have to change the pattern buttonhole spacing if you have made pattern alterations that change the length or alter the bustline. Respacing may also be necessary if you have chosen buttons that are larger or smaller than the pattern indicates. Buttonholes should be spaced so they occur in the areas of greatest stress. When they are incorrectly spaced, gaps can form, spoiling the look.

For front openings, place buttonholes at the neck and the fullest part of the bust. On double-breasted jackets and coats, however, buttons should be placed somewhat below the fullest part of the bustline to avoid placing two buttons in awkward locations. Place a buttonhole at the waist for coats, overblouses, and princess-seamed dresses or jackets. To reduce bulk, do not place a buttonhole at the waistline of a tucked-in blouse or belted dress. Buttons and buttonholes should end about 5" to 6" (12.5 to 15 cm) above the hemline of a dress, skirt, or coatdress.

To evenly respace buttonholes, mark the locations of the top and bottom buttons. Measure the distance between them. Divide that measurement by one less than the number of buttons to be used. The result is the distance between buttonholes. After marking, try on the garment, making sure the buttonholes are placed correctly. Adjust as necessary.

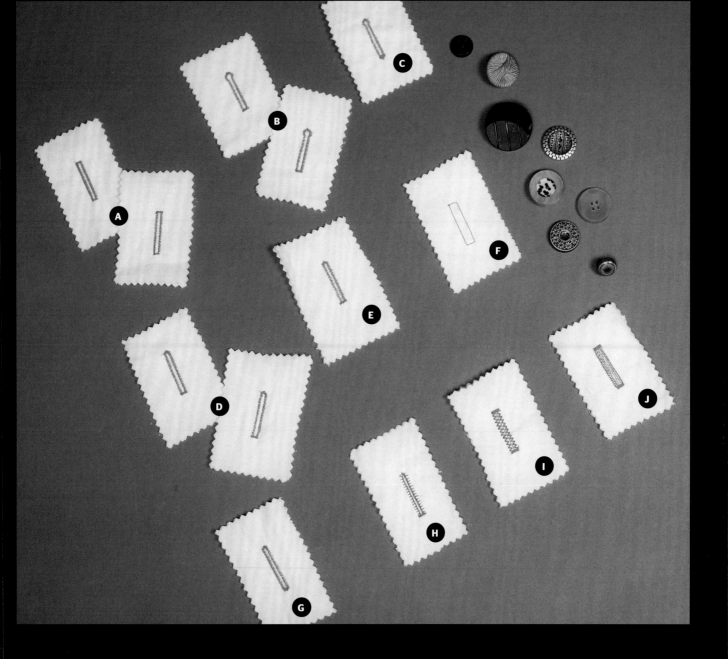

These are common buttonhole options found on newer electronic machines. Except as noted below, most are simply decorative options to be used as desired.

A **Bar-tack Buttonhole** with wide zigzags at each end for a squared-off look.

B **Keyhole Buttonhole** provides extra space at round end for button shanks or heavy threads.

C **Tapered Keyhole Buttonhole** has no bar tack.

D **Round-Ended Buttonhole** with bar-tack at one end only.

E **Round-Ended Buttonhole** with extra-wide reinforced bar tack.

F **Bound Buttonhole Outline** is a guide for making a fabric-bound buttonhole.

G **Dual Round-Ended Buttonhole.**

H **Decorative-Stitch Buttonhole.**

I **Stretch Buttonhole** designed for use on knits and stretch fabrics.

J **Heirloom Buttonhole** looks like the heavier buttonholes made by older nonelectronic machines.

How to Determine Buttonhole Length

Measure width and height of button to be used. The sum of these measurements plus $\frac{1}{8}$" (3 mm) for finishing the ends of the buttonhole is the correct length for a machine-worked buttonhole. The buttonhole must be large enough to button easily, yet snug enough so the garment stays closed.

Test proposed buttonhole. First, make a slash in a scrap of fabric the length of the buttonhole minus the extra $\frac{1}{8}$" (3 mm). If button passes through easily, length is correct. Next, make a practice buttonhole with a scrap of the garment fabric, facing, and interfacing. Check length, stitch width, density of stitching, and buttonhole cutting space.

How to Mark Buttonholes

Place pattern tissue on top of garment, aligning pattern seamline with garment opening edge. Insert pins straight up through the fabric and then the pattern piece at both ends of the buttonhole. Gently lift off the pattern tissue.

At this point, you have three ways to mark the buttonholes:

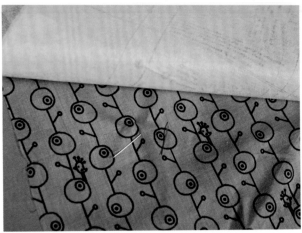

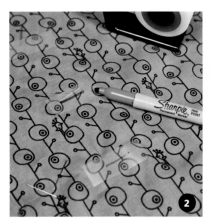

1 **Use a water-soluable textile marker** and draw a line between the pins that are poking through the fabric.

2 **Lightly adhere clear tape** over the pins. With pencil or marking pen, draw a line on the cellophane tape between where the pins come through the fabric. After marking, pull tape halfway off to unstick pins and remove pins from underneath.

3 **Mark the pinholes with textile pencil** and then machine or hand baste between where the pins are sticking through the fabric. Baste lines perpendicular to the buttonholes to assure that they are aligned in a neat row.

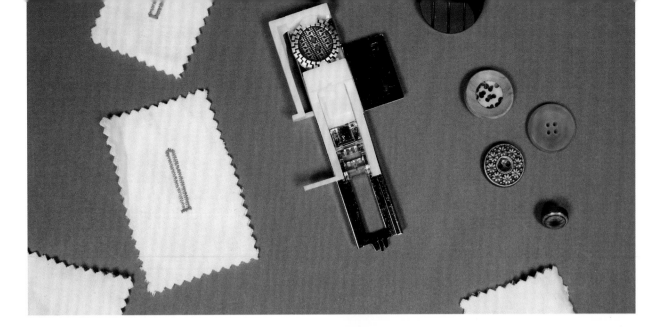

Machine-Made Buttonholes

Machine-made buttonholes are appropriate for most garments, especially casual apparel. There are three ways to make buttonholes with a sewing machine: built in (usually two- or four-step), over-edge, and one step. Always make a test buttonhole with appropriate interfacing before making the buttonholes on your garment. The test buttonhole also reminds you at which point your machine begins the buttonhole stitching, so you can position fabric correctly.

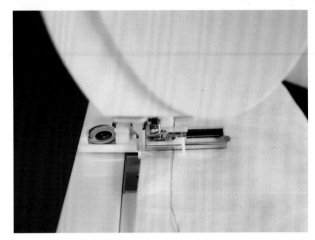

Built-in buttonholes are made with a combination of zigzag stitching and bar tacks. Even the simplest zigzag machines will have a built-in mechanism that stitches this type of buttonhole in two or four steps. The four steps are zigzag forward, bar tack, zigzag in reverse, bar tack. A two-step buttonhole combines a forward or backward motion with a bar tack. Consult your machine manual for specific directions, because each machine varies. The advantage of this buttonhole is that it allows you to adjust the density of the zigzag to suit the fabric and size of the buttonhole, especially for buttons that are larger than one-step buttonhole attachments. Use spaced zigzag stitches on bulky or loosely woven fabrics and closer stitches on sheer or delicate fabrics. Similarly, if your machine does not have a built-

in buttonhole function or you have misplaced your machine's one-step buttonhole attachment, you can create this buttonhole by carefully stitching each line individually.

Overedge buttonholes are an adaptation of the built-in or one-step buttonhole. This buttonhole is stitched with a narrow zigzag, cut open, and then stitched a second time, so the cut edge is overedged with zigzag stitches. The overedge buttonhole looks like a hand-worked buttonhole. It is a good choice when the interfacing is not a close color match to the fashion fabric.

One-step buttonholes are stitched all in one step, using a special foot and a built-in stitch available on many

machines. They can be stitched with a standard-width zigzag, or a narrow zigzag for lightweight fabrics. Often, the button is placed in a carrier in back of the attachment and guides the stitching, so the buttonhole fits the button perfectly. Many machines have a lever near the needle that is pulled down and stops the forward motion of the machine when the buttonhole reaches the correct length. All buttonholes are of uniform length, so placement is the only marking necessary.

If buttonholes do not have to be respaced because of pattern alterations, make the buttonholes after attaching and finishing the facings but before joining to another garment section. This makes for less bulk and weight to handle at the machine.

How to Make Buttonholes

Built-in buttonholes. Place fabric under buttonhole foot; align starting point with needle and center foot over mark. (Steps shown separately, but buttonhole is stitched continuously, moving machine to new setting at each step.)

1 **Set dial or lever selector** at first step. Slowly stitch several stitches across end to form bar tack.

2 **Stitch one side** to marked end.

3 **Stitch several stitches across end** to form second bar tack.

4 **Stitch other side** to first bar tack to complete buttonhole. Return to starting position and make a few fastening stitches.

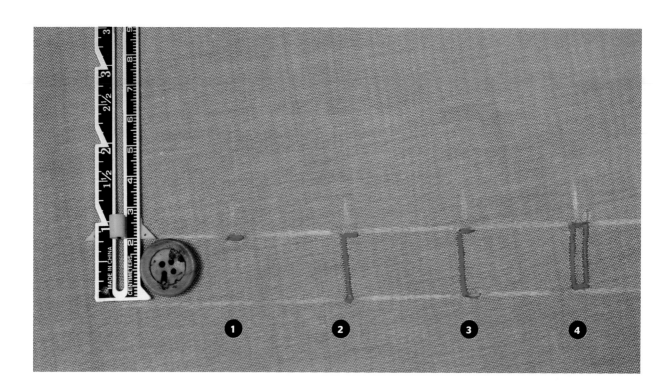

TIP

A crooked or mis-stitched buttonhole can often detract from an otherwise perfectly sewn item. To make it easier to remove the tiny zigzag stitches of a buttonhole, carefully weave a very thin silk pin or very thin sewing needle under the stitches on one side of the material. Then, use a razor blade or craft knife to carefully scrape the threads covering the pin to break the fibers. Pick out the broken threads from the reverse side.

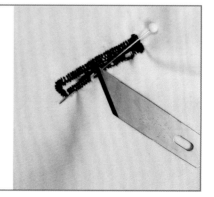

How to Open a Buttonhole

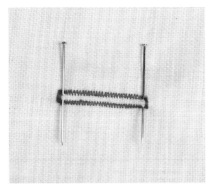

Insert straight pins at each end of buttonhole in front of bar tacks to prevent cutting through ends.

Insert point of small, sharp scissors or a seam ripper into center of buttonhole and carefully cut toward one end, then the other.

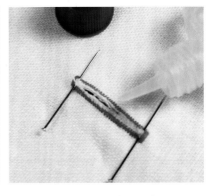

Strengthen the cut edge and prevent raveling by applying liquid fray preventer to the edge. Test fabric on a sample first to make sure the fray preventer does not stain.

TIPS

Always test your choice of buttonhole on a scrap of material first, layered and interfaced to match the section carrying the final buttonholes. Also, cut the test buttonhole and make sure your choice of button fits through.

Because a buttonholer presser foot is longer than other presser feet, it exerts less direct pressure at the point of stitching. As such, some materials do not feed well while being stitched with a buttonhole attachment. If you find that your material is not taking the stitches evenly or not moving under the needle properly, first try adjusting the presser foot pressure. If that doesn't fix the problem, try pinning a bit of water soluble sew-in embroidery stabilizer to both the front and back of your material. Once the buttonhole is stitched, the stabilizer is easily torn away and any bits left under the stitches will disappear in the wash.

Overedge buttonhole

Stitch buttonhole with narrow zigzag. Cut buttonhole open.

Reposition in exact position as first stitching. Adjust zigzag to wider stitch. Stitch second time over cut edge of buttonhole.

One-step buttonhole

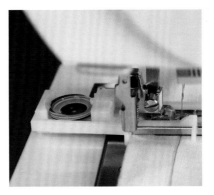

Place button in attachment carrier. Check machine manual for proper stitch setting. Buttonhole is made the correct length and stitching will stop automatically.

Buttons are decorative and functional. More than any other closure, the variety and options for buttons allow you to individualize your garment. There are two basic kinds of buttons: sew-through and shank.

Sew-through buttons are usually flat, with two or four holes. When they are merely decorative, they can be sewn so they lie directly against the garment. On all other applications, sew-through buttons need a thread shank. A shank raises the button from the garment surface, allowing space for the layers of fabric to fit smoothly when it is buttoned.

Shank buttons have their own shanks on the underside. Choose shank buttons for heavier fabrics, as well as when using button loops or thread loops.

Choose buttons that match not only the color and style of your fabric, but also match your fabric's weight and care requirements.

Color. The color of buttons is usually matched to the fabric, but interesting fashion looks can be achieved by coordinating or contrasting colors. If you are unable to find an appropriate color match, make your own fabric-covered buttons with a kit.

Style. Select small, delicate buttons for feminine garments; clean, classic styles for tailored clothes; and novelty buttons for children's clothes. Rhine-stone buttons add sparkle to a velvet garment. Try leather or metal buttons with corduroy and wool tweeds.

Weight. Match lightweight buttons to lightweight fabrics. Heavy buttons will pull and distort lightweight fabrics. Heavyweight fabrics need buttons that are bigger or look weightier.

Care. Choose buttons that can be cared for in the same manner as the garment, whether it's washable or should be dry cleaned.

The back of the pattern envelope specifies how many and what size buttons to purchase. Try not to go more than ⅛" (3 mm) smaller or larger than the pattern specifies. Buttons that are too small or too large may not be in proper proportion to the edge of the garment. Button sizes are listed in inches, millimeters, and lines. For example, a ½" button is also listed as 13 mm and line 20; a ¾" button, as 19 mm and line 30.

When shopping for buttons, bring a swatch of fabric with you to assure a good match. Cut a small slit in the fabric so a button on the card can be slipped through, giving you a better idea of how it will look when finished.

Sew on buttons with doubled All purpose thread for lightweight fabrics and heavy-duty or topstitch thread for heavier fabrics.

How to Mark Button Location

Mark button placement by lapping the buttonhole side of garment over the button side, matching centerlines. Pin garment closed between buttonholes.

Insert pin straight through buttonhole and into bottom layer of fabric. For vertical buttonholes, insert pin in center of buttonhole. For horizontal buttonholes, insert pin ⅛" (3mm) from the end closest to the garment edge.

Carefully lift buttonhole over pin. Insert threaded needle at point of pin to sew on button. Mark and sew buttons one at a time, buttoning previous buttons for accurate marking.

How to Sew on a Shank Button

Cut a length of thread 30" (76 cm) long and run it through beeswax to strengthen it. Fold thread in half. Thread folded end through a crewel needle. Knot cut ends of thread. Position button at pin mark on the garment centerline, placing shank hole parallel to the buttonhole.

Secure thread on right side with small stitch under button. Bring needle through shank hole. Insert needle down into fabric and pull through. Repeat, taking four to six stitches through the shank. Secure thread in fabric under button by making a knot or taking several small stitches. Clip thread ends. If a shank button is used on a heavy fabric, it may also need a thread shank. Follow instructions for making a thread shank on a sew-through button, page 184.

How to Hand Sew a Sew-through Button

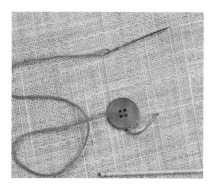

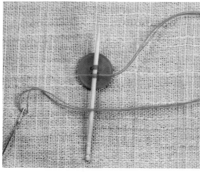

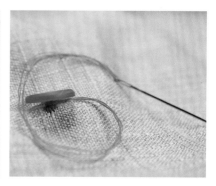

Thread needle as for shank button (page 183) and position button at pin mark. Place holes in button so they line up parallel to buttonhole. Bring needle through fabric from underside and up through one hole in button. Insert needle into another hole and through the fabric layers.

Slip a toothpick, match, or sewing machine needle between thread and button to form shank. Take three or four stitches through each pair of holes. Bring needle and thread to right side under button. Remove toothpick.

Wind thread two or three times around button stitches to form shank. Secure thread on right side under button by making a knot or taking several small stitches. Clip threads close to knot.

TIP

On jackets and coats, you can add a small, clear button on garment wrong side to anchor the main button. A small button, as shown, will protect this stress point better than interfacing, especially on heavy clothes.

How to Machine Sew a Sew-through Button

1 **Attach button foot and special plate** to cover feed or drop feed. Button will be stitched with close zigzag stitching. Regulate stitch width and tension as directed in machine manual. Many machines also have a button sew-on function.

2 **Position button under foot.** Lower needle into center of one buttonhole by turning handwheel toward you. Lower presser foot. Turn handwheel until needle rises out of button and is just above foot. Insert match or toothpick to make slack to form shank.

3 **Set zigzag stitch width** regulator so that stitch width equals the space between holes in button. Proceed slowly until you are sure you have the correct width. Take six or more zigzag stitches. Clip threads with 8" (20 cm) extra thread. Thread bobbin thread into a needle and stitch bobbin thread to right side. Wind the bobbin and top thread two or three times to form a shank. Secure threads with a knot or several small stitches.

Snaps are available as regular sew-on snaps, gripper-type snaps, or snap tape.

Sew-on snaps are suitable for areas where there is little strain, such as at the neckline or waistline to hold the facing edge flat when buttons are used, at the waistline of blouses, or at the pointed end of a waistband fastened with hooks and eyes. Sew-on snaps consist of two parts: a ball and a socket. Select a size that is strong enough to be secure, but not too heavy for the fabric.

Gripper-type snaps are attached with a special plier tool or a hammer. They have more holding power than a sew-in snap and will show on the right side of the garment. Gripper snaps can replace button and buttonhole closures in sportswear.

Snap tape consists of snaps attached to pieces of tape. The tape is stitched to the garment with a zipper foot. Snap tape is used in sportswear, home decorating, and for the inside seam of infant and toddler pants.

How to Attach Sew-on Snaps

Position ball half of snap on wrong side of overlap section, ⅛" to ¼" (3 to 6 mm) from the edge so it will not show on the right side. Stitch in place through each hole, using single strand of thread. Stitch through facing and interfacing only, not through to right side of garment. Secure thread with two tiny stitches.

Mark position of socket half of snap on right side of underlap section. Use one of the following methods: If there is a hole in center of ball half, insert pin from right side through hole and into underlap section. If there is no hole in ball, rub tailor's chalk on ball or dot ball with ink and press firmly against underlap.

Position center of socket half over marking. Stitch in place in same manner as ball half, except stitch through all layers of fabric.

What has teeth, but cannot bite and can be sewn down the back, up the front, on sleeves, cushions, pockets, pants, pillows, and purses? Zippers, of course! No closure is quite as functional and practical as a zipper. Conventional zippers are the most commonly used zippers. They are closed at one end and sewn into a seam. Conventional zippers can also be purchased as "endless," by the yard or foot, for long zipper applications like cushions or sleeping bags, or, if you sew frequently, as a way to save money. Invisible, separating, purse, heavy-duty, and fashion zippers are also available for different uses.

Patterns will specify the type and length zipper to buy. When selecting a zipper, unless you want the zipper to be a contrasting design element, choose a color that closely matches your fabric. Also consider the weight of the zipper in relation to the weight of the fabric. Choose synthetic coil zippers for lightweight fabrics, because these zippers are lighter and more flexible than metal zippers. If you cannot find a zipper of the correct length, buy one that is slightly longer than you need and shorten it using the directions on the page 189.

There are several ways to insert a zipper. The method you choose depends on the type of garment and the location of the zipper in the garment. The following pages contain instructions for the lapped, centered, and fly-front applications for conventional zippers; two methods for inserting separating zippers; and instructions for inserting an invisible zipper. There are variations of each of these applications. The methods shown are just a few of the many ways to insert zippers; these are quick and easy, featuring time-saving tools such as fabric glue stick, basting tape, and cellophane tape. Inserting a zipper always requires using a zipper presser foot. Invisible zippers require a separate presser foot for proper insertion.

Zippers should be pressed to remove any creases before adding to your garment. Most zippers have polyester tapes and are not subject to shrinkage. If you happen to have a zipper with cotton tape, preshrink it in hot water before application. This will prevent the zipper from puckering once the item is laundered. For best appearance, the final stitching on the outside of the garment should be straight and an even distance from the seamline. Stitch both sides of the zipper from bottom to top, and turn the pull tab up to make it easier to stitch past the slider.

Separating zippers can be inserted with zipper teeth covered or exposed. A sport zipper with chunky plastic teeth is lightweight for activewear. These zippers are also sturdy and easy to operate, making them a good choice for young children's apparel.

Purse zippers feature two sliders and two closed ends, allowing the user to open and close the zipper anywhere along the coil to make handbag access more flexible.

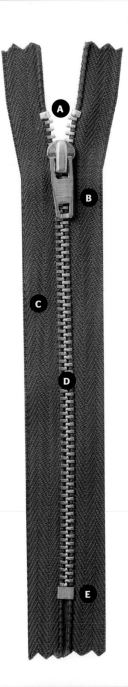

Parts of the Zipper

A. Top stop is the small metal bracket at the top that prevents the slider from running off the tape.

B. Slider and pull tab is the mechanism that operates the zipper. It locks the teeth together to close the zipper and unlocks the teeth to open the zipper.

C. Tape is the fabric strip on which the teeth or coil are fastened. The tape is sewn to the garment.

D. Teeth or coil is the part of the zipper that locks together when the slider runs along it. It may be made of nylon, polyester, or metal.

E. Bottom stop is the bracket at the bottom of the zipper where the slider rests when the zipper is open. Separating zippers have a bottom stop that splits into two parts to allow the zipper to be completely opened.

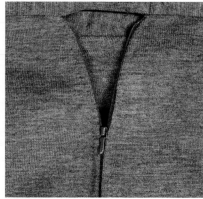

Lapped application totally conceals the zipper, making it a good choice for zippers that do not perfectly match the fabric color. It is most often used in side seam closings of dresses, skirts, and pants.

Centered application is most frequently used for center front and center back closings. Attach facings before inserting the zipper. Waistbands should be applied after the zipper is inserted.

Fly-front zipper is often found on pants and skirts, and occasionally on coats and jackets. Use the fly-front application only when the pattern calls for it, because it requires the wider underlap and facing usually included in the pattern.

Invisible zippers provide a garment closure that is inconspicuous, revealing only the pull tab. They are an excellent alternative to traditional zippers for center back or side installations. A special presser foot is required for inserting an invisible zipper. This foot unrolls the coil; after stitching, the coil and fabric roll to the inside, concealing the zipper.

How to Shorten a Zipper

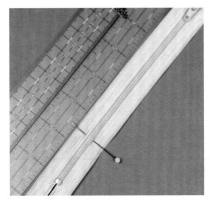

Measure desired length along the coil, beginning at top stop. Mark with pin.

Machine zigzag across the coil at pin to form new bottom stop.

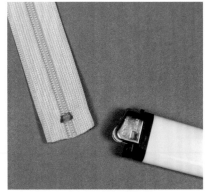

Cut off excess zipper and tape. Run the edge of the polyester zipper tape quickly over a flame to seal it.

How to Insert a Lapped Zipper

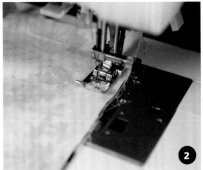

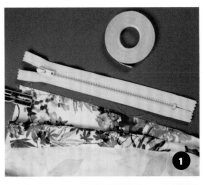

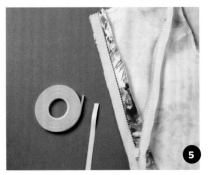

1 **Check seam opening** from wrong side to make sure top edges are even. Length of opening should be equal to length of zipper coil plus 1" (2.5 cm). Pin seam from bottom of opening to top of garment.

2 **Machine baste on seamline** from bottom of the opening to top of the garment, removing pins as you stitch.

3 **Clip basting stitches** every 2" (5 cm) to make basting easier to remove after zipper is inserted.

4 **Press seam open.** If zipper is in side seam of skirt or pants, press seam over a press mitt or tailor's ham to retain shape of hipline.

5 **Place open zipper face down** on right-hand side of seam allowance (top facing you). Position zipper coil directly on seamline with top stop 1" (2.5 cm) below cut edge. Turn pull tab up. Pin, tape, or glue right-hand side of zipper tape in place.

6 **Attach zipper foot** and adjust needle to left side. Machine baste close to edge of coil, stitching from bottom to top of zipper with edge of zipper foot against coil. Remove pins as you stitch.

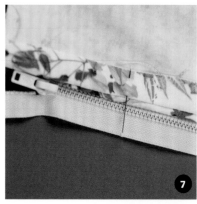

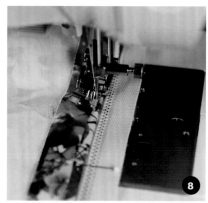

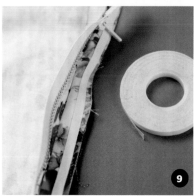

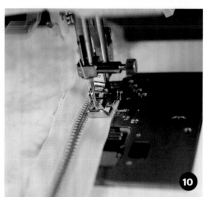

7 **Close zipper and turn** face up. Smooth fabric away from zipper, forming narrow fold between zipper coil and basted seam.

8 **Adjust zipper foot to right** side of needle. Starting at bottom of zipper tape, stitch near edge of fold, through folded seam allowance and zipper tape.

9 **Turn zipper over** so face side is flat against opposite seam allowance. Make sure pull tab is turned up to lessen bulk while stitching. Pin or tape in place.

10 **Adjust zipper foot to left** side of needle. Starting at top of zipper, machine baste through tape and seam allowance only. This holds seam allowance in place for the final stitching.

11 **Topstitch ½" (1.3 cm) from seam** on outside of garment. To aid straight stitching, use transparent tape placed with edge ½" (1.3 cm) from opening and stitch along edge. Starting at seamline, stitch across bottom of zipper, pivot at edge of tape and continue to top. Remove tape.

12 **Pull thread at bottom** of zipper to wrong side and knot. Remove machine basting in seam.

13 **Press,** using a press cloth to protect fabric from shine. Trim zipper tape even with top edge of garment.

How to Insert a Centered Zipper (Using Tape or Glue Stick)

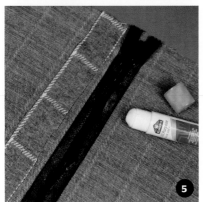

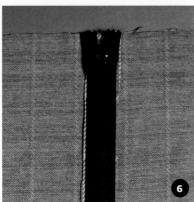

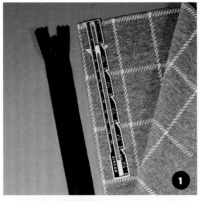

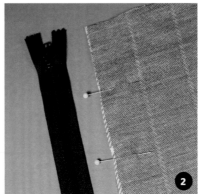

1 **Check seam opening** on wrong side to make sure top edges are even. Length of zipper opening should be equal to length of zipper coil plus 1" (2.5 cm).

2 **Pin zipper opening** in seam from bottom of opening to top of garment.

3 **Machine baste** on seamline from bottom of opening to top of garment. Clip basting stitches every 2" (5 cm) to make basting easier to remove.

4 **Press seam open.** Finish raw edges if fabric ravels easily.

5 **Apply basting tape** or lightly apply glue stick on face side of zipper.

6 **Place zipper face down** on seam, with zipper coil directly on seamline and top stop 1" (2.5 cm) below cut edge (keep pull tab up). Press with fingers to secure zipper. Let glue dry for a few minutes.

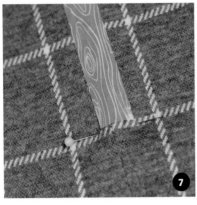

7 **Spread garment flat, right side up.** Mark bottom of zipper with pin. Apply ½" (1.3 cm) wide tape over the center of the seamline. Do not use tape on delicate or napped fabrics; choose whatever marking method will do no damage.

8 **Attach zipper foot and adjust to left** of needle. Topstitch zipper from right side, starting at seam at bottom of tape.

9 **Stitch across bottom of zipper,** pivoting at edge of tape. Stitch up side of zipper to top edge, using edge of tape as a guide.

10 **Adjust the zipper foot to right** side of needle. Begin again at seam at bottom of tape and stitch across bottom of zipper.

11 **Pivot and stitch up** side of zipper, using edge of tape as a guide.

12 **Remove tape.** Carefully remove machine basting in seamline.

13 **Press,** using a press cloth to protect fabric from shine. Trim zipper tape even with the top edge of the garment.

How to Insert a Fly-front Zipper Before Stitching the Pants Seams

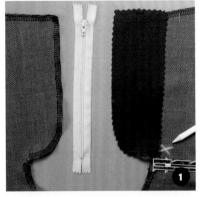

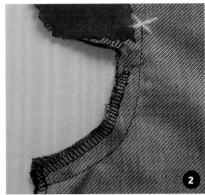

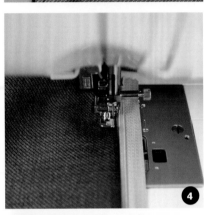

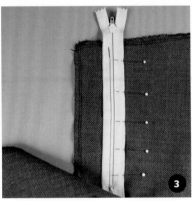

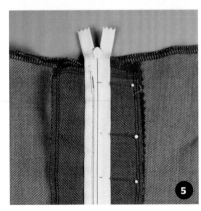

1 **Cut interfacing 1¾"** (4.5 cm) wide by the length of the fly facing, using pinking shears. Fuse to wrong side of overlap facing. Mark bottom of zipper opening and choose a zipper 1" to 2" (2.5 to 5 cm) longer than the finished zipper opening. Finish raw edges of fly facings. Press fold on overlap facing at center front.

2 **Stitch front crotch seam,** using short stitches, and ending at bottom of zipper opening; backstitch three or four stitches.

3 **Place closed zipper face down** on underlap facing, with edge of zipper tape at center front and zipper stop ⅛" (3 mm) above bottom of zipper opening. Pin outer edge of zipper tape to facing. Using zipper foot with needle right, stitch zipper tape to facing only. Remove pins.

4 **Flip zipper right side up** and fold underlap facing to wrong side. Press and machine baste next to foldline.

5 **Match center front markings** at upper edge and pin from right side. From wrong side, pin remaining edge of zipper tape to overlap facing only.

6 **With facing held away** from pants and zipper foot set needle left, stitch zipper tape to facing.

7 **Mark stitching line on right side** of

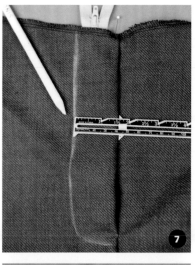

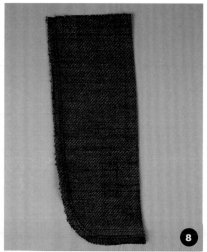

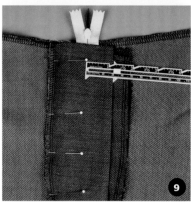

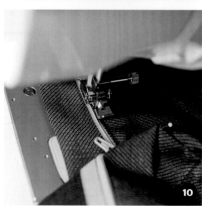

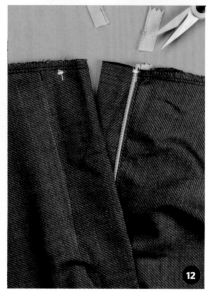

7 **Mark stitching line on right side** of pants, about 1½" (3.2 cm) from center fold. Hand baste next to stitching line, if desired. Stitch with a regular foot, backstitching three or four stitches at center fold. Remove basting. Open zipper.

8 **Cut fly shield** from pants fabric 4" (10 cm) wide by length of fly facing; curve lower edge, if desired. Press fly shield in half lengthwise; finish raw edges.

9 **Place fly shield under zipper** on underlap side, with upper edges matching and folded edge about 1" (2.5 cm) beyond zipper teeth.

10 **Turn to right side and stitch** close to fold along the zipper teeth through all layers with zipper foot set to left needle. Remove basting.

11 **Close zipper and tack** lower edge of fly shield to overlap facing from wrong side. From right side, stitch a bar tack at lower end of zipper opening (shown in white), if desired.

12 **Staystitch with zipper open** across both ends of zipper at upper edge; trim off excess zipper ends. Clip crotch seam allowances below the fly facing to within ¼" (6 mm) of stitching and finish.

How to Insert a Covered Separating Zipper

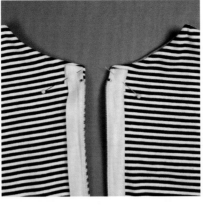

Use basting tape, pins, or glue to secure closed zipper, face up, under faced opening edges. Position pull tab ⅛" (3 mm) below neck (or other edge) seamline. Edges of the opening should meet at center of zipper, covering the teeth.

Open zipper. Turn ends of zipper tape under at top of garment. Pin ends in place.

Topstitch ⅜" (1 cm) from each opening edge, sewing through fabric and zipper tape. Stitch from bottom to top on each side, adjusting zipper foot to correct side.

How to Insert an Exposed Separating Zipper

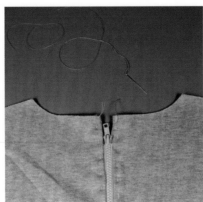

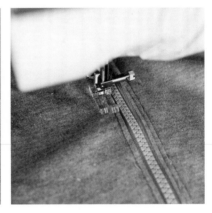

Pin faced opening edges to closed zipper so edges are close to, but not covering zipper teeth, with pull tab ⅛" (3 mm) below neck seamline.

Baste zipper in place with tape ends extending above neck seamline. Turn ends of zipper tape under at top of garment, if facing is already attached. Open zipper. Topstitch close to opening edges on right side of garment, using zipper or topstitching foot and stitching from bottom to top on each side.

To hold zipper tape flat, close zipper and add another line of stitching ¼" (6 mm) from first stitching line on each side. Remove basting stitches.

How to Insert an Invisible Zipper

Invisible zippers can be most easily inserted by stitching them into the garment before stitching any part of the seam.

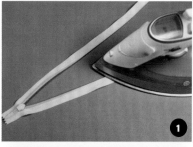

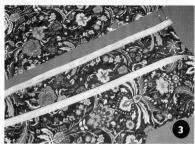

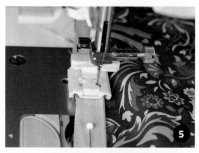

1 **Open zipper.** Steam press zipper tape from wrong side to unroll coils.

2 **Position closed zipper** on the right side of the garment section, with zipper top stop ⅜" (1 cm) from neckline seam; pin-mark garment pieces at upper and lower edges of zipper, making sure the pattern markings are aligned.

3 **Open zipper and position** on right garment section, right sides together, tape edge aligned with fabric edge and ends of zipper aligned to pin marks. Pin or hand-baste zipper tape in place.

4 **Instead of pinning in place,** overedge stitch along the edge of the zipper tape and fabric edge. Place the zipper tape slightly inside while stitching, so that the fabric curls up over the edge of the zipper tape to finish the edge.

5 **Attach invisible zipper foot** to machine and position zipper coil under groove on right side of foot. Slide zipper foot on adapter to adjust needle position so stitching will be very close to the coil. On heavier fabric, set needle position slightly farther from coil.

6 **Stitch, starting at upper edge** of zipper coil, until zipper foot touches the pull tab at bottom, taking care not to stretch fabric. Remove pins as you approach them. Secure thread at ends.

7 **Pin or overedge stitch remaining** side of zipper to left garment section, as in step 3, making sure to align ends of zipper to pin marks.

8 **Close the zipper and stitch** the remainder of garment seam. Use a regular zipper foot to get as close as possible to the zipper seam.

9 **Secure lower end of tape** to seam allowances, using a regular zipper foot.

Sewing Activewear

Elasticized waistbands are comfortable to wear and easy to sew. They complement the stretch of knit fabrics. Some elasticized waistbands are cut-on, which means the waistbands are cut as an extension of the garment at the waistline edge, while others are a separate waistband piece. Choose an application technique according to the fabric, the garment style, and the type of elastic you are using.

Two techniques for cut-on waistbands are included: one with a casing and one with topstitching. Both are appropriate for garments made from lightweight to medium-weight fabrics. Cut-on waistbands with casings give a casual look. Firm braided or woven elastics are well suited for this technique. Because the elastic is not caught in the waistline seam, it can easily be adjusted for a better fit, if necessary. Cut-on waistbands with topstitching give a variety of looks, depending on the type of topstitching. Use an elastic with good stretch and recovery qualities so the elastic will stretch to the circumference of the garment opening, yet retain its fit. Drawstring elastic may be used for this method.

Two additional techniques are included for waistbands that use a separate waistband piece: smooth waistbands and shirred waistbands. When sewing garments from lightweight or medium-weight knits, you may cut the waistband from self-fabric. When sewing bulky fabrics, such as sweatshirt fleece, ribbing is your best choice.

Smooth separate waistbands give the smooth appearance of a traditional waistband when the garment is worn. This waistband style is suitable for a slim-fitting garment made from lightweight or medium-weight knit fabric with moderate stretch. Use a firm 1" or 1¼" (2.5 or 3.2 cm) elastic.

Shirred separate waistbands complement fuller garment styles, such as full skirts, and are especially attractive when used with wider elastics. Shirred waistbands may be topstitched or not, depending on the look you prefer. Firm elastic is recommended for this type of waistband.

In general, cut elastics 2" to 3" (5 to 7.5 cm) less than your waist measurement. Cut soft, lightweight elastics, such as knit elastics, 3" to 5" (7.5 to 12.5 cm) less than your waist measurement. Cut very firm elastics, such as nonroll waistband elastic, equal to, or 1" (2.5 cm) less than, your waist measurement. Mark the elastic, and pin it around your waistline before cutting it. Check to see that the elastic fits comfortably around your waist and pulls over your hips easily.

Multiple rows of topstitching can cause elastic to lose some of its recovery. If you are using a method that calls for topstitching, you may want to cut the elastic up to 1" (2.5 cm) shorter than the guidelines, to ensure a snug fit.

TIPS

Preshrink elastics for casing applications before measuring. Elastics that will be stitched on do not require preshrinking.

Use longer stitches, about eight to nine stitches per inch (2.5 cm), when stitching through the elastic; the stitches will appear shorter when elastic is relaxed. A stitch length that is too short weakens and stretches out the elastic.

Steam the finished waistband after construction, holding the iron above the fabric, to help the elastic return to its original length.

Two Ways to Join the Ends of the Elastic

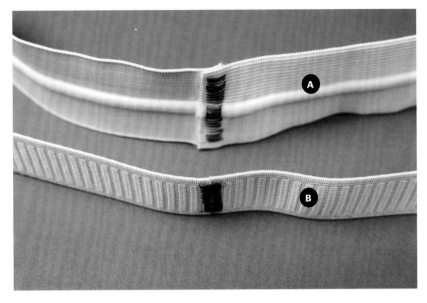

A **Overlapped method.** Overlap ends of elastic ½" (1.3 cm). Stitch back and forth through both layers, using wide zigzag stitch or 3-step zigzag stitch. Use for soft elastics, such as knitted elastic.

B **Butted method.** Butt ends of elastic. Stitch back and forth, using 3-step zigzag stitch or wide zigzag stitch, catching both ends of elastic in stitching. This method is recommended for firm elastics.

How to Sew a Cut-on Waistband with a Casing

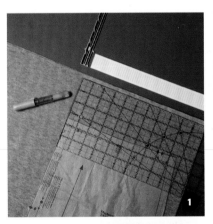
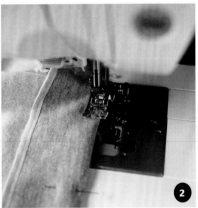
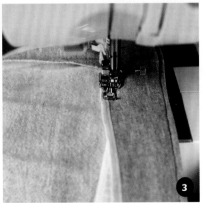
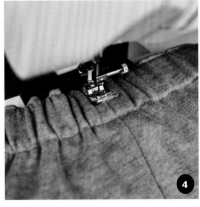

1 **Extend garment pattern pieces** above waistline twice the width of the elastic plus ⅝" (1.5 cm). Cut out garment sections, and stitch together.

2 **Overlock or bind raw edge** at waist, if desired. Fold edge of fabric to wrong side, an amount equal to width of elastic plus ½" (1.3 cm). Edgestitch close to fold.

3 **Join ends of elastic.** Position elastic within folded casing area. Stitch next to elastic, using straight stitch and zipper foot; do not catch elastic in stitching. Shift fabric around elastic as necessary while stitching.

4 **Stretch waistband** to distribute fabric evenly. From right side of garment, stitch in the ditch through all waistband layers, at center front, center back, and side seams, to secure elastic.

How to Sew a Cut-on Waistband with Topstitching

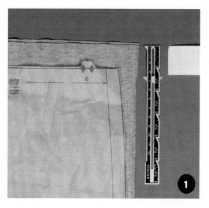

1 **Extend garment pattern** pieces above waistline twice the width of the elastic. Cut out garment sections, and stitch together. Join ends of elastic (page 199).

2 **Divide elastic and garment** edge into fourths; pin mark. Pin elastic to wrong side of garment, with edges even, matching pin marks; overlock or zigzag, stretching elastic to fit between pins. If using overlock machine, guide work carefully or disengage knives to avoid cutting elastic.

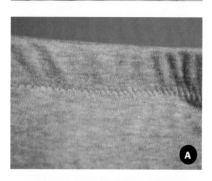

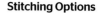

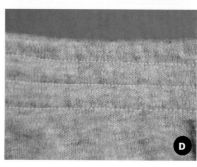

3 **Fold elastic to wrong side** of garment so fabric encases elastic.

4 **From right side of garment,** stitch in the ditch through all waistband layers, at center front, center back, and side seams to secure elastic.

5 **Topstitch through all layers,** stretching elastic as you sew (contrasting thread used to show detail).

Stitching Options

A **Straight stitch or narrow zigzag** close to lower edge of casing, using long stitches.

B **Zigzag close to lower edge,** using medium-to-wide stitches.

C **Double-needle topstitch** close to lower edge.

D **Stitch multiple, even rows** of straight stitching or double-needle stitching.

Drawstring-elastic Method

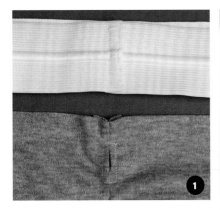

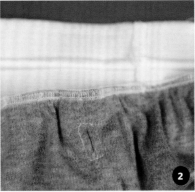

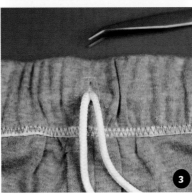

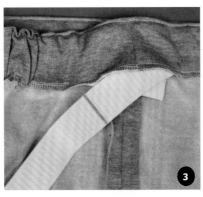

1 **Extend pattern pieces** as in step 1, opposite. Join ends of drawstring elastic, using overlapped method (page 199). Stitch garment sections together, leaving ½" (1.3 cm) opening in center front seam in drawstring area; topstitch around opening to secure.

2 **Follow step 2, opposite.** Zigzag at lower edge of elastic. Fold elastic to wrong side of garment so fabric encases elastic. Straight stitch ¼" (6 mm) from upper and lower edges of elastic, through all layers, stretching elastic to fit.

3 **Pull drawstring through** center front opening. Cut drawstring and knot ends.

Alternate Method

Follow steps 1 and 2, opposite.

1 **Mark elastic to desired length;** do not cut.

2 **Position elastic within** folded casing area.

3 **Stitch next to elastic,** using straight stitch and zipper foot, leaving 2" (5 cm) unstitched; do not catch elastic in stitching.

4 **Pull elastic through** to marking; secure using safety pin. Try on garment to check fit; adjust elastic, if necessary. Cut and join ends of elastic (page 199). Complete waistband stitching. Stitch in the ditch as in step 4, opposite.

How to Sew a Smooth, Separate Waistband

1 **Mark cutting line** on garment section pattern pieces ⅝" (1.5 cm) above waistline. Cut waistband on crosswise grain, twice the width of elastic plus 1¼" (3.2 cm); length of waistband is equal to your waist measurement plus 3¼" (8 cm). Pin ends of waistband together with ⅝" (1.5 cm) seam allowances; check fit over hips.

2 **Join ends of waistband;** press seam open. Divide waistband and garment edge into fourths; pin mark. Pin waistband to right side of garment with raw edges even, matching pin marks. Stitch ⅝" (1.5 cm) seam, using straight stitch or narrow zigzag stitch; if using straight stitch, stretch fabric as you sew.

3 **Join ends of elastic** (page 199). Divide elastic and garment edge into fourths; pin mark. Place elastic on seam allowance of waistband; pin in place, with lower edge of elastic just above seamline. With elastic on top, stitch through both seam allowances, using wide zigzag or multiple zigzag stitch; stretch elastic to fit between pins. Trim seam allowances.

4 **Fold waistband tightly over elastic** to wrong side of garment; pin. Stitch in the ditch along seamline from right side of garment, stretching elastic; catch waistband in stitching on wrong side of garment, but do not catch elastic. Trim waistband seam allowance to ¼" (6 mm) from stitching.

How to Sew a Shirred Separate Waistband

1 **Mark cutting line** on garment section pattern pieces ⅝" (1.5 cm) above waistline. Cut waistband on crosswise grain, twice the width of elastic plus 1¼" (3.2 cm); length of waistband is equal to your hip measurement plus 1¼" (3.2 cm). Join ends of elastic (page 199).

2 **Join ends of waistband** in ⅝" (1.5 cm) seam; press seam open. Divide the waistband and garment edges into fourths; pin mark. Fold the waistband in half lengthwise, wrong sides together, encasing elastic. Baste ½" (1.3 cm) from raw edges, avoiding pins; shift fabric around elastic, as necessary.

3 **Pin waistband to right side** of garment, matching pin marks; if garment is very full, gather waistline edge before attaching waistband. Stitch just inside basting stitches, stretching waistband to fit garment between pins. Trim seam allowances to ¼" (6 mm). Overlock raw edges, if desired.

4 **Stretch waistband to distribute** fabric evenly. From right side of garment, stitch perpendicular to the waistline through all waistband layers, at the center back, and side seams, to secure the elastic. If desired, topstitch through all layers, as on page 200, step 4.

The most common use for ribbing is to finish the edges of knit sportswear garments. Ribbing, which has great crosswise stretch and recovery, enables garment openings to stretch easily when you are getting dressed and return to a neat, comfortable fit during wear. Ribbing is available as yardage and as prefinished ribbed bands.

The width of ribbing yardage ranges from 28" to 60" (71 to 152.5 cm), or 14" to 30" (35.5 to 76 cm) tubular, and is available in several weights. To use ribbing yardage, cut a crosswise strip of the fabric, fold it in half lengthwise, and apply it so the fold becomes the finished edge.

Prefinished ribbed bands have one finished edge and are applied as a single layer. They are available in various widths and lengths, and in different weights and styles.

Ribbing can be used as an edge finish for several styles of necklines, including turtleneck, mock turtleneck, crewneck, and scoop neck. It is also used on sleeves, lower edges of T-shirts and sweatshirts, and waistlines of pants and skirts. The cut width and cut length of the ribbing varies, depending on where it will be used and the desired style.

If using ribbing yardage, the cut width of the ribbing is equal to twice the desired finished width plus ½" (1.3 cm) for seam allowances. If using prefinished ribbed bands, the cut width is equal to the desired finished width plus one ¼" (6 mm) seam allowance.

Many patterns designed for knits indicate what length to cut the ribbing or they provide a pattern piece to be used as a guide for the ribbing pieces. The cut length for ribbing can also be determined by measuring the garment opening at the seamline, see page 204.

For straight, close-fitting edges, the cut length can be determined by pin fitting the ribbing on the body. On straight edges that do not require a close fit, such as the lower edge of a skirt, cut the ribbing slightly shorter than the garment edge. Depending on the stretch and recovery of the particular ribbing you are using, for small area uses, such as cuff or collars, you will want to subtract 1"–2" (2.5–5 cm) from the edge measurement for a snug fit. For skirt, pant, and sweatshirt waistbands, you will want to subtract 3"–6" (7.5–15 cm) for wearing and dressing ease.

To sew ribbed edges, you may use either the flat or the in-the-round method of construction. Flat construction is the fastest method; however, the seams may be noticeable at the edges of the ribbing. For a better-quality finish, the in-the-round method is usually preferred. With this method, the ribbing seams are enclosed for a neater appearance.

If matching ribbing is not available, self fabric, cut on the crosswise grain, can be substituted for ribbing yardage. Use a knit fabric that stretches at least 50 percent crosswise; for example, 10" (25.5 cm) of knit must stretch to at least 15" (38 cm).

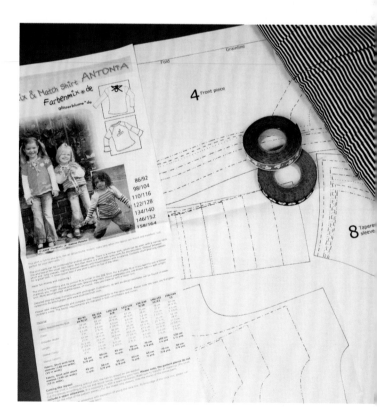

How to Determine the Cut Length

1 Measure seamline of garment opening by standing tape measure on edge. For necklines, cut ribbing as described below. For other garment openings, ribbing is usually cut two-thirds of the measurement plus ½" (1.3 cm). If self fabric is substituted for ribbing, cut it three-fourths of the measurement plus ½" (1.3 cm).

2 Pin-fit ribbing or self fabric around body for straight, close-fitting edges, such as at hiplines, wrists, and ankles. Fold ribbing crosswise for double thickness, and pin ribbing so it lies flat, without gapping; do not distort the ribs. Add ½" (1.3 cm) for seam allowances.

Types of Ribbed Necklines

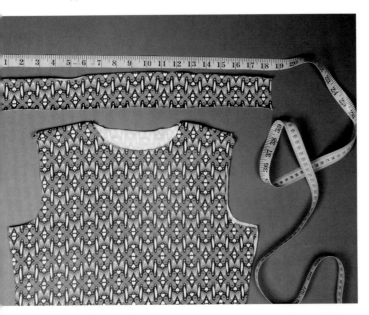

Crewneck garments usually have ribbing with a finished width of 1" to 1¼" (2.5 to 3.2 cm), but they can be as narrow as ½" (1.3 cm) for ladies' scoop-neck shirts and children's and infant wear. The neckline seam usually falls ¾" (2 cm) below the natural neckline. Cut the ribbing two-thirds of the neckline measurement plus ½" (1.3 cm).

Turtleneck garments have ribbing with a finished width of 4" to 6" (10 to 15 cm). The neckline seam falls at the natural neckline. Cut the ribbing the length of the neckline measurement plus ½" (1.3 cm).

Mock turtleneck garments have ribbing with a finished width of 2" to 2³/₈" (5 to 6 cm). The neckline seam falls ½" (1.3 cm) below the natural neckline. Cut the ribbing three-fourths of the neckline measurement plus ½" (1.3 cm).

Scoop-neck garments have rounded necklines, with the edge of the ribbing falling lower than the natural neckline in the front and, sometimes, in the back. Cut the ribbing two-thirds of the neckline measurement plus ½" (1.3 cm). The finished width of the ribbing varies from ¾" to 1" (2 to 2.5 cm).

Self fabric may be used instead of ribbing. For turtlenecks, cut the self fabric the length of the neckline measurement plus ½" (1.3 cm); for crew necks, mock turtlenecks, and scoop necks, cut it three-fourths of the neckline plus ½" (1.3 cm).

How to Sew Ribbed Edges (flat method)

1 **Cut garment pieces,** allowing ¼" (6 mm) seam allowances at garment openings. Stitch shirt front and back together along one shoulder seam. If making a raglan-style shirt, stich front, back and sleeves together, but leave one back shoulder seam unstitched.

2 **If using ribbing yardage** of self-fabric, fold ribbing in half lengthwise, wrong sides together, and press. Divide ribbing and garment opening into fourths; pin mark.

3 **Pin ribbing to right side** of garment, matching pin marks. With ribbing on top, stitch ¼" (6 mm) seam, using narrow zigzag or overlock stitch; stretch ribbing to fit garment opening as you sew. Lightly press seam toward garment.

4 **Trim ribbing.** Stitch remaining garment seam and ribbing closed in one motion, matching ribbing seam and ends carefully.

5 **Secure ribbing seam allowance** in place with a triangular tack. Topstitch around the neckline seam with a stretch stitch, as desired.

How to Sew Ribbed Edges (In-the-Round Method)

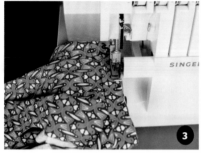

1 **Join ends of ribbing in ¼"** (6 mm) seam into a loop, right fabric sides together. Fold and press ribbing loop in half lengthwise, wrong sides together. Divide ribbing and garment opening into fourths; pin mark.

2 **Pin ribbing to right side** of garment, matching pin marks.

3 **With ribbing on top, stitch ¼"** (6mm) seam, using narrow zigzag or overlock stitch; stretch ribbing to fit garment opening as you sew. Lightly press seam toward garment.

4 **Topstitch close to seamline,** if desired, stitching through garment and seam allowances, using single or double needle. If single needle is used, stretch fabric slightly as you sew.

How to Apply Lapped Ribbing to a V-Neckline

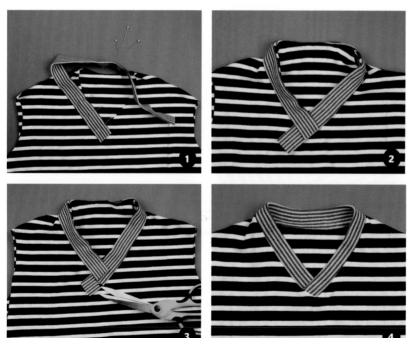

1 **Cut ribbing slightly longer** than the cut edge of neckline. Staystitch on the seamline 2" (5 cm) on either side of the V. Clip carefully to the V.

2 **Pin folded ribbing to right-hand** side of neckline in ¼" (6 mm) seam; leave 1" (2.5 cm) for lapping. With garment on top, begin stitching at center front. Stretch ribbing slightly as you sew.

3 **Stop stitching before reaching point** of V, leaving an opening equal to width of ribbing. Remove garment from machine.

4 **Turn ribbing seam to inside** and then lay garment out flat. Tuck the extensions inside the seam opening with right-hand side overlapping left. Pin ribbing at center front in lapped position. Fold front of garment out of the way. From wrong side, stitch opening closed; pivot at point of V, and stitch free end of ribbing to right-hand seam allowance. Trim extensions close to stitches.

How to Apply Mitered Stitched Ribbing to a V-Neckline (In-the-Round Method)

1 **Sew the shirt front and back** together at the shoulder seams. Add a line of staystitching ⅛" (3 mm) right at the point of the V.

2 **Fold collar piece in half** crosswise and pin. Place the open end of the collar piece under the shirt neckline and trace along the V with a textile marker.

3 **Stitch along the marked V** on the collar piece. Trim away excess material in the V to ⅛" (3 mm) from stitching line. Clip the fabric right at the center of the V on the collar piece. Clip to, but not through, the staystitching right at the V of the shirt neckline.

4 **Press the seam allowances** of the stitched V in the collar piece open with the tip of the iron. Align the two stitching lines of the collar piece V on top of one another to form the miter.

5 **Press the miter and collar** piece in half lengthwise around.

6 **Pin collar piece** in four equidistant places along the neckline. Spread the clipped fabric at the center of the V in the shirt to either side of the V point of the collar piece.

7 **Stitch the collar piece** to the shirt using a stretch stitch. Remove the pins as they approach the knife (serger) or the needle (conventional machine). Begin and end your stitching line at the V point.

8 **Press seam allowance down.** Topstitch with a stretch stitch, as desired.

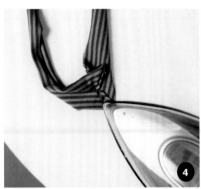

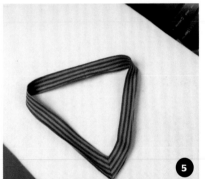

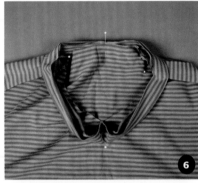

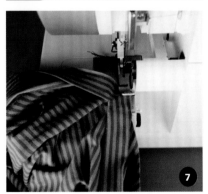

Patterns for swimsuits and leotards are usually closely fitted for comfort and easy motion. A wide range of pattern styles is available. Styles with princess seams are slenderizing. So are patterns with a center panel of a contrasting color; to minimize hips, use a dark color for the side panels. High-cut leg openings on swimsuits and leotards give the appearance of longer legs and a slimmer torso. For a full-busted figure, choose a pattern with a bustline shaped by darts or seams. To fill out a slender figure, use a pattern with shirring, draping, or ruffles. Or choose a simple pattern style and a splashy printed fabric to enhance a slender figure.

By sewing your own swimsuits and leotards, you can make garments that meet your needs. Add a full-front lining to a swimsuit, if desired; this is especially important for light-colored and light-weight fabrics. Or you may line just the crotch area or add a bandeau lining in the bust area. Purchased bra cups may be sewn into the bandeau if firmer support is desired.

Two-way stretch fabric stretches to fit the contours of many different figure types. Select the pattern according to the bust measurement to avoid extensive fitting adjustments at the bustline. If you require different pattern sizes for the hips and the bust, choose a multisize pattern, following the cutting lines for the appropriate sizes and blending the lines in the waistline area.

Adjusting the Pattern

For one-piece swimsuits and leotards, measure your torso length, shown opposite, and compare it to the torso lengths given in the accompanying chart; do not measure the pattern pieces for this comparison, because they will measure less than the actual body measurement. If your torso measurement falls within the range given for your bust size, no pattern adjustment is needed.

If your torso measurement is different from the length given in the chart, first adjust the pattern front an amount equal to one-fourth the difference, then adjust the pattern back the same amount. The total pattern adjustment is only one-half the difference between your torso measurement and the chart; the two-way stretch fabric will be stretched when it is worn, automatically giving you the rest of the length needed. If each pattern piece has two adjustment lines, divide the total amount of adjustment needed equally among all four lines.

Linings can limit the stretch of the swimsuit fabric, so if you are going to line the front of a swimsuit, add an extra ½" (1.3 cm) of length to the front and back pattern pieces.

How to Adjust the Torso Length on the Pattern

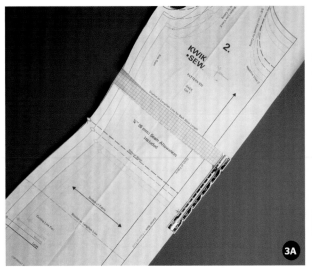

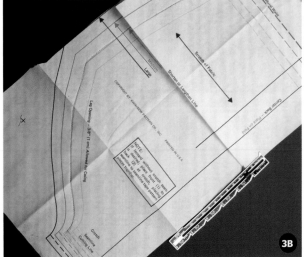

1 Measure torso down chest from indentation at breast bone in front; bring tape measure between your legs and up the back to prominent bone at back of neck. Keep the tape measure snug to duplicate fit of finished garment. It is helpful to have someone help you take this measurement.

2 Determine the difference between your torso measurement and the torso length given in the chart, below, that corresponds to your bust size. The pattern needs to be adjusted an amount equal to one-half the difference; distribute this amount equally among the pattern adjustment lines.

3 Adjust the pattern, adding or subtracting length to the pattern by spreading or overlapping front and back pattern pieces on the adjustment lines. In the example shown here, front and back pieces are lengthened ¼" (6 mm) on each adjustment line for a total adjustment of 1" (2.5 cm).

Comparison of Bust Size and Torso Length

BUST SIZE	TORSO LENGTH
30" (76 cm)	52" to 54" (132 to 137 cm)
32" (81.5 cm)	53" to 55" (134.5 to 139.5 cm)
34" (86.5 cm)	54" to 56" (137 to 142 cm)
36" (91.5 cm)	55" to 57" (139.5 to 145 cm)
38" (96.5 cm)	56" to 58" (142 to 147 cm)
40" (102 cm)	57" to 59" (145 to 150 cm)
42" (107 cm)	58" to 60" (147 to 152.5 cm)
44" (112 cm)	59" to 61" (150 to 155 cm)

Before laying out a swimsuit or leotard pattern, determine which direction of the fabric has the greater amount of stretch. Nylon/spandex knits usually stretch more in the lengthwise direction; cotton/spandex, in the crosswise. For a comfortable fit, lay out the pattern on the fabric so the greater amount of stretch will encircle the body.

Modern swimsuit and dancewear fabrics have excellent recovery properties, which most modern sewing patterns have taken into consideration when grading. Modern swimwear sewing patterns will have less wearing ease calculated into the grading in order achieve a snug, figure-hugging fit. Therefore, it is important to select fabrics especially made for swim and dancewear.

Swimsuits and leotards are fast and easy to sew. Most styles have only a few seams and edge finishes. Stitch the side seams and crotch seam first; then try on the garment and adjust the fit as needed.

If a one-piece swimsuit or leotard is too long in the torso, shorten it at the shoulder seams; if this raises the neckline, the neck opening can be trimmed as necessary. If the armholes are too small, causing the garment to bind under the arms, enlarge them by trimming the openings. Leg openings should fit smoothly; if they are too large, take in the side seams at the lower edge, tapering the seams gradually. Stitch the shoulder seams after the fitting, and apply the elastic (pages 214-215).

HOW TO SEW A BASIC ONE-PIECE SWIMSUIT OR LEOTARD

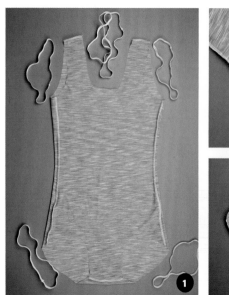

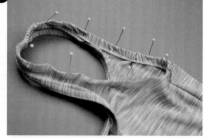

1 **Stitch crotch seam**, applying crotch lining if desired. Stitch side seams. Check garment for fit. Apply full-front lining, if desired. Stitch shoulder seams. Apply elastic to garment openings.

2 **Add and finish** elastic at all open edges as described above and pages 214 and 215.

HOW TO SEW A BASIC TWO-PIECE SWIMSUIT

You'll find a few unique measurements helpful for a two-piece garment. Take a crotch measurement, from the lower back, between the legs to a point on the abdomen where the top edge should rest. Take a bust measurement around the torso. Take a breast measurement beginning at approximately the top of the armpit to underneath the breast. Also take a measurement from the side of the breast at the thickest part to the breast bone.

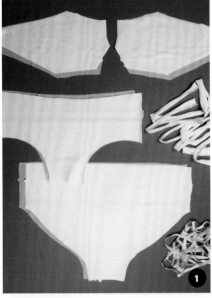

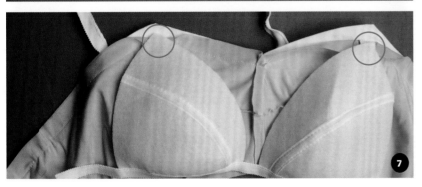

1. **Cut out pieces** of the swimsuit outer and lining. Stitch seams of top outer and lining.

2. **Pin straps in place** between outer and lining.

3. **Machine-baste lining** to right side of swimsuit top, basting a distance equal to width of elastic from raw edges, catching straps in the stitching line. If lining material is somewhat thick, trim lining close to the stitching. Most lingerie and swimwear lining materials are very thin and do not require trimming. However, if you are using the same fabric as the swimsuit outer for the lining, you may want to trim the lining at the seam allowance.

4. **Center boning, if used,** on side seam allowance, positioned so the ends will curve away from body. Stitch over previous stitches along inner edge of boning.

5. **Apply elastic to edges** of swimsuit top (pages 214-215), as neccesary. Most specialty Lycra/spandex elastane swim fabrics have enough elasticity and recovery that adding elastic to the edges of a bikini top may not be necessary.

6. **Stitch lining to outer bikini top** along top edge only, catching straps in the seamline.

7. **Tack pre fabricated bra support** or boning to lining seam allowance, if used (see circles).

8. **Hem the bottom edge** of the turned bikini top, catching the elastic edge of the bra support piece in the seam. See step 7 on page 215.

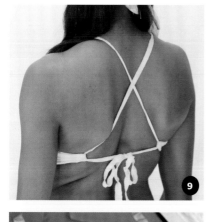

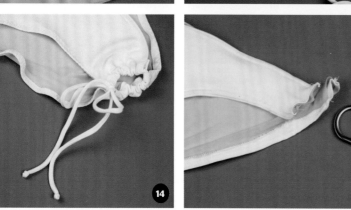

9 **Fold over the right and left bikini top** torso pieces to form two casings and stitch. The straps of the bikini top will be fed through these casings and tied in back for a secure fit and closure.

10 **Stitch center back seam** of the swimsuit bottom (if present). Stitch bikini bottom front to bikini bottom back at the crotch seam. Do the same to lining pieces. Baste lining to outer along seam allowance or use basting spray.

11 **Apply elastic to the leg openings.**

12 **Apply elastic to the top front** edge and the back top edge.

13 **Fold over the four side edges** to form casings and stitch.

14 **Thread string ties** through casings.

15 **Alternately, add decorative rings** and stitch casings closed.

HOW TO MAKE STRING TIES

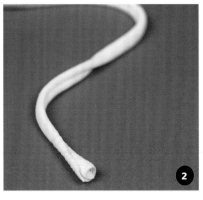

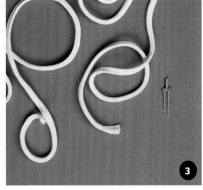

1 **Cut strips of fabric** approximately 1" (2.5 cm) wide parallel to the courses (from selvedge to selvedge).

2 **When stretched, the strips will curl** inward, forming tubes of material with the fabric wrong side facing out. If using a printed fabric, use a coordinating solid for the string ties.

3 **Install a twin needle** and stitch along the string with the fabric edge facing down.

ADJUSTING FOR A GOOD FIT

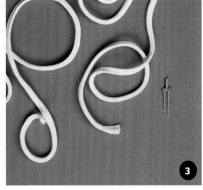

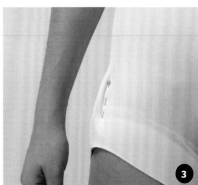

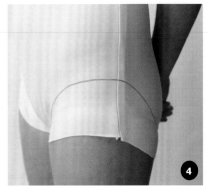

1 **Adjust shoulder seams** for snug fit if garment is too long in torso. Adjust neck opening if shoulder adjustment raised the neckline, marking adjustment with chalk, then trimming on marked lines.

2 **Adjust armhole openings** if the garment binds under the arms, marking the adjustment with chalk or textile marking pen, then trimming away excess fabric.

3 **Adjust side seams,** if necessary, so leg openings fit snugly before the elastic is applied.

4 **Adjust leg opening** to desired height by marking with chalk or textile marking pen and trimming.

To stabilize edges and to ensure a snug fit on swimsuits and leotards, use elastic at necklines, armholes, waistlines, and leg openings. Elasticized edges also allow you to slip the garment on and off easily. Although elasticized edges do self adjust to your figure, do not depend on them to solve fitting problems.

If you have not adjusted the neckline, armhole, or leg openings, cut the elastic to the lengths specified by the pattern. If you have changed the size of the openings, follow the guidelines given in the chart below. Most patterns print the cutting information for the elastic on the guide sheet or provide a cutting guide on the pattern tissue. If using a pattern with several views, be sure to cut the elastic for the style you have chosen; for example, a high-cut leg opening requires longer elastic than a standard leg opening.

Latex swimwear elastic (trade name Fulflex) or transparent elastic tape (trade name Mobilon) may be used. Both types of elastic have excellent stretch and recovery and are chlorine resistant and salt resistant. Polyester-cord-covered elastic is more widely available and may also be used, but will be bulkier. Fulflex and Mobilon elastics can be cut shorter, but can also be cut to the same length as the garment opening and still hug the wearer snuggly. Polyester cord covered elastic will need to be cut shorter. See table.

Most patterns call for $3/8$" (1 cm) elastic for adult swimwear and $1/4$" (6 mm) elastic for children's.

TIP

When stitching the elastic to the edge of your opening with an overcast stitch, place the elastic just inside the edge of the fabric ($1/32$"–$1/16$" or 1-2 mm). That way, as you stitch the overcast stitch, the fabric will curl up around the edge of the elastic for a cleaner look.

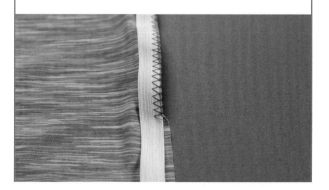

Guidelines for Cutting Elastic (polyester-cord-covered elastic)

TYPE OF EDGE	LENGTH TO CUT ELASTIC
Leg opening	Measurement of leg opening minus 2" (5 cm) for adult's garment or minus 1" (2.5 cm) for the child's.
Upper edge of two-piece swimsuit bottom	Measurement of upper edge minus 2" to 3" (5 to 7.5 cm), depending on desired fit. Check to see that elastic fits comfortably over hips.
Armhole	Measurement of armhole.
Neckline	Measurement of neckline. Or for a snug fit on V-necked, low, or scoop necklines, use elastic 1" to 3" (2.5 to 7.5 cm) shorter than neckline.

How to Apply Elastic to Neckline or Waistline Openings

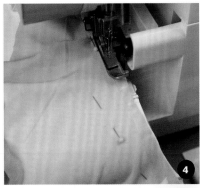

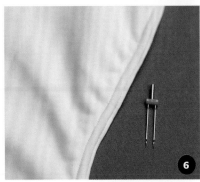

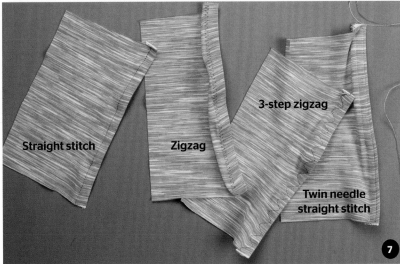

Straight stitch

Zigzag

3-step zigzag

Twin needle straight stitch

1 **If using polyester cord elastic,** join ends of elastic, using overlapped method (page 199). Because polyester cord elastic is cut shorter, divide this elastic into fourths; pin-mark, with one pin next to joined ends of elastic. Divide garment opening into fourths; pin mark. Seams may not be halfway between center front and center back. If using Fulflex (latex elastic) or Mobilon (transparent poly elastic), you will not need to pin mark, and can stitch directly to the garment.

2 **Pin elastic to wrong side** of fabric, matching edges and pin marks. Place joined ends at center back of neckline or waistline.

3 **Stitch outer edge of elastic** to the garment, using overlock or narrow zigzag stitch; stretch elastic to fit between pins. If your elastic is shorter than the opening to which it is stitched, the seam creates waves, which won't be seen when worn. Fulflex and Mobilon, if cut to the opening length, will lay flat.

4 **If using overlock machine,** guide work carefully or disengage knives to avoid cutting elastic.

5 **Fold elastic toward inside** of garment, encasing it in garment fabric.

6 **Stitch through all layers,** ¼" (6 mm) from folded edge using twin needle. You may use long straight stitches, but remember to stretch as you sew to allow for easing of the thread when the item is worn. When the elastic is relaxed, straight stitches will appear much shorter.

7 **Or use a stretch stitch,** such as a zigzag stitch, 3-step zigzag stitch, or topstitch

   Leg openings. Join ends of elastic (page 199). Pin elastic to leg opening, with joint at side seam. Keep elastic relaxed on garment front; remaining elastic will stretch to fit the back of leg opening. Follow steps 3 to 5, stretching elastic as you sew.

selection, which you will need for all your sewing projects.

With a few basic sewing skills, you can create accents in your living spaces that are a real reflection of you. Create new room "wardrobes" of window treatments, table fashions, accent pillows, and slipcovers. Or even replace and recover the cushions on a flea market treasure. "Rustic Mid-Century Hollywood Bohemian Meets Chic Nantucket Zen Monk"? Why not? You are the interior designer!

Home decorating projects also make wonderful gifts. A quick knife-edge pillow as a welcome for the new neighbors moving in, beautiful handmade bed linens for a newlywed couple, or a set of pretty table linens for a good friend are easy to sew, and, because they were made with your own hands, will surely bring a smile to the recipient for many years.

Decorator Fabrics

Decorator fabrics have characteristics not found in fashion fabrics. For example, stain-resistant and permanent press finishes are often applied to decorator fabrics, since they must go for long periods of time without being cleaned. When cleaning is necessary, most decorator fabrics must be dry cleaned to avoid shrinkage.

The weave pattern, fiber content, and weight of the fabric will have an impact on the finished appearance and durability of home décor items. For window treatments, these fabric characteristics will also determine how they control light, privacy, sound, and heat insulation.

Lightweight open weaves include casements, laces, eyelets, and sheers. Often these fabrics are woven in 118" (300 cm) widths, with the width intended to run vertically, allowing you to make floor-length sheer curtains without seams. Novelty sheers can have interesting textural features, sometimes arranged in stripes or grids. Most sheers are made of polyester for strength and stability, though they may also contain other fibers. Natural fibers, including cotton and linen, are also used for sheer and lightweight fabrics.

Medium-weight fabrics include a wide range of fiber contents and weave structures. Their strength is determined by the closeness of the yarns in the weave. Satin weaves are woven so that warp yarns float on the surface over two or three weft yarns, giving the fabric subtle sheen. Jacquard weaves, including damasks, tapestries, and brocades, have woven-in designs. Novelty weaves, often in solid colors, feature textural interest created by complicated weave patterns. These fabrics are very versatile in any decorating scheme. Decorator pile fabrics, such as suede, corduroy, velvet, and chenille, have interesting surface textures and are usually heavier than their apparel fabric counterparts.

Decorator fabrics for the interior are often made of man-made and natural fibers, including cotton, linen, silk, and wool. Natural fibers are breathable, comfortable, and easy to sew. Synthetic fibers and blends offer greater durability. For outdoor use, manufacturers offer water-repellent, fade-resistant, acrylic or polyester decorator fabrics that look and feel much like interior fabrics. They are colorfast and are treated to resist stains, mildew, and fading.

In addition, when purchasing decorator fabrics, you may encounter terms not used with garment fabrics:

Railroaded: This refers to the way the design is printed on, or woven into, a decorator fabric. If the design runs from selvedge to selvedge, the design is considered railroaded. Think of stripes, for example: If they run across the width of the fabric—like railroad ties—then the fabric is railroaded. If the stripes run up and down the length of the fabric, then the fabric is not railroaded. If the print is a damask running up the length of the fabric like wallpaper, it is not railroaded. On the other hand, if a flower border print is growing along the selvedge, then the fabric is railroaded. Railroaded fabrics are more efficient for upholstery applications, but they are unsuitable for most drapery applications, where a horizontal seam is undesirable.

Custom backing: To increase durability, prevent fraying, and reduce seam slippage, a custom backing may be fused onto your decorator fabric. Typically, it is a polyester tricot backing bonded to the reverse side of the fabric. Frequently, a custom backing will reinforce silks, felts, chenilles, and other fabrics for upholstery use. A custom backing adds bulk and may not be appropriate for drapery applications. Despite the added bulk, a custom backing does not affect the way the fabric looks.

Insulating linings are sold under a variety of trade names and are typically a cotton/polyester blend, often with a suede-like surface. These provide the greatest amount of light, sound, and heat insulation. These insulating linings are a good choice for older homes with drafty windows and doors. With regular use, they can help keep heating bills down, too. These materials are heavier than other linings, so select curtain rods or other hardware that will bear the extra weight. Also make certain your hardware is anchored more securely than would otherwise be necessary.

Vinyl linings are a good choice for areas of the home where an extra measure of sound, light, and heat insulation are required. Because vinyl can withstand regular cleaning with household cleaners, vinyl linings can be used in areas of the home requiring regular disinfecting, such as nurseries or bedrooms for individuals with compromised immune systems.

With the exception of drapery sheers, fabrics intended for upholstery and décor use will be tagged with their measure of durability.

Fabric durability is measured several ways. "Double rubs" is a measure of the strength of an upholstery fabric, which approximates the back-and-forth abrasion of regular sitting and standing. 3,000 double rubs is considered one year's worth of use on an upholstered seat. 15,000 or more double rubs is considered heavy duty; 9,000–15,000 double rubs is medium duty; and 3,000–9,000 is considered light fabric duty.

The Martindale method is a standard accepted by many international textile and decorating associations and is widely accepted as a good measure of durability and pilling. If your fabric was milled, for example, in Europe or Asia, very likely the Martindale measure will be indicated. The Martindale method is considered to better resemble real life, because the Martindale method uses a figure-eight motion. The number of cycles that the fabric can withstand before showing an objectionable change in appearance is counted. 20,000 Martindale cycles is considered general commercial use and is appropriate for most home applications.

You may also encounter the Wyzenbeek measure. The Wyzenbeek abrasion test is used primarily in North America and was adapted for textiles from the tire manufacturing industry.

Though considered a stringent test, the Wyzenbeek does not as closely measure real life conditions as well as other methods because it tests the material in only the warp direction (in the length-wise direction), and then in the weft direction (the filling direction). The number of cycles before yarn breaks occur or when "noticeable wear" appears is measured. 15,000 Wyzenbeek cycles is considered general commercial use and is appropriate for most home applications.

Similar to interfacings for garment sewing, drapery and upholstery projects have their own types of supporting materials, which help the item function as you would like it to.

Drapery lining: There are a variety of specialty lining fabrics just for draperies, each functioning a bit differently, depending on how you want your draperies to perform. Different linings will provide different levels of privacy, shade, and noise and heat. All linings will protect your curtain fabric from ultraviolet damage to some degree. Most linings are wrinkle resistant and will help keep your main curtain fabric from wrinkling. Some lining materials are water repellent and are a good choice for rainy parts of the world to prevent water streaks. Drapery linings are most often 54" (160 cm) wide and sold on rolls, making them easier to use for drapery projects. Most linings are white or ecru, however, black is also available.

Sateen linings are either a cotton or cotton/polyester blend. They have a very dense weave and smooth, almost shiny surface. If you have chosen a printed fabric for your curtains, when light shines through the material, very often the weave of the fabric becomes clearly visible and competes with the printed design. Very tightly woven drapery lining like a sateen lining will counteract that effect. This type of drapery lining will continue to allow some light to shine through and will provide some amount of heat insulation. It will protect your curtain fabric from fading and Sun rot longer than without a lining.

Muslin linings can be made of cotton or, more recently, a cotton/bamboo blend. These do not have the sheen of a satin fabric. Muslin linings perform much like a sateen lining.

Blackout linings are very dense materials, either woven or nonwoven polymers, often with a black core and either white, beige, or black surfaces. Blackout linings do not allow any light to penetrate and provide both sound and heat insulation. These are a good choice for private areas of the home, such as bedrooms, or for use in home theaters and home offices, where reduced light is more conducive to watching movies or working in front of a computer. However, blackout linings may block too much light in more public spaces of the home, like the living room or kitchen, making them cavelike.

Fabric Preparation

Preshrink any dry-clean-only fabrics by steaming. Move the iron evenly along the grainlines, hovering just above the surface of the fabric. Allow the fabric to dry before moving it. Preshrink washable fabrics by washing and drying in the same way you intend to care for the finished item.

After preshrinking, straighten the cut ends of the fabric. Mark the other cutting lines, using the straightened edge as a guide. Before cutting full-width pieces of fabric for large home-décor projects, such as tablecloths, curtains, or bed covers, pin mark the placement of each cut along the selvage. Mark out pieces for smaller projects, such as pillows or napkins, with chalk. Double check your measurements and inspect the fabric for flaws. To ensure that large décor items will hang or lay straight, the fabric lengths must be cut on-grain. This means that the cuts are made along the exact crosswise grain of the fabric. Patterned decorator fabrics are cut following the pattern repeat rather than the grainline so make sure the fabric you buy is printed on grain.

TIP

Often, decorator fabrics ravel more than apparel fabrics. Although the edges of a fabric in a decorator project will very often never see the light of day, for ease of sewing, it is recommended to finish the edges of decorator fabrics that tend to ravel easily. Woven polyester fabrics, such as indoor/outdoor fabrics, may be cut with a hot knife, which cuts and seals the edge by melting the fibers in one motion.

How to straighten decorator fabrics

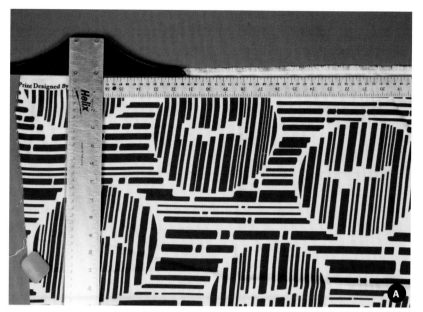

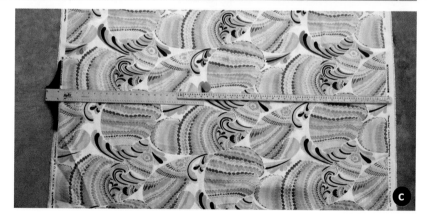

A **For tightly woven fabrics without** a matchable pattern, mark straight cuts on the crosswise grain, using a carpenter's square or T-square. Align one edge to a selvage and mark along the perpendicular side.

B **For loosely woven fabrics,** such as linen tablecloth fabric, pull out a yarn along the crosswise grain, from selvage to selvage. Cut along the line left by the missing yarn.

C **For tightly woven patterned** decorator fabric, mark both selvages at the exact same point in the pattern repeat. Using a long straightedge, draw a line connecting the two points. If you will be stitching two or more full widths of fabric together, make all the cuts at the same location in the repeat. This usually means that you cut the pieces longer than necessary, stitch them together, and then trim them to the necessary length.

Patterned decorator fabrics are designed to match at the seam. Cuts are made across the fabric, from selvage to selvage, following the pattern repeat rather than the fabric grain, so it is very important to purchase fabric that has been printed on grain.

Fabrics that are printed slightly off grain can usually be corrected by stretching diagonally, unless they have a polished finish.

If the print is noticeably off grain, you can use this fabric for smaller projects, such as pillows or totes. Avoid off-grain fabrics for draperies.

The pattern repeat is the lengthwise distance from one distinctive point in the pattern, such as the tip of a particular petal in a floral pattern, to the same point in the next pattern design. Some patterned fabrics have pattern repeat markings (+) printed on the selvage. These markings indicate the beginning of each pattern repeat, and they are especially helpful for fabrics that include several similar designs.

When sewing large items such as curtains or duvet covers, extra yardage is usually needed to match the pattern. Add the amounts needed for any hems, rod pockets, headings, ease, and seam allowances to the finished length, to determine how long the lengths of fabric need to be. Then round this measurement up to the next number divisible by the size of the pattern repeat to determine the cut length. For example, if the pattern repeat a is 24" (61 cm), and the needed length b is 45" (115 cm), the actual cut length c is 48" (122 cm). To have patterns match from one panel to the next, each panel must be cut at exactly the same point of the pattern repeat.

To calculate the amount of fabric needed, multiply the cut length by the number of fabric widths required for the project; add one additional pattern repeat so you can adjust the placement of the pattern on the cut lengths. This is the total fabric length in inches (centimeters); divide this measurement by 36" (100 cm) to determine the number of yards (meters) required.

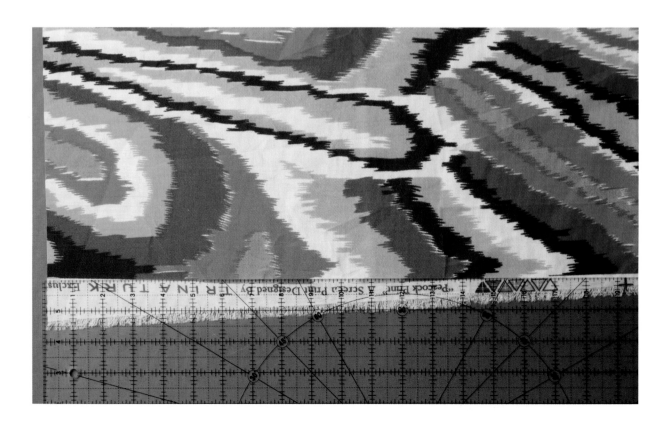

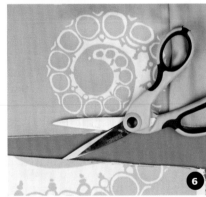

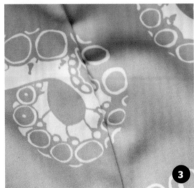

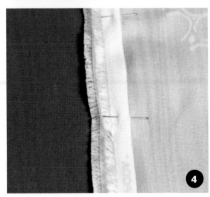

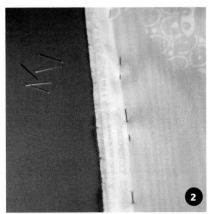

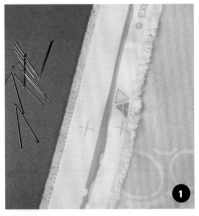

1 **Place two fabric widths** with right sides together, aligning the selvages. Fold back the upper selvage until the pattern matches. Adjust the top layer slightly up or down so that the pattern lines up exactly. The printing may be just slightly off center and the selvedges may not align. Press the foldline.

2 **Unfold the pressed selvage,** and pin the fabric widths together, inserting the pins in and parallel to the foldline.

3 **Turn the fabric over,** and check the match from the right side. Make any necessary adjustments.

4 **Repin the fabric** so the pins are perpendicular to the foldline. Stitch the seam following the foldline; remove the pins as you come to them.

5 **Check the match** from the right side again. Make any necessary adjustments. Trim away the selvages, cutting the seam allowances to ½" (1.3 cm).

6 **Trim the entire fabric** panel to the necessary cut length, as determined in the project instructions. (Remember your initial cut length for the patterned fabric included extra length to accommodate the pattern repeat.)

All seams in home décor sewing are ½" (1.3 cm) unless otherwise specified. To secure straight seams, backstitch a few stitches at each end. For most projects, avoid using the selvage as a seam allowance edge. It will make the seam pucker and may shrink more than the fabric body when steamed or laundered. The exception to this rule is stitching long seams in loosely woven fabrics such as casements or laces. Long seams tend to pucker in some fabrics. Or the top fabric tends to get "snowplowed" by the presser foot, causing the fabrics to misalign at the end of the seam. To prevent this, practice taut sewing. As you sew, pull equally on the fabric in front and back of the needle as if the fabric were in an embroidery hoop. Do not stretch. Pull the fabric taut, and let it feed through the machine on its own. Similarly, you may use an even feed (feeder) presser foot.

The following seams are the most commonly used seams for home decorator sewing.

Seams for Home Décor Sewing

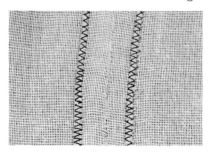

Plain seam, pressed open, is suitable for almost every fabric and application when you plan to enclose the seam or cover it with lining. If the seam allowances will be exposed or if the item will be laundered often, finish the seam allowances with an overcast zigzag or overlock stitch.

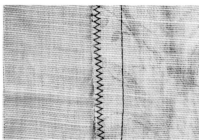

Plain seam, pressed to one side, is most commonly used for window treatments. The seam allowances are pressed toward the return edge of the curtain (away from the center of the window). Finish the seam allowance edges together, especially if the item will not be lined or if the fabric tends to ravel.

4-thread or 5-thread safety stitch on a serger trims the seam allowances to a uniform width while stitching a seam and overcasting the seam allowances together. Use this stitch for curtains or any item where the seam allowances are exposed.

Narrow zigzag stitch is used for long seams in loosely woven fabrics or laces. The zigzag allows the seam to relax slightly and prevents puckers. If removing the selvages would cause excessive raveling, leave the selvages on and clip them up to the stitching line every 1" to 6" (2.5 to 15 cm) to allow them to relax.

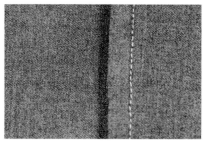

French seam eliminates raw edges by encasing them. It is especially suitable for lightweight, sheer, and loosely woven fabrics when the item will be laundered or exposed to abrasion. This seam is also used for fashion sewing, however, for home décor sewing, where the seam allowances are only ½" (1.3 cm), two ¼" (6 mm) seam allowances are sewn.

Slipcovers

Without going through the expense and effort of reupholstering your furniture, with basic sewing skills, slipcovers allow you to transform your furniture and create a whole new look for your room. Consider slipcovers "wardrobe" pieces for your living spaces: Have everyday slipcovers, but then also sew up special-occasion slipcovers. Slipcovers also protect your furniture from wear, tear, and ultraviolet damage, and with a toss in the washer or trip to the drycleaner, all evidence of sticky toddler fingers and muddy puppy paws disappears.

Laying Out and Cutting the Fabric

Whenever possible, lay out all the pattern pieces on the fabric before you start to cut. This allows you to rearrange the pieces as necessary to make the best use of the fabric.

When using a patterned fabric, matching may be required. When seaming widths of fabric together, the pattern should be matched. If a patterned fabric with a one-way design is used, be careful to lay the pieces in the correct direction of the fabric.

Center large motifs in a print fabric on the top and bottom of the cushion for a traditional look. Or place overscale designs anywhere you like for an on-trend, eclectic look. It is nearly impossible to match a fabric pattern across all the seams in a slipcover. Instead, focus on matching the pattern in the areas that are most visible, such as the seam between the seat and chair back and the seam between the seat front and the skirt front.

Dining Chair Slipcovers

These two-piece, optionally reversible seat covers can serve a number of functions: They can protect the up-holstery and wood, especially when young children are about, change things up in your décor or add a fun touch to celebrating a special occasion. Choose either elegant lacing with grommets for a decadent look or buttons for a more tailored appeal. Make the skirt long enough just to cover the seat, or all the way down to the floor. The instructions are for chairs with rounded seat corners: For chairs with square corners, you may place darts in the corners or pleats.

Because the amount of fabric needed depends on your chair size and the fabric design size, make the pattern first so you'll know how much fabric to buy.

When making covers for two or more chairs, you'll want to center the same motif on each seat cover. If you like fabric with large motifs, such as the damask shown here, take the pattern with you when you shop for fabric.

YOU WILL NEED

- muslin to make the pattern
- decorator fabric
- buttons (self cover or other)
- grommets and decorative upholstery cording (optional)
- bias tape
- sewing thread

Option 1: Create a button band down the back of the chair for a tailored look.

Option 2: Lacing cord through grommets to fit the slipcover to the chair.

For the chair seat (chair with armrests)

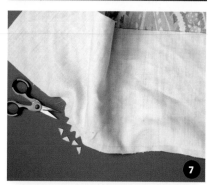

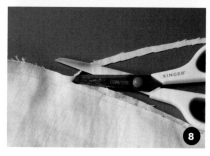

1. **Pin muslin around your chair** seat. With a marker, trace the outline of the chair seat top. Clearly mark the posts for the armrests and the seat back. Measure the front and back halfway points and mark them.

2. **Cut the muslin pattern out** and place it back on the chair. Note on the muslin where you may require more material.

3. **Trace a more accurate pattern** piece. Make it a pattern piece to be cut on the fold for symmetry. On the outside of the pattern piece, with the aid of a seam gauge, mark a cutting line ½" (1.3 cm) past the edge. If you plan on including welting in any of the seams, and depending on the thickness of your fabric, you may want a wider seam allowance. For the seat back posts and the armrest posts, mark a cutting line ½" (1.3 cm) inside the cutouts.

4. **Cut two pieces of fabric** for the chair seat cover top.

5. **Decide how long** you would like the chair skirt to hang. Cut rectangular pieces for the seat cover chair skirt across the grain as follows:

   Chair skirt front (Cut 2, one for the face and one for the reverse): Distance from the front edge of the left armrest post to the right armrest post plus 10" (25.5 cm), by length of chair skirt plus 1" (2.5 cm).

   Chair skirt back (Cut 2, one for the face and one for the reverse): Distance from the left edge of the left back seat post to the right edge of the right back seatpost plus 10" (25.5 cm), by length of chair skirt plus 1" (2.5 cm).

   Chair skirt side (Cut 4, two from the face fabric and two from the reverse): Distance from the back edge of the left armrest post to the front edge of the left back seatpost plus 1" (2.5 cm), by the length of the chair skirt plus 1" (2.5 cm).

6. **Center the skirt front piece** on the front seat edge, pin and stitch.

7. **Clip any round corners** up to the seam allowance. Trim square corners at an angle.

8. **Grade the seam allowances** to reduce bulk.

9. **Center the skirt back** piece on the back seat edge, pin, and stitch.

10. **Stitch the skirt side pieces** to the chair seat sides.

11. **Repeat steps** 6 through 10 for the reverse fabric pieces.

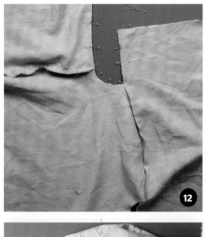

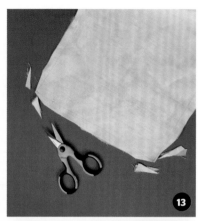

12 **Pin the two sides** of the chair seat along all edges, right sides together, and stitch. Leave an opening for turning along the bottom of one skirt piece.

13 **Trim all corners.**

14 **Turn the seat cover** right side out. Use a point turner in the corners. Press the encased seams.

15 **Turn the seam allowances** of the opening toward the inside, press, pin, and stitch the opening closed.

16 **Mark and stitch buttonholes** on the front skirt piece and back skirt piece flaps.

17 **Mark the button placement** under the buttonholes. Stitch buttons on both sides of the seat cover on the side pieces.

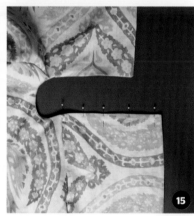

TIP

Depending on the width of your fabric, you may have to piece together fabric to accommodate the size of your chair. It is best to piece the extra material for the back piece in the center of your fabric, where it will end up in hidden in the pleats. If extra material is required for the front, add it to both the right and left sides.

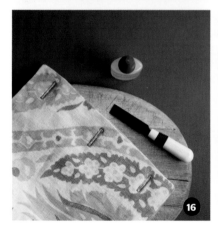

For laced chair leg ties (this works best with an upholstered chair with a seat cushion)

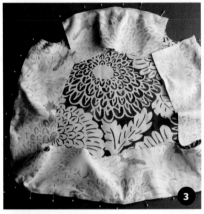

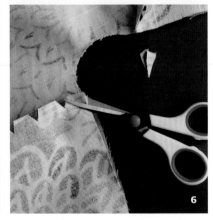

1 **Measure the side of the chair** from the top to the bottom of the seat. Add 1" (2.5 cm) to the length. This will be the length of the skirt.

Chair skirt front/side piece (Cut 2, one for the face fabric and one for the reverse): From the left edge of the left seat back post, around the front, to the right edge of the right seat back post plus 1" (2.5 cm), by length of chair skirt plus 1" (2.5 cm)

Chair skirt back (Cut 2, one for the face and one for the reverse): Distance from the right edge of the left back seat post to the left edge of the right back seat post, by length of chair skirt plus 1" (2.5 cm)

2 **Cut the seat cover top** as instructed on (page 229), both top fabric and reverse. Cut the skirt pieces, two each for front/side piece and back piece.

3 **Stitch the skirt front/side piece** to the seat cover top, right sides together, with a ½" (1.3 cm) seam allowance. Stitch the back piece to the seat cover top, right sides together, with a ½" (1.3 cm) seam allowance. Repeat for the reverse pieces.

4 **Press the seam allowances up** toward the center of the seat. Clip the round corners.

5 **Lay the top piece** on the reverse side piece right fabric sides together and pin. Stitch the two halves of the seat cover together with a ½" (1.3 cm) seam.

6 **Do not stitch around the U-shaped** area around chair post openings and the adjoining ends of the seat cover skirt piece. Clip the excess material at the seam allowances to reduce bulk.

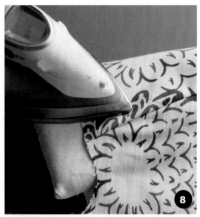

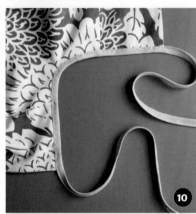

7 **Turn the seat cover right side out** through one of the openings.

8 **Press** the encased seams.

9 **Cut and press 130"** (330 cm) double-folded bias tape for each chair seat cover. Cut the strips on the true bias. Depending on the weight of the material you are using for the slipcover, you may need to cut the bias strips wider than 1½" (4 cm). Unfold one edge and center a piece of 65"-long (165 cm) bias tape in the chair post opening, pin to the opening and along the edges of the seat skirt and stitch to the edge of the opening right along the first fold of the bias tape. Fold the bias tape over the stitched line and over the fabric edge to the opposite chair seat cover side and pin.

10 **Beginning at one dangling end** of the bias tape, stitch the two halves of the bias tape together with a straight stitch.

11 **Once you reach the seat** cushion cover, change your stitch to a zigzag or three-step zigzag stitch and continue stitching, catching the seat cushion cover between the bias tape in your stitching line. Switch back to a straight stitch and continue stitching the opposite side of the dangling bias tape. Repeat for the opposite chair post opening and piece of bias tape. Knot the ends of the ties.

12 **Place seat cushion cover** on your chair and tie or lace the ties around the back legs, as desired.

For the seat back (with armrests)

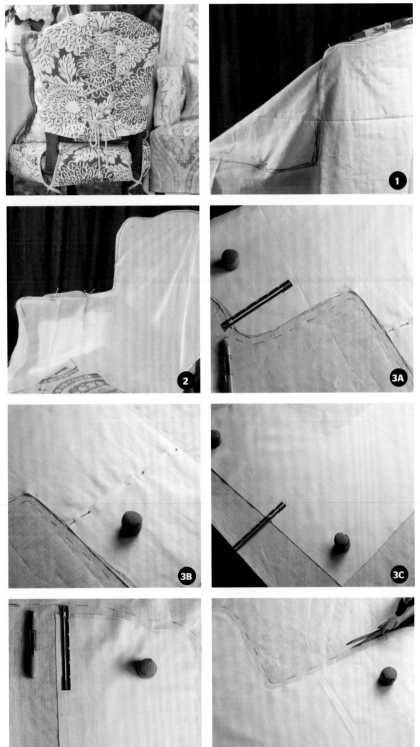

1. **Pin muslin** around your chair back. With a marker, trace the outline of the chair from the back. Trace along the chair back and along the armrest, down to the chair seat. Measure the top and bottom halfway points and mark them. Move the muslin to the front of the chair. Align the center marks with the center of the front of the chair. Trace the inner line of the armrest with your marker. The inner line of the armrest should be shorter than the outside curve.

2. **Cut the muslin pattern** pieces out and place them back on the chair. Note on the muslin where you may require more material.

3. **Trace a more accurate pattern** pieces. Make a pattern pieces to be cut on the fold for greater symmetry.

   Fold your fabric along the grain. Pin the pattern piece along the armrest to adjust for the shorter inside curve. Place the front slipcover piece with your pattern piece on the fold. On the outside of the pattern piece, with the aid of a seam gauge, mark a cutting line ½" (1.3 cm) past the edge and cut the slipcover front on the fold. Cut the front slipcover piece.

4. **Remove the pins i**n the armrest of the pattern piece and lengthen the piece to accommodate the longer outer curve. Place the muslin pattern piece on your fabric 5" (12.5 cm) away from the fold. Mark a line perpendicular from the fabric fold to the top and bottom edges. Above this line and continuing around the pattern piece, with the aid of a seam gauge, mark a cutting line ½" (1.3 cm) past the edge. Cut the slipcover back on the fold..

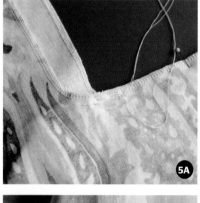

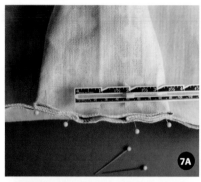

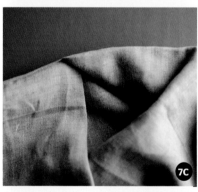

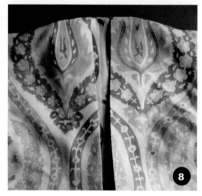

5 **Stitch basting stitches** along the curve of the armrest on the back slipcover piece and gather the material so that the armrest back is the same length as the armrest front. This will help the slipcover fit around the armrests.

6 **Pin the slipcover front** to the back beginning along the armrest and working your way up the sides.

7 **OPTION 1:** Form two pleats 3" (7.6 cm) apart with the extra material on the slipcover back and pin.
OPTION 2: Form two overlapping pleats right at the center of the slipcover to form a button placket.

Stitch the front to the back along the armrests and the chair back and catch the pleats in your stitching line. Notch the round corners and trim excess fabric from the pleats to reduce bulk. Finish the edges to prevent raveling (non-reversible slipcover only). Press the seam allowance open.

8 **OPTION 1:** Place the slipcover over your chair back and pin the pleats so they form two straight lines following the slope of the chair back. Remove the slipcover from chair and press the pleats in place.
OPTION 2: Place the slipcover over your chair back and pin the pleats so they form a nice straight button band. Remove the slipcover from chair and press the button band pleats in place.

9 **OPTION 1:** With a textile marker, mark the locations for the grommets along the pleats. Set the grommets.
OPTION 2: With a textile marker, mark the locations for the buttonholes along the top button band pleat and stitch. Stitch buttons under the buttonholes.

10 (non-reversible slipcover): Hem the bottom edge with a ½" (1.3 cm) blind-stitch hem. (reversible slip cover): Place the slipcover reverse inside the slipcover face fabric with right sides together and pin along the bottom edge. Stitch the two halves together along the bottom edge and leave a small opening for turning. Turn the slipcover right side out. Press the bottom encased seam and press the seam allowances of the turning opening toward the inside. Stitch the turning opening closed with a straight stitch edge stitch.

11 (OPTION 1): Place the slipcover top over your chair. Lace upholstery cord, stitched double-folded bias tape, or sturdy ribbon through the grommets and tie.

For the seat back (no armrests)

1 Pin muslin around your chair back.

2 With a marker, trace the outline of the chair. Measure the top and bottom halfway points and mark them.

3 Cut the muslin pattern pieces out and place them back on the chair. Note on the muslin where you may require more material.

4 Trace a more accurate pattern piece. Make a pattern piece to be cut on the fold for greater symmetry.

5 For the piece that wraps around the inside of the chair, place your pattern piece on your fabric folded along the grain.

6 On the outside of the pattern piece, with the aid of a seam gauge, mark a cutting line 1/2" (1.3 cm) past the edge and cut the slip cover front on the fold.

7 For the piece that wraps around the back of the chair back, place the muslin pattern piece on your fabric 5" (12.5 cm) away from the fold. This extra 5" (12.5 cm) is used to make the closure. Mark a line perpendicular from the fabric fold to the top and bottom edges. Above this line and continuing around the pattern piece, with the aid of a seam gauge, mark a cutting line ½" (1.3 cm) past the edge. Cut the slipcover back piece on the fold.

8 Depending on the fabric you are using you may stitch a few basting stitches and gather at the curves for greater ease.

9 For a slipcover with grommets and lacing, pin the slipcover back to the front beginning along the sides. Form two pleats 3" (7.6 cm) apart with the extra material on the slipcover back and pin.

10 For a slipcover with a button closure, overlap two 1 1/2" (3.8 cm) pleats at the center top of the slipcover to form a placket. Stitch the front to the back and catch the pleats in your stitching line.

11 Clip the round corners to the seam line and grade or trim excess fabric from the pleats to reduce bulk. Finish the trimmed edges to prevent raveling (non-reversible version).

12 Press the seam allowances open. Turn the slipcover right side out. Hem the bottom with a ½" (1.3 cm) blindstitch hem (non-reversible version).

13 Place the slipcover over your chair back and pin the pleats so they form two straight lines following the slope of the chair back. Remove the slipcover from chair and press the pleats in place. Bond interfacing on the reverse side along the pleats at the grommet or button stress points if required.

With a textile marker, mark the locations for the grommets or buttonholes along the pleats. Set the grommets or stitch buttonholes.

Attach buttons (button placket version). Place the slipcover on the chair and lace bias tape, upholstery cord, or sturdy ribbon through the grommets and tie.

Pillows and Cushions

While pillows and cushions are somewhat different, the sewing techniques for both are mostly the same. The difference most often comes down to size, the inserts and types of closures. Pillows are often smaller, have a loose filling, such as poly fiber fill or down and don't necessarily maintain their shape.

Cushions tend to be larger, have a solid foam core and retain their shape. Both pillows and cushions come in several basic styles and their variations: knife-edge, mock box, flange, box, and bolster. Each of these styles can incorporate any one of several different closure options, such as a concealed zipper (page 258), an invisible zipper (page 260), hook-and-loop tape (page 262) or buttons. Similarly, both pillows and cushions can be given structure and style by adding welting or decorative trim. Before embarking a larger project, such as making new slipcovers for the sofa cushions, practice new techniques on smaller pillows, first. In the instructions for the covers, *pillow* and *cushion* may be used interchangeably.

Because of their larger size, cushions are most often covered in slipcovers. Slipcovers are removable and are placed over cushion inserts or directly over existing slipcovers. Freshed up any space with new slipcovers on window seats, garden furniture, the boat or camper. Make slipcovers for your sofa and chair cushions to replace worn upholstery.

Or place slipcovers right over existing slipcovers to protect treasured upholstery fabrics from everyday wear and tear.

Most cushions fall into one of the three styles: knife-edge, waterfall (bullnose), and boxed. Any of these styles can be fitted flush to the front of the chair or T-shaped, resting in front of the chair arms.

Boxed and knife-edge cushions can be sewn with or without welting at the seams. See page 264 for instructions on making and attaching welting. Knife-edge cushions on chairs or sofas usually have a welted seam around the center on sides where the cushion is exposed. If there are hidden sides, such as for a knife-edge seat cushion on a wing chair, the hidden sides are often constructed with a boxing strip. Waterfall cushions are sewn with one continuous piece of fabric wrapping over the front, from top to bottom. This style has a boxing strip around the sides and back and is usually made without welting.

To make it easier to insert the cushion, you will most often install a zipper across the back of the slipcover and extending about 4" (10 cm) onto each side. For cushions that are exposed on three sides, install a zipper only across the back of the slipcover. Use upholstery zippers, which are available in longer lengths, or purchase an endless zipper, which you can cut to size. For boxed and waterfall cushions, the tab of the zipper will be concealed in a pocket at the end of the zipper opening. This is an upholsterer's technique that gives a professional finish. For slipcovers intended for outdoor use, hook-and-loop tape closures might be better than metal zipper closures.

Pillows get their shape from the choice of filling. Different brands and types of filling vary in quality and properties: some clump less, others recover better, some are springier, others requiring fluffing. Some have hypoallergenic or antimicrobial properties, some are easily tossed in the washer, others require special handling. Options for loose filling include poly fiber fill, goose down and down-feather mixes, polystyrene foam pieces or new-generation synthetic foams, such as memory foam. In addition, a growing industry of Earth-friendly and cruelty-free options are making stuffing options such as coir (coconut fiber), kapok pod fibers, shredded natural rubber, and buckwheat husks more widely available. Kapok pod fibers, for example, are harvested from live trees and mimic the characteristics of goose down.

Pillow covers and slipcovers can be made to fit either prefabricated pillow inserts or pillow inserts of your own making. Forms are great for pillows that will be laundered, because they are easily inserted and removed through a closure. Premade standard sized inserts for square, rectangular, round and cylindrical pillows are widely available. For pillows in nonstandard sizes and shapes, you can make fitting forms from muslin and fill them with the loose stuffing of your choice. If you want the pillow to be plump and firm, plan the finished size to be at least 1" (2.5 cm) smaller than the pillow form size. If you prefer that your pillow be softer and less plump, plan the finished size to be the same as the form.

If your premade form is high through the center and the filling that doesn't reach the corners, open a seam and adjust the filling. If you want more or less plumpness, add or remove some loose fiber fill before sewing the form closed. For pillows without removable inserts, stuff the filling directly into the pillow cover. Forms are available in knife-edge squares from 10" to 30" (25.5 to 76 cm), rectangles, rounds, and bolsters.

Cushions inserts are often made from a piece of high-density polyurethane foam surrounded by a layer of thick poly fiber batting called cushion wrap. Cushion inserts containing a variety of materials such as coir, down, wool felt and latex have their own stability and recover properties and can also be purchased from specialty suppliers.

Knife-edge Pillows and Cushions

Well-loved or found textiles that have outlived their original purpose make great materials for making or embellishing throw pillows. Leaving the moth-eaten bits behind, these treasured vintage serapés have a second life as bright and bold conversation starters. The fringes have been left on as an added bit of interest.

On the left, a square pillow made using the shaping technique; on the right, a pillow made with two regular squares, resulting in a pointy "dog ear."

Knife-edge pillows or cushions have a front and a back that are the same size and shape and are joined by a single seam around the perimeter. If desired, that seam can also incorporate a decorative element, such as welting, fringe, or a ruffle. Knife-edge pillows and cushions can be almost any shape you wish, though some shapes are better suited to this style than others. Round knife-edge pillows or cushions, for instance, will pucker around the edge.

Square and rectangular knife-edge pillows and cushions are best sewn not from actual squares or rectangles, but from an ever-so-slight octagon shape. Squared pieces of fabric will result in "dog ears" (pointy corners) when they are stuffed, because they are thicker in the center than around the edges. Prevent pointed dog ear corners using the following shaping technique:

How to Make a Knife-edge Pillow or Cushion

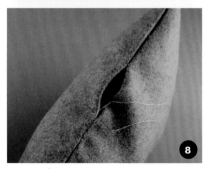

1 **Determine the desired finished size** of your pillow or cushion and add 1" (2.5 cm) in both directions for seam allowances. If the cushion is rectangular, fairly flat, and soft, like a pillow, cut a cushion cover top to the same dimensions as the original cushion plus 1" (2.5 cm) for seam allowances.

If using a zipper, cut the cushion cover bottom 1" (2.5 cm) longer than the top to allow for ½" (1.3 cm) seam allowances at the zipper closure.

If continuous zipper tape is used, cut the zipper tape with the length equal to at least three-fourths of the cushion width, or purchase a conventional zipper with this approximate length. See page 258 for zipper directions.

2 **Fold the front into fourths.** Mark a point halfway between the corner and the fold on each open side. At the corner, mark a point the distance of your seam allowance from each edge. Trim a gradually tapering sliver of fabric from the marked point on the fabric edge to the marked corner point. Repeat on the adjoining side to shape the corner.

3 **Cut two halves** using the pattern.

4 **Pin the pillow front to the back,** right sides together. Stitch ½" (1.3 cm) seam, pivoting at the corners. Leave an opening on one lengthwise-grain side for stuffing the pillow. If you will be inserting a pillow form, leave an opening about two-thirds the length of the side. For loose stuffing, a smaller opening will do. Trim the corners without cutting into the seam.

5 **Press the seams flat.** Then turn back the upper seam allowance and press with the tip of the iron in the crease of the seam. In the area of the opening, press both seam allowances back.

6 **Turn the pillow cover right side out.** Square up the corners, using a point turner inserted through the opening. Press lightly.

Compress and insert the pillow form, making sure the form sits squarely inside the cover; add fiber fill in the corners, if necessary, or stuff the pillow with the desired stuffing.

7 **Pin the opening closed,** aligning the pressed folds. Edge-stitch by machine.

8 **Or pin the opening closed,** aligning the pressed folds. Slipstitch the opening closed by hand.

TIP

If you are using a heavier weight fabric or a fabric with a pile, cutting may be inaccurate. In this case, it is best to fashion a kraft-paper pattern piece.

1 **Adding welting to the edge** of a knife edge pillow will add interest and also works well to conceal an invisible zipper. Cut fabric strips for the welting long enough to fit the welted section of the cushion. The invisible zipper will be well concealed beneath a welted edge.

2 **Mark the center of the zipper** on the tape and the center on one edge of both the top and bottom pieces. Press the zipper teeth coil flat (page 257). Once the welting is applied, pin one zipper tape to the cushion edge with welting, right sides together. Place the zipper teeth close to the welting.

3 **Use an invisible zipper foot** or a conventional zipper foot, stitch the one zipper tape to the cushion panel. Begin and end stitching the zipper tape within the length of the zipper coil, leaving a small portion of the zipper tape with coil at both ends unstitched to the cushion panel. Zip the zipper closed. Mark the center of the zipper on the opposite side of the zipper tape.

4 **Find the center** on the edge of the opposite cushion panel. Unzip the zipper. Align the center of the zipper with the center of the opposite panel and pin the zipper tape to the opposite cushion panel edge. Stitch this zipper tape to the cushion panel, again leaving that small portion of the zipper tape with coil at both ends unstitched to the cushion panel.

5 **Zip the zipper closed.** Pin the two cushion panels together around the edges, right sides together. Fold the ends of the zipper toward the cushion inside. Begin stitching the two halves of the cushion together, beginning and ending under the invisible zipper ends (arrow).

A flange is flat fabric that extends beyond the stuffed portion of a pillow. A **single** flange is formed from two layers of fabric seamed together around the edge. **Raw-edge** flange pillows are made from two layers of reversible fabrics. Self-lined flange strips can be sewn into the seams of a knife-edge pillow to make a pillow with **contrasting** flanges that are interrupted at the corners. The flange width can vary to suit your pillow's size and design. A good flange width for sofa pillows is 1½" to 2½" (3.8 to 6.5 cm). Unless the fabric is quite stiff, wide flanges tend to flop forward, so that is something to consider if you want to display the pillow standing upright. The easiest way to make a flange pillow is to stitch the opening closed by machine. If you want to be able to remove the pillow form, plan for a plain or decorative overlap closure, a centered zipper closure on the back, or an invisible zipper closure between double flanges.

How to Make a Single Flange Pillow

Add twice the width of the flange to the finished size of the stuffed area of the pillow plus 1" (2.5 cm) to the width and length for ½" (1.3 cm) seam allowances all around.

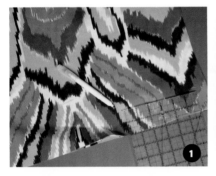

1 **Follow steps 4 to 6** for the knife-edge pillow (page 239) but don't stuff yet. Mark the depth of the flange from the seamed outer edge. Pin the layers together along the marked line to keep them from shifting. Stitch on the marked line, leaving an opening of the same size parallel to the outer opening. Insert the pillow form or stuffing into the inner area.

2 **Topstitch the inner area** closed, using a zipper foot. Slipstitch the flange closed, or edgestitch around the entire flange.

How to Make a Pillow with Contrasting Flanges

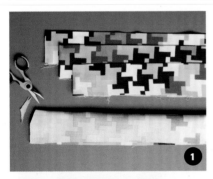

1 **Follow steps 1 to 3** for a knife-edge pillow (page 239). Cut four flange strips the same lengths as the pillow sides and 1" (2.5 cm) wider than twice the desired width of the flange. Fold each strip in half lengthwise, and stitch ½" (1.3 cm) seams across the ends. Turn right side out and press.

2 **Pin the flange strips** to the outer edges of the pillow front, ½" (1.3 cm) from the corners, aligning the raw edges. Baste a scant ½" (1.3 cm) from the edges. Follow steps 4 to 8 for the knife-edge pillow (page 239) to complete. Take care that the finished ends of the flanges do not get caught in the stitching.

instead of a knife edge technique, you can make a pillow in any shape—circles, hearts, stars, anything really—and the pillow will retain the shape of the motif and not pucker along the edges. Standard pillow forms can be used for square box pillows, but to fill the pillow depth more consistently, make the pillow cover with a width and length 2" (5 cm) smaller than the pillow form size. For nonstandard shapes and sizes, make your own pillow insert or stuff loose filling directly into the cover.

To use a premade knife-edge pillow form for a square box pillow, move filling out of the corners and follow steps 3-6 for the corners of the mock box cushion, page 250, stitching on the outside of the form to create a cube shape for the insert.

Box pillows and cushions (also called boxed) have fronts and backs of the same shape and size joined together with a strip of fabric around the sides known as a boxing strip. Using this technique

How to Make a Round Box Pillow

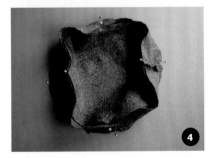

1 **Make a pattern for the pillow** front and back, using a string-and-pencil compass. Add ½" (1.3 cm) seam allowance all around. Cut out the pattern; use it to cut out the pillow front and back.

Multiply the finished diameter by 3.14, and round the measurement up to the nearest fraction of an inch (millimeter) to determine the finished length of the boxing strip (the strip that wraps around the pillow sides); add 1" (2.5 cm) for seam allowances. Cut the boxing strip this length at the the desired width plus 1" (2.5 cm) for seam allowances.

2 **Stitch the boxing strip** into a continuous loop, as in step 2 for the rectangular box pillow. Stitch a scant ½" (1.3 cm) from each edge of the boxing strip. Then clip the seam allowance every ½" (1.3 cm) up to, but not through, the stitching line.

3 **Pin-mark the pillow front,** pillow back, and boxing strip equidistantly into fourths. Pin the boxing strip to the pillow front, right sides together, raw edges even, matching the pin marks. With the boxing strip facing up, stitch a ½" (1.3 cm) seam.

4 **Stitch the other side** of the boxing strip to the pillow back, leaving an opening for turning and stuffing.

How to Handle Inside and Outside Corners on a Box Pillow or Cushion

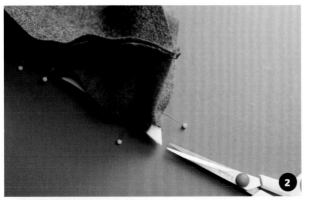

1 **Make a pattern for the pillow** front and back, adding ½" (1.3 cm) for seam allowances all around. Measure the entire outer seamline and add 1" (2.5 cm) to determine the cut length of the boxing strip (the strip that wraps around the pillow sides). Cut the boxing strip to the desired width plus 1" (2.5 cm); piece together, as necessary.

2 **Mark both long edges** of the boxing strip with the lengths of each side of the pillow, using a ⅜" (1 cm) clip into the seam allowances. Do not use a joining seam as one of the marks.

3 **Mark the seam lines at any inner** corners of the pillow front and back. Using short straight stitches, stay stitch on the seamline, about 1" (2.5 cm) on each side of the outer corners, pivoting at the corners. Clip up to, but not through, the stitching lines at the corners.

4 **Pin the boxing strip** to the pillow front, right sides together, raw edges even, matching the clip marks on the boxing strip to the pillow corners.

5 **Stitch ½" (1.3 cm) seam** with the boxing strip facing up in areas of straight lines or outer curves. At each outside corner, stop with the needle down in the fabric, and pivot the fabric. The clip marks will spread, allowing the fabric to turn the corner. Stop stitching within 2" (5 cm) of any inner corners, and resume stitching 2" (5 cm) beyond the corner. Complete the stitching at the inner corners with the boxing strip on the underside. Stitch just to the inside of the staystitching lines.

6 **Pin the other side of the boxing strip** to the pillow back, right sides together, matching the clip marks to the corners. Stitch the seam as in step 5, leaving an opening for stuffing the pillow.

How to Make a Square or Rectangular Box Pillow or Cushion

1. **Determine the finished width,** length, and depth of the pillow. Add 1" (2.5 cm) to the width and length for ½" (1.3 cm) seam allowances all around. Cut out the pillow front and back, aligning sides to the fabric grainlines.

2. **Follow steps 1 to 5 on page 243** to make and install the boxing strip.

3. **Press the seams flat.** On each seam, turn back the upper seam allowance and press with the tip of the iron in the crease of the seam. In the area of the opening, press both seam allowances back.

4. **Turn the pillow cover** right side out. Square up the corners, using a point turner or similar pointed utensil inserted through the opening. Press lightly.

5. **Compress and insert** the pillow form, making sure the form sits squarely inside the cover; add fiber fill in the corners, if necessary, or stuff the pillow with the desired stuffing. Slipstitch the opening closed.

French Mattress Seam Pillows and Cushions

A French mattress seam on a pillow or cushion refers to a lip of fabric around all seamed edges of a box pillow or cushion. To add a French mattress seam to a stuffed pillow, complete making a box pillow, as described above, through step 4.

How to Make a French Mattress Seam Pillow

1 **Pin the edges of all the seams** of a pillow or cushion without an insert, working any stuffing away from the edges as you go.

2 **Topstitch a ½"** (1.3 cm) straight stitch seam around all edges.

How to Make a French Mattress Seam Cushion

Determine the desired finished width, length, and depth of the cushion without including the additional lip of the French mattress seam. Add 2" (5 cm) to the width and length for 3/8" (1 cm) seam allowances and ½" (1.3 cm) mattress-lip edge stitching all around, including ⅛" (3mm) for turn of the cloth. Cut out the cushion top and bottom plates (or faces), aligning edges to the fabric grain lines.

Finished plate width + 2" (5 cm)

Finished plate length + 2" (5 cm)

Cut the boxing strip on grain or cross-grain, with the length equal to the total distance around the pillow plus 7" (18 cm) for end seam allowances and the mattress-lip corner stitching. If the boxing strip will need to be pieced, also allow 1" (2.5 cm) for each ½" (1.3 cm) piecing seam. Cut the width equal to the finished cushion depth plus 2" (5 cm) for 3/8" (1 cm) seam allowances and a ½" (1.3 cm) mattress-lip edge stitching, again including ⅛" (3mm) for turn of the cloth.

Boxing strip length = finished perimeter + 7" (18 cm)

Boxing strip width = finished depth + 2" (5 cm)

YOU WILL NEED

- 3" or 4" (8 or 10 cm) high-density foam cushion form
- 1" (2.5 cm) cushion wrap
- decorator fabric
- webbing for handle (optional)
- sewing thread

---

1 **Piece the boxing strip together,** if necessary, using ½" (1.3 cm) seam allowances. Mark the centers of both long edges of the pieced strip.

2 **Mark the center** on a matching long edge of each plate. The seam that will later join the boxing-strip's unfinished ends will be on the side of the pillow opposite these marked edges.

3 **Match the center** mark on the boxing strip to the one on the pillow front, right sides together, raw edges even, and pin.

4 **Stitch the plate** to the boxing strip from the pinned centers using a ⅜" (1.6 cm) seam, stopping that same distance from the corner's raw edges. Clip the boxing strip to ⅛" (3mm) from the end of the stitching, then align the strip with the next edge of the front plate and continue stitching as before. Clip and re-align the strip at the second corner as before, but only stitch

to just short of the center along this edge of the front. Return to the start and stitch the same away from there around the other sides of the front, again ending just short of the final edge's center.

5 **Overlap the free ends** of the boxing strip so they match the finished length of the front edge, mark a seam line and join them right sides together across the width of the strip. Trim and press open these seam allowances and finish the seam to join the strip completely to the front. Press open all the seam allowances between strip and front and trim the front corners.

6 **To make a secure handle** (Optional) add a strip of webbing (or a turned, pressed tube of your fabric) at the center of one side of the boxing strip. Topstitch the ends of the webbing with crossed rectangles.

7 **Join the pillow back** to the other edge of the strip, starting at the same center point and stitching and clipping exactly as in Step 4, but when you turn the second corner on each side, continue stitching for only a few inches, leaving an opening along this edge large enough to insert the pillow form. Press open all the seam allowances between strip and front and trim the front corners, then turn the cushion cover right side out.

8 **Press the turned seams.** Press the corners on the boxing strip. Press the edges of the opening toward the inside.

9 **Beginning ½" (1.3 cm) from a corner** and ending ½" (1.3 cm) from the next corner on the plate without the opening, edge stitch a line 1/2" (1.3 cm) away from the encased seam to make the French mattress-lip. Repeat for the remaining three sides. Repeat the above for the opposite plate. Leave the opening unstitched.

10 **Stitch the vertical corners** in the same manner, connecting the horizontal seams.

11 **Compress and insert the cushion form,** making sure the form sits squarely inside the cover; add fiberfill in the corners, if necessary. Machine-stitch the opening closed to match as well as possible.

How to Make a Boxed Rectangular Cushion with a Zipper

YOU WILL NEED

- muslin for making patterns
- decorator fabric
- zipper, about 8" (20.5 cm) longer than back edge of cushion
- fabric and cording for fabric-covered welting; or brush fringe for twisted welting
- sewing thread

A boxed cushion is sewn much the same as a boxed pillow, however, a zipper is included in the boxing strip and the opening it fills usually extends beyond the length of the back edge onto both sides for several inches to facilitate putting the cover on and pulling it off the form.

Cut the top and bottom cushion plates 1" (2.5 cm) larger than the cushion size to allow for seam allowances. If the insert is wrapped in cushion wrap, subtract 1" (2.5 cm) for a taut fit.

Measure the original boxing strip between seams and add 1" (2.5 cm) for seam allowances. Cut the boxing strip with the length equal to the total measurement of the front and sides of the cushion. Excess length will be cut off during construction. If piecing is necessary, allow 1" (2.5 cm) for each seam, planning the placement of the seams out of view along the sides of the cushion.

If continuous zipper tape is used, cut the zipper tape 8" (20.5 cm) longer than the back cushion measurement, or purchase an upholstery zipper with this approximate length. See page 189 for how to use continuous zipper tape. Cut two fabric strips for the zipper closure with the length equal to the length of the zipper tape and the width equal to half the cut width of the boxing strip plus ¾" (2 cm).

1 **Make welting** as on page 240. Sew the welting around the outer edge of the cushion top and cushion bottom, following the continuous circle method.

2 **Install the zipper** to the zipper strip as on page 257.

3 **Center the zipper strip** over the back edge of the cushion top, right sides together. Stitch the zipper strip to the cushion top, beginning and ending on the sides about 1½" (3.8 cm) beyond the corners.

4 **Clip into the zipper strip seam allowance** at each corner to allow the fabric to spread, and pivot.

5 **Align the center of the boxing strip to the front** center of the cushion top, matching the print, if necessary. Smooth the boxing strip to the right front corner; mark with a ⅜" (1 cm) clip into the seam allowance. Smooth the boxing strip along the right side of the cushion top; pin the boxing strip to the cushion top up to about 6" (15 cm) from the back corner.

6 **Stitch the boxing strip** to the cushion top, beginning at the side pin and sewing ½" (1.3 cm) seam. For a welted cover, use a welting foot or zipper foot. Match the clip mark to the front corner; pivot the stitching at the corner. Continue stitching the boxing strip to the cushion top, matching the center marks. Clip once into the boxing strip seam allowance at the left front corner; pivot. Stop stitching about 6" (15 cm) from the back left corner.

7 **Pin the end of the boxing strip** to the end of the zipper strip, right sides together where it overlaps the zipper pull end of the zipper strip. matching all cut edges .

8 **Form a small pocket** to hide the zipper pull when the cover is closed.

9 **Cut the opposite end of the boxing strip 1"** (2.5 cm) beyond the point where it overlaps the other end of the zipper strip. Pin the ends together. Stitch ½" (1.3 cm) from the ends stitching slowly over the zipper teeth. Turn the seam allowance toward the boxing strip.

10 **Finish sewing the zipper strip and boxing strip** to the cushion top.

11 **Open the zipper partially.** Pin the boxing strip to the cushion bottom, matching the clip marks to the corners. Stitch. Turn the cover right side out through the zipper opening.

Sewing a Boxed T-cushion Cover

T-cushions are common on wingback, bergère, and other chairs where the chair seat is longer than the armrests. Sofas and loveseats, which have two, three, or more separate seat cushions will have two half T-cushions on the ends. T-cushion slipcovers are sewn as one would a box pillow with a zipper in the boxing strip.

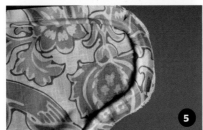

1 **Cut a piece of muslin fabric** about 4" (10 cm) larger than the top of the cushion; mark the grain line at the center of the fabric. Place the muslin over the cushion; pin along the seamline, smoothing out the fabric. Mark the seamline along the pin marks. Remove the muslin. True the seamlines, using a straightedge. Fold the muslin in half to make sure that the cut piece will be symmetrical; make any necessary adjustments. Add ½" (1.3 cm) seam allowances to the pattern.

2 **Cut the pieces,** matching center front of boxing strip to the top plate front.

3 **Press under a ½"** (1.3 cm) seam allowance on one long edge of each zipper strip. Position the folded edges of the strips along the center of the zipper teeth, right sides up. Using a zipper foot, topstitch ⅜" (1 cm) from folds.

4 **Press under 2"** (5 cm) on one short end of the boxing strip. Lap the boxing strip over the zipper strip to cover the zipper tab. Stitch through all layers 1½" (3.8 cm) from the folded edge of the boxing strip.

5 **(Optional) Make and apply welting** as on page 240. Stitch welting to the right side of top and bottom pieces.

6 **Place the boxing strip** on the slipcover top, right sides together; center the zipper on the back edge. Start stitching 2" (5 cm) from the zipper end, crowding the cording. Clip the corners as you come to them; stop stitching 4" (10 cm) from the starting point.

7 Clip to mark the seam allowances at the ends of the boxing strip. Stitch the boxing strip ends together. Trim off excess fabric; finger press the seam open. Finish stitching the boxing strip to the slipcover top.

8 Fold the boxing strip, and clip the seam allowance to mark the lower corners; be sure all corners are aligned with the corners on the slipcover top. Open the zipper.

9 Place the boxing strip and slipcover bottom right sides together. Match the clips of the boxing strip to the corners of the slipcover bottom; stitch. Turn the cover right side out.

10 Fold the cushion to insert it into the cover. Stretch the cover from front to back. Close the zipper. Smooth the cover from center to edges. Stretch the welting taut from corner to corner to square the cushion.

Alternative zipper placement. Install the zipper across the back of the slipcover, without extending it around the sides, if the slipcover will be exposed on three sides.

The mock box pillow or cushion, a variation of the knife-edge style, is cube-shaped with soft, undefined edges. Unlike the knife-edge pillow that tapers in depth toward the outer edges, the mock box pillow is chunkier with a consistent depth from center to sides. The depth is created by stitching a vertical seam in each corner of the pillow cover, which shortens the length and width. The length of that seam determines the pillow depth. The larger the pillow, the deeper it can be. For instance, a large floor pillow can look well-proportioned with a depth of 6" (15 cm), whereas a smaller sofa pillow looks better at a depth of 2½" to 3" (6.5 to 7.5 cm). The perimeter seam circles the pillow halfway between the front and back. If desired, this seam can incorporate welting. Mock box slipcovers are quick to sew and a good choice to slip over existing box sofa cushions.

How to Make a Mock Box Pillow or Cushion

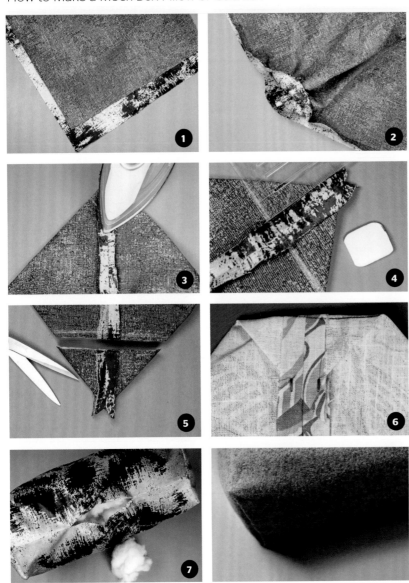

1 **Cut two retangles or squares** of fabric the same size. Use the chart, opposite, for pillow forms. For cushions add the form depth to the form width and length plus 1" (2.5cm) for seam allowances.

2 **Stitch front and back together** with a ½" (1.3 cm) seam allowance. Add a zipper (page 257) or leave an opening for turning in the center of the bottom edge. Press the seam allowances open. Press the edges at the opening back.

3 **Refold the fabric at each corner** so that a new corner is formed with the seams in the center. Pin through the seams from front to back to ensure they are aligned.

4 **Measure and mark half** the desired pillow depth along the seam. Draw a line through the mark perpendicular to the seam, from fold to fold. The length of the line equals the total desired pillow depth.

5 **Stitch on the marked line.** Trim off the corner triangle to reduce bulk.

6 **Or keep the triangle attached** and tack in place with a few stitches.

7 **Turn the pillow right side out** through the opening. Fill the pillow or place a pillow or cushion form inside. Close the opening with hand stitches.

Cut Sizes Needed for Mock Box Pillow

FINISHED SIZE	DEPTH	CUT SIZE	FORM SIZE
10" 10" (25.5 25.5 cm)	2" (5 cm)	13" 13" (33 33 cm)	12" 12" (30.5 30.5 cm)
11½" 11½" (29 29 cm)	2½" (6.5 cm)	15" 15" (38 38 cm)	14" 14" (35.5 35.5 cm)
13" 13" (33 33 cm)	3" (7.5 cm)	17" 17" (43 43 cm)	16" 16" (40.5 40.5 cm)
14½" 14½" (37 37 cm)	3½" (9 cm)	19" 19" (48.5 48.5 cm)	18" 18" (46 46 cm)
16" 16" (40.5 40.5 cm)	4" (10 cm)	21" 21" (53.5 53.5 cm)	20" 20" (51 51 cm)
19" 19" (48.5 48.5 cm)	5" (13 cm)	25" 25" (63.5 63.5 cm)	24" 24" (61 61 cm)
24" 24" (61 61 cm)	6" (15 cm)	31" 31" (78.5 78.5 cm)	30" 30" (76 76 cm)

The chart above shows the cut sizes needed for the finished sizes of mock box pillows that will fit standard pillow forms. Cut sizes include ½" (1.3 cm) seam allowances

How to Make a Custom Cushion Form

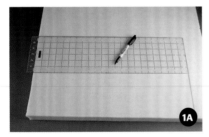

Cut a cushion insert from foam with a serrated edge knife to your desired dimensions.

Wrap the foam in a layer of cushion wrap. Adhere the cushion wrap to the foam with upholstery spray adhesive.

Instead of chemical adhesives, tack the cushion wrap through the foam. You may also wrap cheesecloth around the cushion and stitch the ends together..

TIPS

- To use a knife-edge pillow form inside a mock box pillow, move filling out of the corners and follow steps 3 to 6 for the Mock Box Pillow, stitching from the outside of the form.

- To achieve a good, taut fit over a foam cushion insert, it makes sense to make the insert first and take your measurements from the finished insert.

Bolsters are cylindrical pillows. With their interesting shape, they are a great addition to the "pillowscape" and versatile enough to be used on beds, sofas, chairs, and window seats. In its simplest form, a bolster is merely a rectangle sewn into a cylinder and drawn closed at each end with a drawstring in a casing. An alternative is to tie the ends with decorative cording so the pillow resembles a wrapped candy. In a tailored version, the bolster ends are capped with circles of fabric. The cylinder itself can be pieced together from two or more fabrics and the seams can be embellished with welting or other decorator trims.

Bolster forms are available in several sizes, or you can make your own, following the instructions below.

How to Make a Simple Bolster

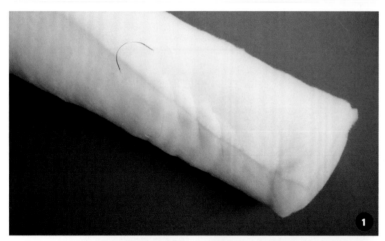

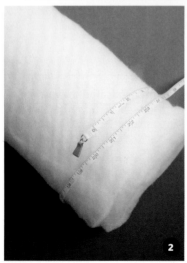

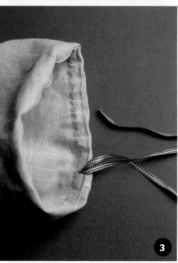

1 **Cut a rectangle of batting** about 1 yd (1 m) long, with the width equal to the desired finished length of the bolster. Roll the batting with the desired firmness (the looser you roll it, the softer the bolster will be) until it is the desired diameter; cut off any excess. Whipstitch the cut end to the roll.

2 **Cut a rectangle of fabric** with the width equal to the circumference of the bolster form plus 1" (2.5 cm) and the length equal to the length of the bolster form plus the diameter plus 1½" (3.8 cm) for casings.

3 **Press under ¼"** (6 mm), then ½" (1.3 cm) on each short end of the fabric to form the casings. Unfold the ends. Fold the fabric in half lengthwise, right sides together. Stitch ½" (1.3 cm) seam on the lengthwise edge, beginning and ending with backstitches ¾" (2 cm) from the ends; press the seam open.

4 **Refold the casings.** Edgestitch along the inner folds; reinforce the stitches at the openings. Turn the bolster cover right side out.

5 **Thread narrow cording** into the casings. Insert the bolster form. Draw up the cording and tie securely. Tuck the cord ends inside the opening, if desired.

TIP

If the bolster form is not completely covered at the ends, place pieces of matching fabric over the ends before tying the cords. The tightness of the drawstring will keep them in place.

How to Make a Candy Wrapper Bolster

1 **Make a bolster form as in step 1,** opposite, for a simple bolster, if necessary. Cut a rectangle of fabric with the width equal to the circumference of the bolster form plus 1" (2.5 cm) and the length equal to the length of the bolster form plus three times the diameter.

2 **Press under ¼"** (6 mm) on each short end; unfold. Fold the fabric in half lengthwise, right sides together. Stitch a ½" (1.3 cm) seam on the lengthwise edge, beginning and ending with backstitches ¾" (2 cm) from the ends; press the seam open.

3 **Refold ¼" (6 mm)** at the open ends. Fold the ends under half the diameter of the bolster. Edgestitch along the inner folds; reinforce the stitches at the openings. Stitch again ½" (1.3 cm) from the fold, forming a casing.

4 **Thread narrow cording** into the casings. Turn the bolster cover right side out. Insert the bolster form. Draw up the cording and tie securely. Tuck the cord ends inside the opening. Tie decorative cording around the gathers at each end, if desired.

How to Make a Tailored Bolster

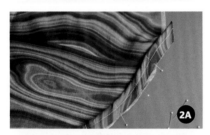

1 **Make a bolster form** as in step 1, opposite, for a simple bolster. Cut a rectangle of fabric with the width equal to the circumference of the bolster form plus 1" (2.5 cm) and the length equal to the length of the bolster form plus 1" (2.5 cm). Cut two circles of fabric for the ends with the diameter equal to the diameter of the bolster form plus 1" (2.5 cm).

2 **Stitch welting to the edges** of the circle pieces using the continuous overlap method.

3 **Fold the rectangle in half lengthwise,** right sides together. Stitch a ½" (1.3 cm) seam on the lengthwise edge, leaving an opening for turning and inserting the bolster form in the middle of the seam; press the seam allowance open. Or insert a zipper into this seam as described on page 258.

4 **Stitch a scant ½"** (1.3 cm) from the outer edge of each end of the cylinder. Clip into the fabric every ½" (1.3 cm) up to, but not through, the stitching line, to allow the material to curve.

5 **Pin a circle to one end,** right sides together, aligning the raw edges. The cylinder ends will fan out at the clips. Stitch a ½" (1.3 cm) seam, keeping the outer edges even. You should be stitching just inside the first stitching line. Repeat at the opposite end.

Waterfall Cushion

A waterfall cushion, sometimes called a bullnose cushion, doesn't have a pillow equivalent. It has three square sides like a box cushion, but the top and bottom plate are one continuous piece, which wraps over the front of the cushion making a rounded edge. A waterfall cushion is used most often as a loose seat cushion on chairs with wrap-around armrests or sometimes as loose sofa back cushions with the rounded edge being on top. It's ideal for fabrics with large scale prints, for which you do not want to break up the design along the front.

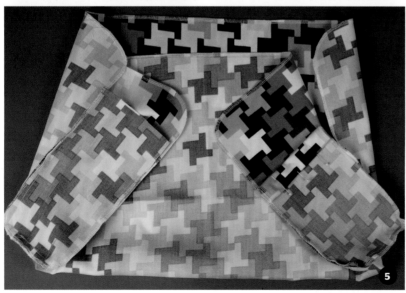

1 **Pin-fit a muslin pattern** for the continuous-wrap top/bottom piece, or simply mark around the form on your final fabric as you wrap it around the form. Add a seam allowance of ½" (1.3 cm) each side and at the ends of the wrap. If your cushion has 1" (2.5 cm) cushion wrap around it, do not add a seam allowance at all; the cushion wrap will compress and create a nice fit.

2 **Cut the wrap-around** cushion top and bottom piece. Mark the end of the piece that will become the cushion top (with a directional print or napped fabric, the fabric will run in the correct direction only on the top). Round the corners.

3 **Cut the side boxing strips** a length equal to the side measurement of the cushion plus 1" (2.5 cm).. If your cushion has wrap around it, do not add a seam allowance. Excess length will be cut off during construction. Round the corners on one end.

4 **Match centers** of the cushion top/bottom piece and centers of the rounded edges and pin right sides together.

5 **Stitch the boxing pieces** to the top/bottom, beginning at the center of the boxing strip. Align the edges and carefully stitch around the tapered corner. Stop stitching 2" (5 cm) before the end of the boxing piece.

6A

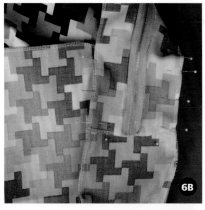

6B

7

8

9

6 **Cut continuous zipper tape** by the back cushion measurement plus 8" (20.5 cm), or purchase an upholstery zipper with this approximate length. Cut two fabric strips for the zipper closure, with the length equal to the length of the zipper tape and the width equal to half the cut width of the boxing strip plus ¾" (2 cm).

Prepare the boxing with the zipper, pinning and basting the two strips together as noted on page 258, steps 2 and 3. Pin the boxing with the zipper to the center of one side of the cushion plate, right sides together. Stitch the boxing with zipper to the cushion plate and stop stitching approximately 2" before the end of the boxing piece.

7 **Fold the back edge** of the side boxing piece under, so that it covers approximately 1" (2.5 cm) to 1½" (3.3 cm) of the zipper end and pin to the zipper piece, so that the zipper piece is under the side boxing piece. Trim any excess side boxing material.

8 **Stitch the cushion seam** over the end of the side boxing piece and over the zipper piece from the fabric right side. Stitch a line approximately ¾" to 1" (2 to 2.5 cm) below the folded edge of the side boxing to make a little pocket to conceal the zipper pull. Repeat for the opposite side of the cushion and zipper piece.

9 **Once the boxing is stitched** to one side of the plate piece, unzip the zipper halfway for turning. Stitch the opposite cushion plate side to the boxing. Turn the cushion right side out through the zipper.

Pillows that are used for comfort, tossed about, and handled a lot need closures that will allow you to easily remove the stuffing so the covers can be laundered or dry cleaned occasionally. The options include conventional zippers, invisible zippers, and lapped closures.

The pillow style influences the closure choice as well as the closure location. Invisible zippers, for instance, work well in the seams of plain knife-edge pillows or mock box pillows, especially when the pillows are decorative on both sides. If a knife-edge pillow has welting or ruffles, though, it can be more difficult to insert a zipper in the seam. A conventional zipper or lapped closure in the pillow back would be easier in such cases. If a box pillow needs a zippered closure, it is usually applied into a section of the boxing strip so that the pillow is reversible. Flange pillows that require removable covers can have zippered, lapped, hook-and-loop tape, or buttoned closures in the back or decorative buttoned closures in the front.

Sometimes, the closure is the main decorative feature of the pillow. Items borrowed from the fashion world—like fancy buttons, toggles, frogs, buckles, and fabric or ribbon ties—give these home décor pieces a couture touch.

Zippers

Conventional polyester zippers (not the separating kind) can be inserted in a seam between pieces of the pillow back. The seam can be centered in the pillow back or placed close to one edge so that it is less visible; the seam allowances hide the zipper teeth. Invisible zippers are usually placed in the seam between the pillow front and back, where they almost disappear, but they can be placed anywhere you prefer with very unobtrusive results.

Make the zipper closure long enough so that removing and inserting the pillow form will not strain the zipper ends. As a general rule, use a zipper that is at least three-fourths the pillow width. Zippers can be shortened, if necessary, following the directions on page 189.

For a typical application, cut the pillow back 1" (2.5 cm) wider than the front to allow for ½" (1.3 cm) seam allowances at the closure. Fold the pillow back in half, right sides together, if you want the closure to be centered in the pillow back. Fold one edge in 1¾" (4.5 cm), if you want the closure near one edge. Press.

HOW TO INSERT A CONVENTIONAL ZIPPER

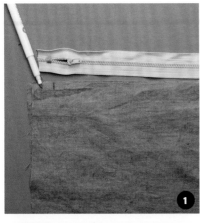

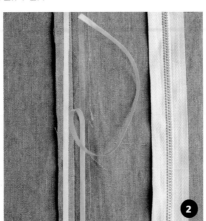

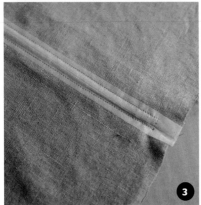

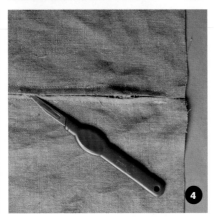

1 **Mark the fold** at the location of the zipper stops. Stitch ½" (1.3 cm) from the fold, from the pillow edge to the first mark; backstitch. Machine baste to the second mark. Shorten the stitch length again and backstitch; then stitch to the opposite edge. Cut on the fold; press the seam allowances open.

2 **Center the closed zipper** face down over the seam, with the stops at the marks. Glue baste, use basting tape or pin to the seam allowances only. Finish the seam allowances with an overcast stitch, catching the zipper tape in the stitches.

3 **Spread the pillow back** flat, right side up. Mark the top and bottom of the zipper coil with pins. Center a strip of transparent tape over the seam from pin to pin. Topstitch a narrow rectangle along the edges of the tape or through the tape, using a zipper foot. Stitch slowly as you cross the zipper teeth just beyond the stops. Remove the tape. Pull threads to the underside and knot. Remove the basting stitches.

4 **Finish the pillow,** following the general directions for the pillow style. Rather than leave an opening for turning, simply open the zipper before stitching the final seam.

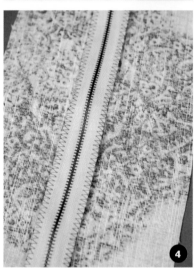

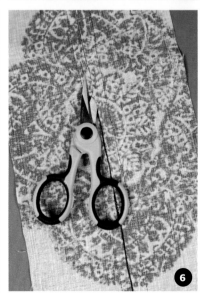

1. **Purchase a zipper** or cut a piece of endless zipper that is about 2" (5 cm) shorter than one side of a square box pillow or one-third the circumference of a round pillow. Cut a boxing strip for the zipper section 2" (5 cm) wider than the desired finished width of the boxing strip and equal in length to the zipper tape. Cut a boxing strip for the remaining pillow circumference 1" (2.5 cm) wider than the desired finished width and about 6" (15 cm) longer than the remaining circumference.

2. **Pin the boxing/zipper strip** in half lengthwise, right sides together. Machine baste ½" (1.3 cm) the seam down the fold. Cut along the fold and press the resulting seam allowances open.

3. **Center the closed zipper face down** over the seam. Glue baste or pin to the seam allowances only.

4. **Finish the seam allowances** with an overcast stitch, catching the zipper tape in the stitches.

5. **Turn the zipper strip face up.** Center a strip of ½" (1.3 cm) tape over the entire seam. Topstitch along the edges of the tape from end to end, using a zipper foot (no need to cross the zipper). Remove the tape.

6. **Remove the basting stitches.**

7. **Stitch one end of the boxing strip** with the zipper to the remaining boxing strip. Fold the boxing strip piece up over the end of the zipper to form a pocket to conceal the zipper pull. Pin the cut end to the bottom of the zipper strip, right sides together. Trim the boxing/zipper strip to the finished pillow circumference plus a small fold to conceal the zipper pull. Stitch ½" (1.3 cm) seam, stitching slowly over the zipper teeth.

HOW TO USE ENDLESS ZIPPER

Zipper sold by the yard or sold on a roll is an economical and efficient way to have a zipper exactly the length you need.

1. **Prepare two ends** for the zipper from project fabric. Cut a length of zipper to the correct length.

2. **Flame the ends** of the cut zipper to prevent the tape material from fraying.

3. **Insert the teeth into the pull.** With practice, this becomes easier.

4. **Pin the fabric ends** to the ends of the zipper.

5. **Stitch the zipper to the fabric.** Zigzag over the teeth to create a secure stop.

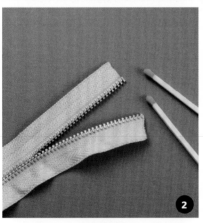

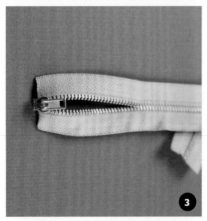

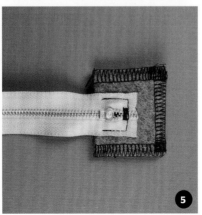

How to Insert an Invisible Zipper in the Middle of a Pillow Back

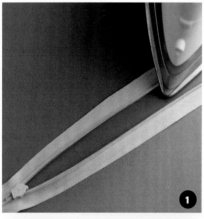

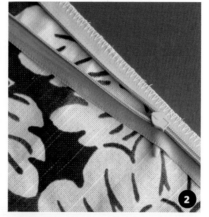

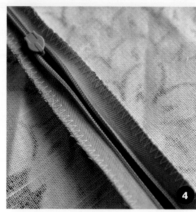

1 **Shorten zipper as needed** so it's at least 1" (2.5 cm) less than the finished back length from top stop to new bottom stop (see page 189).Open the zipper; press open the zipper tape from the wrong side to unroll the coils.

Measure the width of one of the pressed-open zipper tapes. Cut the pillow back from the front pattern adding twice this measure to the width on the sides parallel to the seam you want for the zipper, creating the right seam allowances at the closure. Cut the back piece along the seamline.

2 **Position the open zipper** on one of the pillow back pieces, right sides together, with the zipper coil aligned to the seamline and the top stop just below the crossing seam line. Glue baste or pin in place. Finish the seam allowance, catching the zipper tape in the stitches.

3 **Insert the top of the zipper coil** into the appropriate groove of invisible zipper foot. Slide the zipper foot on the adapter to adjust the needle position so stitching will be very close to the coil; on heavier fabrics set the needle position slightly away from the coil. Stitch, starting at the top of the zipper, until the zipper foot touches the pull tab at the bottom.

4 **Repeat steps 2 and 3** on the other back piece.

5 **Close the zipper and stitch** the remainder of the seam; use a regular zipper foot to get as close as possible to the zipper seam (see page 196).

6 **Finish the pillow** with a general purpose presser foot, following the general directions for the pillow style. Rather than leave an opening for turning, simply open the zipper before stitching the final seam.

Lapped Closures

A lapped closure is simply two hemmed edges that overlap, similar to that on a button-down shirt, and, as on shirt fronts, the range of edge finishes and closure options is extensive. The edges can be held together with fasteners, such as hook-and-loop tape, snap tape, or buttons. If the edges are overlapped slightly deeper, fasteners are not even necessary. Closures that are strictly functional can be placed in the center of the pillow back or near one side. On the other hand, decorative closures showing off fancy buttons or toggles can be positioned on the pillow front.

How to Sew a Plain Lapped Closure

1 Cut two pieces for the pillow back with the length equal to that of the finished pillow plus 1" (2.5 cm) and the width equal to half the finished pillow width plus 3½" (9 cm). Press a 1" (2.5 cm) double-fold hem in one long edge of each back piece. Stitch along the inner fold of each piece.

2 Overlap the hemmed edges 2" (5 cm), right sides up. The inner folds will align. Baste across the hem ends. Follow the general pillow directions to complete the pillow. Rather than leave an opening for turning, turn the pillow right side out through the overlapped hems.

How to Sew a Buttoned Closure

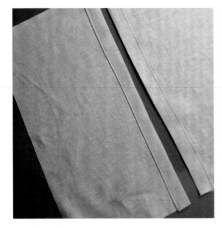

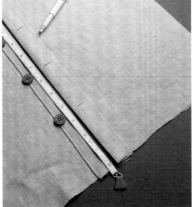

Follow step 1 for the plain lapped closure, but stitch both hems in place after deciding whether you want the hem allowance on the outside or inside, for one or both edges when finished. In this case, the allowances will face one another with the upper layer facing inward.

Stitch the desired number of evenly spaced buttonholes parallel to, and down the center of, the hem of one pillow back piece (or front piece, if closure is decorative). Overlap the hems and mark the button placement through the center of each buttonhole onto the underlapped hem. Sew on the buttons.

Button the hems. Baste across the hem ends. Finish the pillow, following the general directions for the pillow style. Rather than leave an opening for turning, unbutton the hems to turn the pillow right side out.

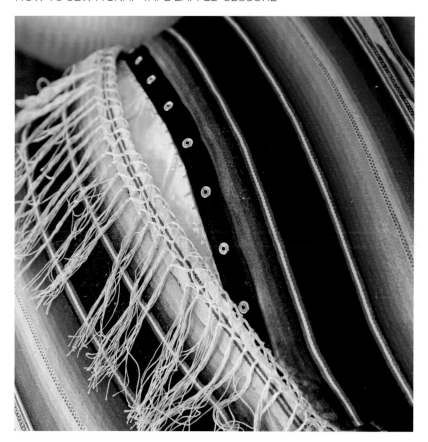

Follow the directions for the plain lapped closure, but extend the snap tape sides into the seam allowances at the ends of the opening. Be sure the snaps align before stitching.

HOW TO SEW A HOOK-AND-LOOP TAPE LAPPED CLOSURE

1   **Follow step 1 for the plain** lapped closure, but add only 3" (7.5 cm) to half the finished width. Press a 1" (2.5 cm) double-fold hem in one long edge of each back piece. Stitch along the inner fold of one piece.

2   **Cut strips of ¾"** (2 cm) hook-and-loop tape 3" (7.5 cm) shorter than the hemmed side. Center the loop side of the tape on the right side of the stitched hem. Stitch around the outer edges of the tape.

3   **Unfold the hem edge** of the other pillow back piece. Center the hook side of the tape on the right side of the fabric, between the two pressed folds; stitch around the outer edges of the tape. Refold the hem, and stitch.

4   **Overlap the hems** and seal the tape. Baste across the hem ends. Follow the general pillow directions to complete the pillow. Rather than leave an opening for turning, unseal the tape to turn the pillow right side out.

The seams around a pillow are the perfect place for decorative accents. While defining the pillow's lines, accents such as fabric-covered welting and twisted-cord welting also lend stability and give the pillow a tailored, classic look. Ruffles soften the pillow lines and create a casual, romantic appearance. Fringes, in every style imaginable, add texture, movement, and interest to your accent pillows.

Welting

Welting is the general term used for a type of trim made from cording encased in fabric when used in larger, home décor sewing projects, while the same thing is called "piping" when used on smaller projects or garments. The cording used to make welting is available in many sizes, beginning at $^2/_{32}$" and sold in increments of $^1/_{32}$". A medium-sized cording that would be used for most home décor projects, such as slipcovers or placemats would be $^4/_{32}$" to $^6/_{32}$". In metric markets, cord is sold by the millimeter diameter or by a number, with the largest diameter having the number 8. Cording is also available in a variety of natural and man-made materials. Choose a cording diameter that will complement the pillow's size and shape and work well with the pillow fabric. Choose a cord material that will serve the pillow's function, for example, use poly foam cording for outdoor-use pillows or boat seat slipcovers. Narrower welting is more tailored and well suited to small pillows made with lightweight fabrics. Thicker welting is more casual and more prominent in the overall design of the pillow. In order to round corners and fit curves smoothly, fabric strips for making welting are cut on the true bias. However, consider the look you want to achieve: Striped fabrics, for example, when cut on the bias will create welting with a candy-cane look, which you may or may not like. You may, instead, prefer to match the stripes over the welting and compensate for the lack of bias ease by round tapering corners or creasing the welting at the corners.

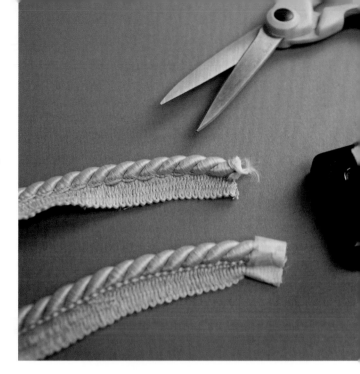

Twisted cord welting, also called lip cord, is an ornate alternative to fabric-covered welting and is available in a wide range of styles, colors, and sizes. A welt tape, or lip, is attached to a decorative cord for sewing into a seam. From the right side of the welting, the inner edge of the lip is not visible. For easier stitching and a neat appearance on the pillow front, the welting is applied to the pillow back first, right side up. The ends of the welting can be twisted together to join them inconspicuously.

Decorative trims, including twisted welting, tend to ravel easily. Before cutting these trims in the fabric store, the clerk should wrap the trim with tape and cut through the center of the taped area. Likewise, when you begin a project, wrap the trim with tape before cutting to a workable length. Before making final cuts, saturate the trim with liquid fray preventer or fabric glue and allow it to dry completely, then cut through the center of the sealed area.

HOW TO MAKE FABRIC-COVERED WELTING

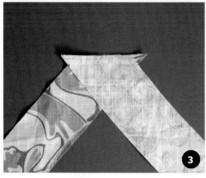

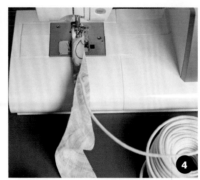

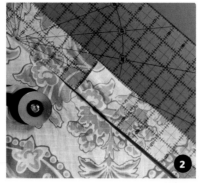

1 Wrap your fabric around your cording to measure where the cutting line should be.

2 Fold the fabric diagonally, aligning the cut end to the selvage. Cut bias strips parallel to the fold 1" (2.5 cm) wider than the cording circumference. For a thicker fabric, you may want to cut a more generous welting seam allowance such as ⅞" (2 cm).

3 Piece strips together to a length a few inches (cm) longer than the distance to be welted. Be sure to align at seam lines, not raw edges.

4 Fold the fabric strip over the cording, right side out, aligning the raw edges. Using a cording or zipper foot, begin stitching approximately 1½" (4 cm) in from the end and machine baste with the needle stitching on the cord side. Do not crowd the cord with your stitching line, since you'll be stitching between it and these stitches twice more. Keep the cording straight, free and smooth as you sew.

5 Stitch the welting to the right side of the pillow, starting 2" (5 cm) from the end of the welting and aligning the raw edges; stitch inside the previous stitching line. Clip the welting at corners, easing around curves.

6 Stop stitching 2" (5 cm) from the point where the ends will meet. Cut off one end of the welting so it overlaps the other by 1" (2.5 cm). Remove the stitching from one end of the welting and trim the ends of the cording so they just meet.

7 Fold under ½" (1.3 cm) of fabric on the overlapping end of the welting. Lap it around the other end; finish stitching the welting to the edge.

8 Finish the pillow, following the general directions. On seams that carry welting, use a cording foot or zipper. With the wrong side of the welted piece facing up, stitch inside the previous stitching line, crowding the stitches against the welting.

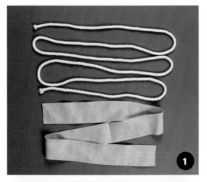

1. **Cut a piece of fabric** on the true bias to the correct final length, plus approximately 1" (2.5 cm) to make up for loss at trimming. Cut a piece of soft, flexible cording twice as long as the final piece of fabric-covered cording.

2. **Use a zipper foot** and place the needle to the left and do not crowd the cord. For thicker cord, place the needle on the right of the zipper foot. Stitch the fabric casing with a straight stitch.

3. **Tack the cord to the fabric** at the end of the fabric, which sits at the middle of the cording piece.

4. **Trim the seam allowance** as close to the stitching line as possible without cutting the thread.

5. **Hold the opposite end** of the cord and pull firmly, but gently, to turn the cord right side out.

6. **Trim the turning cord** from the resulting fabric cord and save for another use.

7. **Knot the fabric cord ends** as desired.

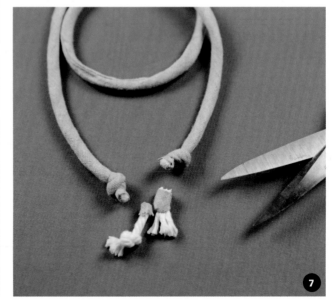

HOW TO ATTACH TWISTED-CORD WELTING (LIP CORD)

1 **Pin the twisted welting** to the pillow back, right sides up, with the beginning and end along one side (not at a corner). Mark each corner with a pin. Remove the trim. Hand-tack the lip to the cord ¼" (6 mm) from each side of each pin. Cut away ½" (1.3 cm) of lip at each corner mark. This will make it easier to attach the welting as it rounds the corners.

2 **Stitch the twisted welting** to the pillow back, right sides up, using a zipper foot; align the edge of the welt lip to the raw edge of the fabric. Round the cord at the corners and stitch only on the fabric. Leave 1½" (3.8 cm) unstitched between ends; leave 3" (7.5 cm) tails.

3 **Loosen the cord from the lip** in the area of the join. Trim the lip ends so they overlap 1" (2.5 cm).

4 Separate the cord plies; wrap the end of each ply with tape. Arrange the plies so those on the right turn up and those on the left turn down.

5 **Insert the plies on the right,** under the crossed lip ends, twisting and pulling them down until the welting is returned to its original shape. Secure in place using tape. Twist and pull the plies on the left over the right plies until the twisted ends look like continuous twisted welting from both sides. Tape in place.

6 **Position the zipper foot on the left** of the needle, if possible. Place the pillow back to the right of the needle; this will allow you to stitch in the direction of the cord twists. Machine baste through all layers to secure the welting. If you are unable to adjust your machine to stitch in this position, remove the presser foot and stitch manually over the thick cords. Be sure the presser foot lever is down so the thread tension is engaged.

7 **Finish the pillow,** following the general directions for the style. On seams that carry twisted welting, use a zipper foot. With the wrong side of the welted piece facing up, stitch inside the previous stitching line, crowding the stitches against the welting.

Ruffles

Because they will be visible from both sides, self-lined ruffles are best for pillows. Taper square pillow corners, before attaching ruffles. Then round the corners rather than pivoting sharply. The finished pillow will appear square and the ruffles will lie more smoothly around the corners.

HOW TO MAKE RUFFLES

1 **Cut strips of fabric** for the ruffles on the lengthwise or crosswise grain of the fabric, twice the desired finished width plus 1" (2.5 cm). Piece enough strips together to reach a length two to three times the pillow circumference; piece the strips together in diagonal seams to reduce bulk.

2 **Stitch the ends** of the ruffle strip together in a diagonal seam, forming a circle. Fold the strip in half lengthwise, right sides together. Press the fold, if desired, or leave it unpressed for softer ruffles.

   Finish and prepare the raw edges for gathering in one step by using a zigzag stitch and over a gathering cord, such as crochet cotton or dental floss, within the ½" (1.3 cm) seam allowance.

3 **Fold the ruffle into fourths.** Make a ⅜" (1 cm) clip into the seam allowances at each fold. Arrange the ruffle on the right side of the pillow front, with the zigzagged cord on top and raw edges even. For a square pillow, match the clips to the corners of the pillow front; for a rectangular pillow, match the clips to the centers of the sides; for a round pillow, match the clips to quarter-marks along the outer edge. Pin at the marks.

   Pull up the gathering cord until the ruffle fits the areas between the marks. Distribute the fullness evenly, allowing extra fullness at the corners so the ruffle can fan out. Pin the ruffle in place. Secure the gathering cord by wrapping the ends around pins.

4 **Machine baste the ruffle** to the pillow front, stitching just inside the gathering row.

5 **Finish the pillow,** following the general directions for the style. On seams that have ruffles, with the wrong side of the ruffled piece facing up, stitch just inside the previous stitching line.

Fringes

Fringes, traditionally made of silk but available most commonly in synthetics, elevate simple throw pillows to luxury room accessories. Fringes are the caviar of interior décor: a delicate, textural, and slightly decadent something extra that makes anything better. Fringes come in many variations and thicknesses, from simple brush fringes to opulent onion tassel fringes. There are almost limitless variations of basic trims, which might include beads, feathers, varying loops, gimp cording, and so on. If you like luxurious detail in your décor, trims will become your fast friend..

HOW TO ATTACH FRINGES

Fringe without decorative heading: Taper the corners on square-corner pillows. Machine baste the fringe to the right side of the pillow front, placing the heading within the ½" (1.3 cm) seam allowance and the fringe facing inward. At the ends, cut the fringe between the loops and hand stitch the cut ends to prevent raveling; butt the ends together. Finish the pillow following the general directions for the style

Fringe with decorative heading: Before stuffing the pillow, pin the fringe around the front outer edge of the finished pillow cover, aligning the inner edge of the heading to the outer edge of the pillow. Miter the heading at corners. If the heading is thick or textured, use paper-backed, two-sided fabric adhesive. Secure a thin, flat heading using fabric glue or paper-backed fusible adhesive strips.

Bed and Bath

YOU WILL NEED
- Decorator fabric for each pillow sham (see chart opposite)
- sewing thread
- masking tape

Flanged Pillow Shams

Flanged shams transform ordinary bed pillows into custom designer pillows. They can be made to fit standard-size, queen-size, king-size, or Euro square pillows. An overlapping closure in the center of the back makes it easy to insert and remove the pillow. Select decorator fabric to coordinate with your duvet or bedspread or stitch up luxury natural linen shams for a timeless look and sleeping comfort.

Cutting Directions
Cut a sham front and two sham back pieces according to the measurements given in the chart, opposite.

How to Sew a Pillow Sham

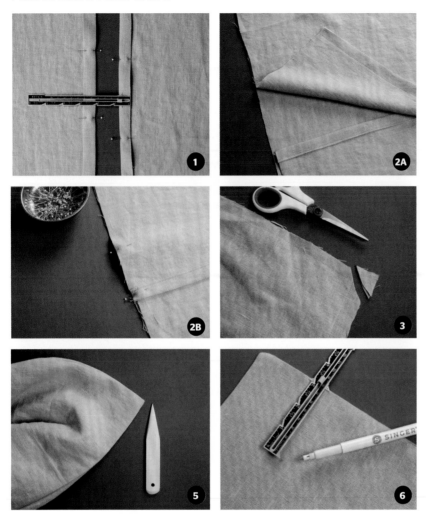

1. **Press ½"** (1.3 cm) double-fold hems on one long edge of each back piece (these will be the vertical, over-lapping edges). Stitch the hems.

2. **Place the sham back** pieces over the sham front, right sides together, aligning the cut edges and overlap-ping the back hemmed edges 3" (7.5 cm).

   Pin the layers together around the outer edge.

3. **Stitch ½"** (1.3 cm) from the edge, piv-oting at the corners. Trim the seam allowances diagonally at the four corners to remove excess bulk.

4. **Insert a heavy cardboard tube** or a seam roll into the opening and place it under the seam. Press the seam allowances open, applying light pres-sure with the tip of the iron down the crease of the seam.

5. **Turn the pillow sham** right side out, reaching in through the overlap to pull out each corner. Insert a point turner or similar tool into the sham, gently pushing the points out to form perfect corners.

6. **Press the seamed edges.** Edge stitch as desired. With the front fac-ing up, pin the layers together about 3" (7.5 cm) from the four sides. Mark small dots 3" (7.5 cm) from the cor-ners of the shams to help you know when to pivot.

7. **Place a piece of masking tape** on the bed of your machine 3" (7.5 cm) to the right of the needle, parallel to the seam allowance guide. Stitch the pillow sham flange, guiding the seamed edge along the tape and pivoting at each corner.

PILLOW SIZE	CUT SIZE OF FRONT	CUT SIZE OF EACH BACK
Standard 20" × 26" (51 × 66 cm)	27" × 33" (68.5 × 84 cm)	27" × 19" (68.5 × 48.5 cm)
Queen 20" × 30" (51 × 76 cm)	27" × 37" (68.5 × 94 cm)	27" × 21" (68.5 × 53.5 cm)
King 20" × 36" (51 × 91.5 cm)	27" × 43" (68.5 × 109 cm)	27" × 24" (68.5 × 61 cm)

These pretty, simple, and easy-to-make pillowcases have ties for an eye-catching designer touch on an otherwise humdrum household item. Sleep on the smooth side and just flip it over when you make the bed: Who needs extra decorative throw pillows? Sewn from neutral linen, these pillowcases are modern and rustic in equal measure. Or use colorful broadcloth remnants to freshen up your bedroom look in a jiffy. Below are instructions for a standard-size U.S. bed pillow. Adjust the fabric measurements for Euro squares or king pillows, as needed.

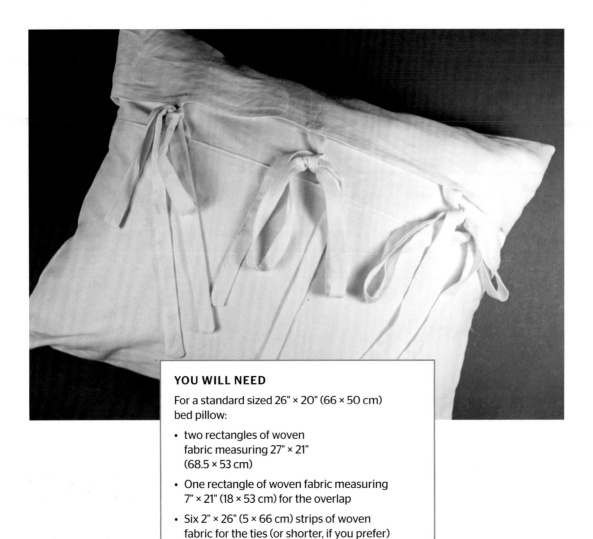

YOU WILL NEED

For a standard sized 26" × 20" (66 × 50 cm) bed pillow:

- two rectangles of woven fabric measuring 27" × 21" (68.5 × 53 cm)

- One rectangle of woven fabric measuring 7" × 21" (18 × 53 cm) for the overlap

- Six 2" × 26" (5 × 66 cm) strips of woven fabric for the ties (or shorter, if you prefer)

How to Make a Sweet Dreams Pillowcase

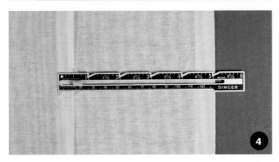

1 **Fold the strip pieces** in half lengthwise. Stitch one short end and both long open edges together. Clip the corner for a smooth turn. Turn the ties right side out and press.

2 **Press one long edge** of the overlap piece ½" (1.3 cm) toward the fabric wrong side. Mark the folded edge at the center and at 8" (20.5 cm) to the left and right of center. Place open ends of three of the ties under the pressed fold at the marks. Fold up the edge again ½" (1.3 cm) and pin.

3 **Arrange the ties** to hang down from the hem and pin. Edgestitch along both edges of the double-folded hem and catch the ties in the stitching line.

4 **Stitch a ½"** (1.3 cm) double-folded hem along the top edge of the underlap piece. Press a ½" (1.3 cm) deep pleat 5" (13 cm) down from the top hem of the underlap piece. The inside of the pleat should face up, like a pocket, toward the double-folded hem made in a previous step.

5 **Mark along the pleat** at the center and 8" (20.5 cm) to the left and right of the center mark. Tuck the open edges of the remaining three ties into the fold of the pleat and pin.

6 **Edgestitch** along the pleat edge, and catch the ties in the stitching line. Turn the underlap piece over and edgestitch along the opposite edge of the pleat to secure each of the underlap ties in two places.

7 **Place the pillowcase** front right fabric side up on your work surface. Place the overlap piece on the pillow front and pin right sides together. Place the underlap piece along the top edge and over the underlap piece and pin right sides together.

8 **Stitch all the way around** the pillow with a ½" (1.3 cm) seam. Finish the seam allowances. Clip the corners for a smooth turn. Turn the pillowcase right side out, press seams, and insert pillow.

TIP

Adapt the cord-covering technique on page 266 for strip turning by stitching the strip around and across a cord starting not in the middle but at one end, so the strip turns onto itself as you pull the cord through it.

Duvet Cover

A duvet cover keeps a duvet or comforter clean and is easily removed for laundering. The sewing steps are fairly simple; the difficulty comes in handling large expanses of fabric. Set up a card table next to your sewing machine station to help with the task. Duvet covers usually require two or more widths of fabric sewn together for the front and back: one full width down the center with equal partial widths along the sides. Choose a lightweight, firmly woven, washable fabric. Consider how the fabric feels against the skin and whether the sleeper has any sensitivities to any materials. Natural fibers will breathe better, releasing excess heat and moisture for a more comfortable sleep.

How to Sew a Duvet Cover

1 **Measure your duvet or comforter** to determine the finished size of the cover. Use the formulas below to determine the cut length and cut width of the pieces and the amount of fabric you will need. If you are using a print that requires matching, allot for extra material. We are using numbers for a queen-size duvet cover; yours may be different.

2 **Measure and mark** the location of each cut along the selvage. Cut the pieces, following the cutting guidelines below. If you do not have to match a pattern, cut away the selvages. Cut one front and one back piece in half lengthwise.

Pin a half-width piece to the full-width front piece, right sides together, along the lengthwise edges. Match the pattern, if necessary, following the guidelines on page 243. Stitch ½" (1.3 cm) seam. Repeat for the other side. For a patterned fabric, finish the seam allowances and press them open. Alternately, you may finish the seam allowances by stitching them together, then pressing the seam allowances toward the center of the duvet and topstitching for an extra line of defense against the seam ripping.

3 **Measure and cut** the duvet front to the exact cut width, as determined in the chart. Be sure to trim equal amounts from each side.

4 **Repeat steps 2 and 3** for the duvet cover back. Mark a line 12" (30.5 cm) from the lower edge of the back. Cut on the marked line.

5 **Press a 1½"** (3.8 cm) double-fold hem in the upper edge of the small back piece. Stitch the hem.

Press and stitch 1½" (3.8 cm) double-fold hem on the lower edge of the strip from the back piece.

Finished length of the duvet cover	86" (218.5 cm)	To find the number of widths needed		2
Add 1" (2.5 cm) for seam allowances	+ 1" (2.5 cm)	Multiply the number of widths		2
		by the cut length of the front		87" (221 cm)
To find the cut length of the front*	= 87" (221 cm)			
Finished length of the duvet cover	86" (218.5 cm)	To find the amount needed for the front	=	174" (442 cm)
Add 8" (20.5 cm)	+ 8" (20.5 cm)	Multiply the number of widths		2
		by the cut length of the back		94½" (240 cm)
To find the cut length of the back*	= 94½" (240 cm)			
Finished width of the duvet cover	86" (218.5 cm)	To find the amount needed for the back	=	189" (480 cm)
Add 1" (2.5 cm) for seam allowances	+ 1" (2.5 cm)	Add the amount needed for the front		174" (442 cm)
		to the amount needed for the back	+	189" (480 cm)
To find the cut width of the cover	= 87" (221 cm)	to find the total amount needed	=	363" (922 cm)
Divide the cut width	87" (221 cm)	Convert to yards (meters); round up	=	10⅛ yd. (9.25 m)
by the fabric width	54" (137 cm)			
Round up to the next whole number	1.6			

*If you buy a fabric with a pattern repeat, the cut lengths must be rounded up to the next number evenly divisible by the pattern repeat length. In our example, if the repeat length is 7" (18 cm) the cut lengths are 91" and 98" (231 and 249 cm) instead of 87" and 94½" (221 and 240 cm). Proceed with your figures using the revised cut lengths.

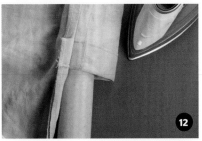

6 **Mark placement and length** for buttonholes on the hem of the small back piece, centered between the fold and stitching line. Place outer marks 6" (15 cm) from each side and the others spaced about 10" to 12" (25.5 to 30.5 cm) apart.

7 **Sew buttonholes** over the marked lines. Apply liquid fray preventer to the buttonholes.

Allow to dry and then cut the buttonholes open.

8 **Overlap the hemlines** of the back pieces 1½" (3.8 cm), and pin them together at the outer edges. Mark the placement for the buttons on the hemline of the large back piece. Sew buttons over the marks.

9 **Button the back pieces** together. Place the duvet cover back over the front, right sides together, aligning the outer edges. Pin the layers together. Fold a 20" (51 cm) piece of twill tape in half. Align the folded edge to the outer edge of the duvet cover ½" (1.3 cm) from the corner, and pin in place. Repeat at each corner.

10 **Stitch a ½"** (1.3 cm) seam around the edge of the duvet cover, pivoting at each corner and catching the folded end of the twill tape in the stitching. Trim the seam allowances diagonally at the four corners to remove excess bulk. Avoid cutting through the twill tape. Unbutton the opening. Insert a heavy cardboard tube or a seam roll into the opening and place it under the seam. Press the seam allowances open, applying light pressure with the tip of the iron down the crease of the seam.

11 **Stitch a plastic ring at each corner** of your duvet or comforter. Spread the duvet or comforter out over your new duvet cover and tie the twill tape to the rings at each corner. Now turn the duvet cover right side out, encasing the duvet or comforter inside.

YOU WILL NEED
- fabric for top and back of duvet
- sewing thread
- buttons, ½" to ⅝" (1.3 to 1.5 cm)
- twill tape
- 4 small plastic rings

Bed skirts hide the box springs and legs of a bed frame. Gathered skirts give a soft effect; pleated skirts are more tailored. Both styles cover the sides and foot of the bed, and can be made with split corners (to accommodate bed posts and foot boards) or continuous corners (for beds without footboards).

Gathered skirts can be made with one layer or two. When making a two-layered skirt, prepare the panels separately and then gather them together as one piece. The weight of the fabric and the desired look will determine the fullness of the skirt. Allow up to three times fullness for very lightweight, semisheer fabric, if you want a full look. Double fullness works better for medium-weight fabric.

Pleated skirts have box pleats at the foot corners and centers of each side. You may also want to add a pleat in the center of the foot and three to four along the sides as an added detail. The directions that follow allow for 6" (15 cm) pleats. There is a 1" (2.5 cm) double-fold hem at the lower edge and front edges.

Store-bought bed skirts are attached to a plain fabric deck that slides between the mattress and box spring. The directions for the pleated skirt incorporate a deck, which can be made from muslin, broadcloth, or a flat sheet. When you make your own bed skirt, you can sew it to a fitted sheet, which keeps the skirt from shifting out of position. The directions for the gathered skirt show how to attach it to a fitted sheet. Both styles can be made either way.

Cutting Directions

For gathered dust ruffle length, cut two pieces each the length of the box spring times the desired fullness, plus 4" (10 cm) for 1" (2.5 cm) double-fold side hems. Cut one piece the width of the box spring times the desired fullness, plus 4" (10 cm) for 1" (2.5 cm) double-fold hems. The skirt depth is equal to the distance from the top of the box spring to the floor plus 4" (10 cm).

For pleated skirt, cut the deck 1" (2.5 cm) wider and 1" (2.5 cm) longer than the box spring. Cut bed skirt on lengthwise grain of fabric. Cut two pieces the length of the box spring plus 18" (46 cm). Cut one piece the width of the box spring plus 18" (46 cm). Bed skirt depth equals distance from top of box spring to floor minus ¼" (6 mm), plus 2½" (6.5 cm) for the seam and hem.

YOU WILL NEED

- decorator fabric
- fitted sheet or muslin, broadcloth, or flat sheet for deck
- thread
- cord, optional
- shirring tape, optional

How to Sew a Gathered Bed Skirt

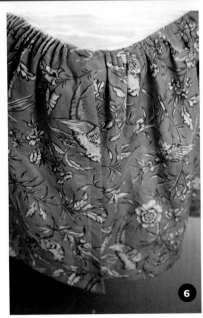

1 **Stitch 1"** (2.5 cm) double-fold hem along lower edges of the three pieces, then turn under and stitch 1" (2.5 cm) double-fold hem on both ends of each piece. Mitered corners are optional.

2 **Gather 1"** (2.5 cm) from upper edge with ruffler attachment a, two-string shirring tape b, two rows of basting c, or zigzag stitching over a cord d.

3 **Place fitted sheet** on box spring. On sheet, mark upper edge of box spring. Mark every 12" (30.5 cm) along this line for matching to skirt. Mark upper edge of skirt every 24" (61 cm) if using double fullness; every 36" (91.5 cm) for triple fullness.

4 **Pin right sides of skirt** pieces along three sides of sheet, raw edges on marked line, and hems overlapping at corners. Match markings on skirt pieces to markings on sheet. Pull up gathers to fit.

5 **Remove sheet** from box spring, keeping skirt pinned in place. Stitch 1" (2.5 cm) from raw edge of skirt.

6 **Turn skirt down** over lower edge of sheet. Topstitch ½" (1.3 cm) from seam, stitching through skirt and sheet.

How to Sew a Pleated Bed Skirt

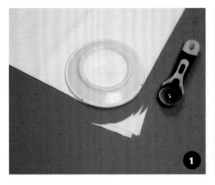

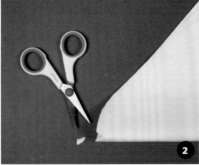

1 **Fold deck in half lengthwise** then crosswise so corners are together. Using saucer as a guide, cut corners in gentle curve.

2 **Fold curved corners in half** to determine centers; mark fold with ¼" (6 mm) clips. Also, mark center of each side with clip.

3 **Stitch skirt pieces,** right sides together, on narrow ends, with shorter piece in center.

Stitch 1" (2.5 cm) double-fold hem on lower edge of skirt and on unstitched narrow ends of skirt pieces, as in step 1.

4 **Pin skirt to deck,** right sides together, with stitching of side hem at clip on one end of deck . Form 6" (15 cm) pleats at clips on sides and corners of deck. Seam will fall inside pleats.

5 **Remove skirt** and machine-baste pleats. Reposition skirt on deck. Pin with right sides together. Clip center of corner pleats. Stitch ½" (1.3 cm) seam.

6 **Press seam allowance** toward deck. Press ¼" (6 mm) double-fold hem at open end of deck; stitch hem. Topstitch the skirt seam allowance to deck. Press pleats.

For beds with footboards and posts, attach three separate bed skirt pieces to the sides and front of your deck or fitted sheet. For tailored bed skirts, add 2" (5 cm) in width for each side piece and 4" (10 cm) to the front piece to accommodate the additional double side hems.

A bathroom shower curtain is easy to sew. You can choose fabric to coordinate with your fixtures, tile color, and towels. This shower curtain has grommets along the upper hem, spaced to align with the grommets in a standard shower curtain liner. Join the fabric panels with a French seam to give the curtain a neat appearance from both sides. To make the shower curtain washable, select a washable fabric and preshrink it before you cut it. Polyester outdoor fabrics are a good choice to resist mildew.

Cutting Directions

Cut two full-width pieces 82" (208.5 cm) long. Curtain will be trimmed to necessary cut width in step 2.

YOU WILL NEED

- 4⅝ yd (4.25 m) fabric
- water-soluble fabric marker
- twelve grommets, size 0 or ¼" (6 mm) and attaching tool
- thread to match the fabric

How to Sew a Shower Curtain

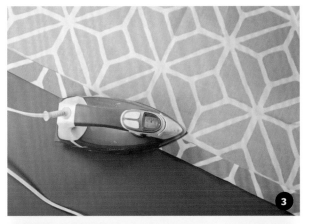

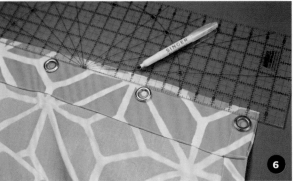

1   **Cut away the selvages** of your decorator fabric evenly. Join the two lengths together using a French seam (page 119). The total seam allowance width is ½" (1.3 cm), so use ¼" (6 mm) seams for each pass.

2   **Cut one vertical edge** of the shower curtain so the total width is 76" (193 cm). The finished width of a standard shower curtain is 72" (183 cm). This allows 2" (5 cm) on each side for hemming.

3   **Press a 3"** (7.6 cm) double-fold hem into the upper edge and a 2" (5 cm) double-fold hem into the side edges. Unfold the fabric at the upper corners.

4   **Trim out the excess fabric** from the inner layer, as shown, trimming to within ³/₈" (1 cm) of the fold. Refold the upper edge, and pin; stitch the upper hem.

5   **Press a 3"** (7.6 cm) double-fold hem into the lower edge. Unfold the hem and trim excess fabric from the side hem. Stitch the hem.

6   **Mark the placement** for twelve evenly spaced grommets along the upper hem, using a fabric marker. Position them ¾" (2 cm) from the upper edge with the outer marks centered in the side hems. Read the manufacturer's directions for attaching the grommets, and test the technique on a sample of fabric folded several times. Attach the grommets.

This simple and highly versatile item can be used any number of ways: As a laundry hamper, storage tote, reusable grocery bag, or beach tote. The easily sewn oval shape allows for storage in a narrow areas, such in a bathroom or mudroom. Choose a sturdy fabric such as denim or canvas twill. Polyester outdoor fabric is a good choice to resist mildew when making a laundry hamper or beach tote.

TIP

Because the bottom of the bag needs to be a perfect fit to the upper portion, it makes sense to cut and sew the upper portion in its entirety before cutting the bottom section from your fabric. That way, you will have the exact measurement to fit the upper portion of your bag.

YOU WILL NEED

- 2 yd (1.8 m) sturdy fabric
- water-soluble fabric marker
- heavyweight fusible interfacing
- welting cord
- thread to match the fabric

How to Sew a Space-saver Hamper or Tote

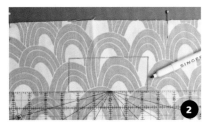

1 **Cut four rectangles** of fabric measuring 36 × 30 (91 × 76 cm) each, two pieces from the outer fabric and two pieces from the lining fabric.

2 **For both halves** of the bag upper, place the lining material on the main fabric, right sides together, and secure in place with several pins. Measure down 2" (5 cm) from the center of the top edge on the lining side and mark a rectangle 5" × 2" (12.5 cm × 5 cm).

3 **Stitch around this drawn rectangle** with a straight stitch. Cut a slit through the center of stitched area beginning and ending approximately ¾" (2 cm) from the side edge. Snip V's toward the corners.

4 **Cut two pieces of heavyweight** interfacing approximately 7" × 4" (18 cm × 10 cm). Draw a rectangle in the center of each measuring 5" × 2" (12.5 cm × 5 cm). Place the interfacing over the cut slits and fuse to the material.

5 **Once the interfacing has adhered,** turn the sides of the bag through the slits.

6 **Press the encased seams** around the resulting handle holes. Edgestitch ⅛" (3 mm) around the edge of the handle holes.

7 **Stitch the bag lining** pieces along the sides of the fabric, right sides together. Turn the bag and stitch the bag outer pieces along the side seams fabric, right sides together.

8 **Reach between the two layers** with thumb and forefinger and at the top edge, grab the side seams of both lining and outer and pull them through, so that portion of the bag is wrong side out. The finished handle holes will prevent you from turning the bag completely inside out. Stitch the lining to the outer along the top edge fabric, right sides together, as far as you can on that side, approximately up to the side edges of the handle holes. Turn that side of the bag right side out. Repeat for the other side of the bag.

TIP

For stiff sides, cut pieces of heavyweight fusible interfacing to fit the entire side of the tote. Cut the heavyweight interfacing 1" (2.5 cm) shorter on each side to allow for the seam allowance.

9 **Press the upper encased seams,** taking care to press under the seam allowances over the handle holes. Edgestitch all the way around the top of the bag at ⅛" (3 mm).

10 **Take the measurement** of the bottom opening. Pin your tape measure into a loop at this exact measurement. Place the pinned and looped tape measure on the fabric wrong side and within the tape measure, place two small, round equally sized plates. Trace around the two plates with a water soluble textile marker. Connect the two sides of the resulting circles to form an oval.

11 **Cut out this piece** and use it as a pattern to cut a piece from the heavyweight interfacing. Trace the pattern onto the lining fabric, add ½" (1.3 cm) seam allowance all around and cut on the new line.

12 **Prepare a piece of welting** for the bottom edge as described on page 264. Stitch the welting to the bottom outer piece, overlapping ends as described.

13 **Fuse the leather-weight** interfacing to the bottom outer piece wrong side.

14 **Separate the bag** upper lining from the bag upper outer fabric, so that the fabric wrong side is showing. Pin the bag bottom outer to the bag upper outer, right sides together, and stitch, crowding the welting in the stitching line as you go.

15 **Stitch the bag lining** bottom to the bag lining upper, right sides together. Leave an opening in the stitching line for turning. Turn the bag right side out. Stitch the opening closed.

Table Fashions

Eating a meal together is the most universal way we communicate and connect with people the world over. Therefore, setting a table with linens you made yourself offers an opportunity to show the people in your life how much they mean to you. Table linens protect your furniture while adding color and interest to your setting. While made almost obsolete by their single-use paper cousins, cloth napkins are coming back strong to the family dining table, as a more cost-effective, environmentally considerate and, frankly, better choice for the job at hand. When you sew your own tablecloths, no longer will they be too long on the sides and too short on the ends: You can make tablecloths to fit the exact size and shape of your table. Cotton, linen, bamboo, and blends of these natural fibers are excellent choices to withstand a good deal of wear and washing.

Selecting Fabrics

You may find a small selection of 72" (183 cm)-wide tablecloth fabrics in basic colors at the fabric store or online. In most cases, you simply buy the length you need and hem the edges for a quick tablecloth. Many decorator fabrics are good choices for tablecloths, but they are not wide enough to provide the needed coverage in one fabric width, so you must piece widths together. Avoid a center seam by using a full fabric width in the center and stitching narrow, equal side panels to it.

The length of the tablecloth from the edge of the table to the bottom of the cloth is called the drop. The usual drop length for tablecloths is 10" to 12" (25.5 to 30.5 cm), which is at or near chair seat height. Be sure to include the drop length in your measurements.

Three common drop lengths are short, 10" to 12" (25.5 to 30.5 cm); mid-length, 16" to 24" (40.5 to 61 cm); and floor length, 28" to 29" (71 to 73.5 cm). Short cloths end at about seat height and are good for everyday use. Mid-length cloths are more formal. Floor-length coverings are impractical for dining and are used, for example, on buffet and decorator tables.

Round tablecloth. Measure the diameter of the table then determine the drop length of the cloth. The size of the tablecloth is the diameter of the table plus twice the drop length plus 1" (2.5 cm) for a narrow hem allowance. A narrow hem is the easiest way to finish the curved edge of a round tablecloth.

Square or rectangular tablecloth. Measure the length and width of the tabletop, then determine the drop length of the cloth. Add twice the drop length measurement to both length and width measurements to find the finished tablecloth size. To find the cut size, add 1" (2.5 cm) to each measurement for a narrow hem or 4" (10.2 cm) for a wider hem.

Oval tablecloth. Measure the length and width of the tabletop then determine the drop-length of the cloth. Add twice the drop length measurement to both length and width measurements to find the finished tablecloth size. To find the cut size, add 1" (2.5 cm) to each measurement for a narrow hem. Because oval tables vary in shape, mark the

finished size with the fabric on the table. Center the fabric on the table and keep it in place with weights. Then use a hem marker or cardboard gauge to mark the drop length evenly around the curves.

There are two ways to finish the edge of a round tablecloth: a ¼" (6 mm) double-fold hem or by adding fabric-covered welting. To determine the yardage for a round tablecloth, divide the tablecloth diameter by the fabric width minus 1" (2.5 cm). Count fractions as one width. This is the number of widths you need. Then multiply the number of widths by the diameter and divide by 36" (100 cm) to find the total yards (meters).

Cutting Directions

The cut size of the tablecloth is the diameter of the table plus twice the drop length. Add 1" (2.5 cm) for a narrow hem allowance. If you want to finish the edge with welting, the cut size is the same as the finished size. Determine where you want the seams in your tablecloth, using one of these options:

Option 1. Use one seam when the diameter of the tablecloth is less than one-and-one-half times the fabric width. Subtract the fabric width from the tablecloth diameter. Cut a strip on the lengthwise grain of one fabric piece that is 2" (5 cm) wider than this measurement.

Option 2. Use two seams when the diameter of the tablecloth is more than one-and-one-half times the fabric width. Cut one fabric piece in half lengthwise.

TIP

To ease the material around a curved hem without puckering, run a basting stitch within the seam allowance before stitching the hem. When doing so, increase the thread tension enough so to that the edge of the fabric curls inward. Or, finish the edge of your material with a four-thread overlock stitch. Increase the thread tension on the needles until the material edge curls inward.

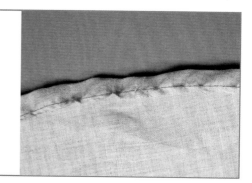

How to Cut a Round Tablecloth

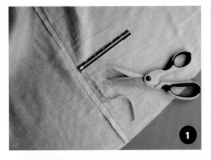

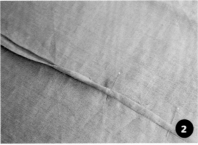

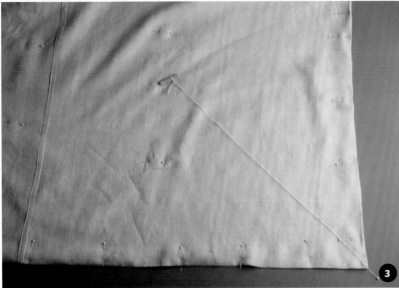

1 **Join fabric panels,** right sides together, with ½" (1.3 cm) seams to form a square.

2 **Sew a flat-fell seam** (page 120) for a reversible tablecloth.

3 **Fold square into fourths.** Pin layers together to prevent slipping. Tie a string to a marking pencil. Pin the other end of the string to the center folded corner of the fabric a distance from the pencil equal to the cut radius of the tablecloth. Mark the arc. Cut on the marked lines; remove the pins.

How to Sew a Narrow Hem

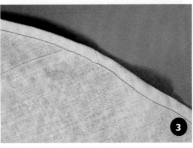

1 **Stitch around tablecloth ¼"** (6 mm) from edge.

2 **Press under on stitching line.** Press under ¼" (6 mm) again, easing fullness around curves.

3 **Edgestitch** close to folded edge.

How to Sew a Welted Hem

1 **Multiply diameter of tablecloth** by 3.12 to determine length of welting needed. Cut and join bias strips, right sides together, to cover welting.

2 **Cover cording and attach** to right side of cloth. Zigzag seam and press to back of tablecloth. Topstitch ¼" (6 mm) from welted seam.

Square and Rectangle Tablecloths

Make tablecloths the desired width by joining widths of fabric as necessary, using full widths in the center and partial widths on the edges. Straighten the crosswise ends of fabric to square the corners. You may use plain, French, or over-edge seams for tablecloths that are not reversible. Use flat-fell seams for reversible tablecloths.

Hem the edges with double-fold hems of ¼" (6 mm) to conserve fabric. Or use 1" (2.5 cm) double-folded hems for more weight. Mitering is the neatest way to square the corners because it covers raw edges. To determine the amount of fabric you need, divide the total width of the tablecloth by the width of your fabric minus 1" (2.5 cm) for seam allowances. Count the fractions as one width. Multiply this figure, which is the number of panels needed, by the total length of the tablecloth. Divide this number by 36" (100 cm) to get the total yards (meters) needed.

Cutting Directions

The cut length of the tablecloth is the length of the tabletop plus twice the drop length plus 4" (10 cm) for the 1" double-folded hems.

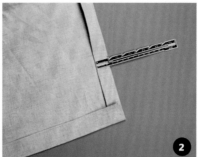

1 **Press under 2"** (5 cm) on all four edges of the cloth. Unfold.

2 **Turn each edge in,** aligning it with the first fold line. Press the outer fold.

3 **Unfold.** Press each corner diagonally to a point where the creases intersect.

4 **Trim off corner diagonally** from one fold line to the other.

5 **Refold hem,** encasing raw edge. Pin. At corners, creases will meet, forming the miter.

6 **Use glue stick** to hold folds in place.

7 **Edgestitch** along inner fold. Pivot at corners. Press.

Placemats

Add fun and variety to your table setting with reversible octagonal placemats. These placemats are lined to the edge and can be made with two different fabrics. Welting sewn into the outer edge adds a bit of structure. For ease of application, choose welting no larger than $3/16"$ (4.5 mm).

How to Sew a Reversible Placemat

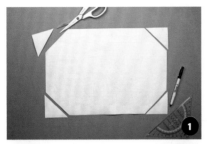

1. **Draw a 13" × 19"** (33 × 48.5 cm) rectangle on paper. Mark point 3½" (9 cm) from each corner. Draw diagonal lines across each corner connecting marks. Cut off corners.

2. **Preshrink fabrics** (page 104). To preshrink welting, wrap it into large loops and tie in the middle with a large, loose knot. Soak welting in warm water, squeeze out excess moisture. Place in net laundry bag or nylon stocking before tossing in dryer. Press the flat edge of the welting when dry.

3. **Cut front and back** for each placemat, using pattern. Make sure edges are parallel to grainlines.

4. **Pin welting to right side** of the placemat front. Keep welting relaxed.

5. **Clip into seam allowance** of welting at each corner of placemat at exact point where welting must bend. Clip to—but not through—stitching line, so that welting seam allowances spread open and lie flat. Sew welting to placemat front as for welted pillow (page 264).

6. **Pin placemat front over back,** right fabric sides together, encasing the welting between layers and aligning outer edges. Stitch just inside first stitching line, leaving an opening for turning along one side.

7. **Trim seam allowances** diagonally at each corner. Turn back and press seam allowances ½" (1.3 cm) from the edge of the opening.

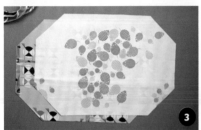

8. **Turn placemat right side out** through opening. Use point turner to push out corners. Press placemat up to welting as you smooth and tug welting out to the edge with your fingers. Slipstitch the opening closed.

TIP

If one fabric has a light background and the dark patterns from reverse fabric can be seen, fuse lightweight interfacing to the fabric wrong side of your lighter fabric to prevent the reverse fabric from showing through.

Napkins

Napkins add the finishing touch to your table. Because napkins are quick and easy to sew, you can choose fabrics to match each occasion or meal. Making your own linen napkins costs a fraction of what they cost to buy finished and this little bit of luxury makes a treasured gift.

Standard finished napkins generally range between 14" or 18" (35.5 or 46 cm) square, however there are different napkin sizes for different uses.

Choose a medium-weight simple woven fabric. Before cutting the fabric, square the fabric ends. For fringed napkins, square the ends by pulling a thread.

Napkin hems can become a design element. Try different decorative stitches and threads on your sewing machine. The hemming techniques shown here can also be used for tablecloths or single-layer placemats.

NAPKIN TYPE	INCHES	CENTIMETERS
Cocktail	6" × 6"	15 × 15 cm
Hor d'oeuvres	13" × 13"	33 × 33 cm
Lunch	18" × 18"	46 × 46 cm
Lunch	20" × 20"	51 × 51 cm
Dinner	22" × 22"	56 × 56 cm
Dinner	24" × 24"	61 × 61 cm

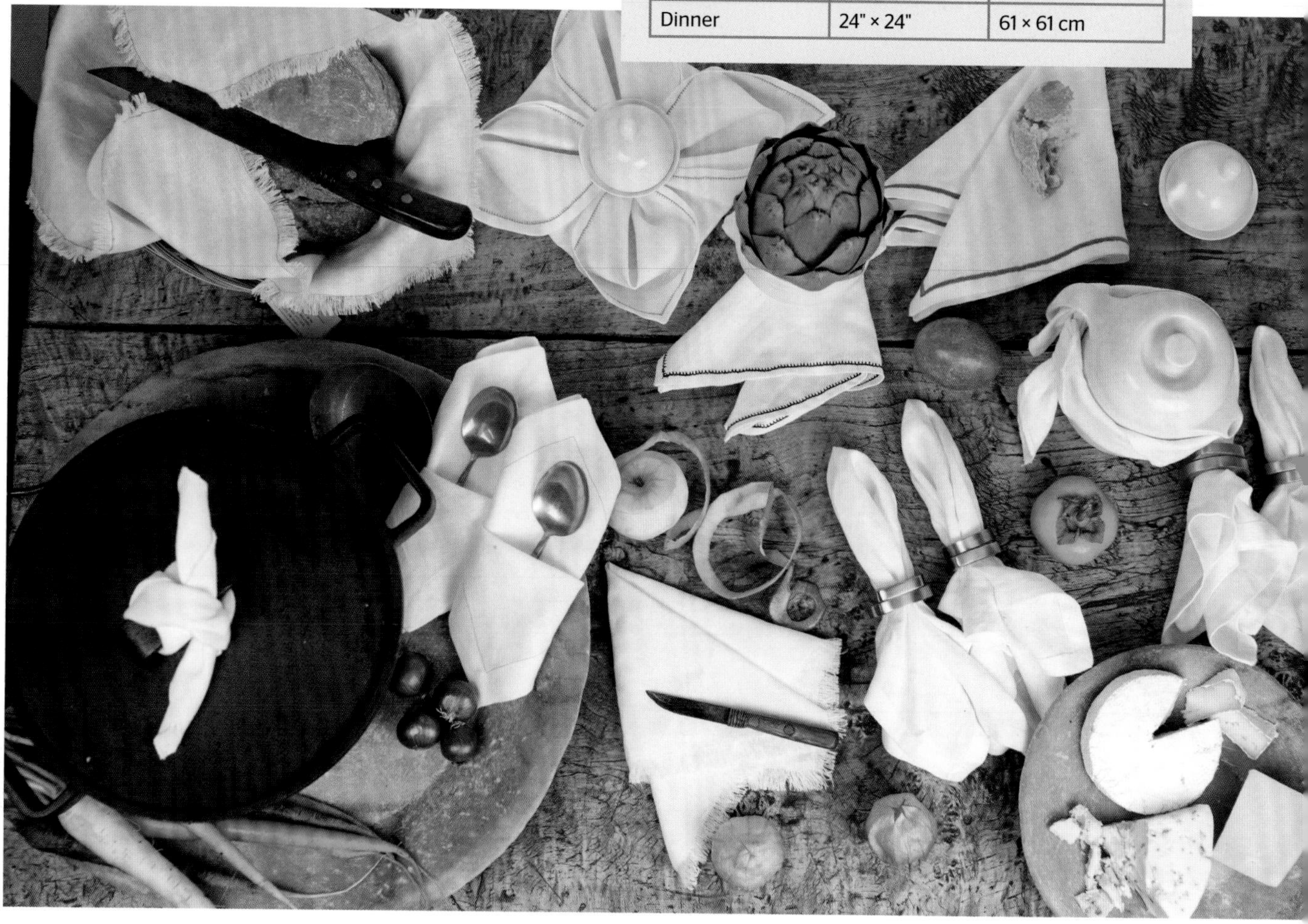

Cutting Directions

Cut most napkins 1" (2.5 cm) larger than the finished size. This will allow for a ½" (1.3 cm) single-folded hem. One yard (meter) of 36" wide fabric (100 cm) yields four 17" (43 cm) napkins. A piece of fabric 45" (115 cm) square yields nine 14" (35.5 cm napkins). Please allow for more or less fabric, respectively, if you are making, for example, double-folded mitered hems or rolled hems.

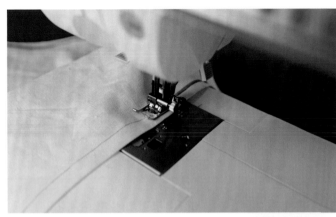

Satin Stitch. A bold satin stitched line creates a luxury napkin look suitable for any formal table. Turn under ½" (1.3 cm) on all sides. Edgestitch along raw edge to use as a guide. Use wide, closely spaced zigzag stitches from napkin right side over the edgestitching line.

Zigzag Overedge. This is a simple napkin finish that conserves fabric. Pressing under the edge helps prevent the zigzag line from curling the fabric. Trim loose threads from napkin edge. Press under a scant ⅛" (3 mm). Stitch over the pressed edge, using wide, closely spaced zigzag stitches. An overedge foot or special-purpose foot helps to maintain zigzag width.

Decorative Stitch. This is your opportunity to try out those different decorative stitches on your machine. Press under ¼" (6 mm) and stitch. From the napkin right side, stitch with a decorative stitch, using straight stitch line as a guide. Blanket stitch (shown) gives a hemstitched look. If you are using a decorative stitch that has a lot of zigzagging, which may pucker the fabric, you may try stabilizing the your fabric with a wash-out water-soluble stabilizer before stitching.

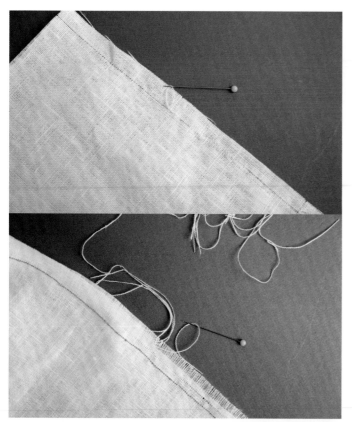

Fringe. These napkins are formal and casual in equal measure and add a bit of texture to your table setting. Cut napkins on a pulled thread to straighten edges. Stitch ½" (1.3 cm) from raw edges with short straight stitches or narrow, closely spaced zigzag. Pull out threads up to the stitching line.

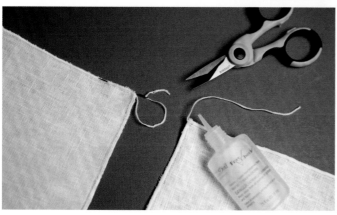

Serged Edge. These napkins are quick to make and conserve fabric. The line along the very fabric edge allows you a chance to add a bit of color. Using wooly nylon in one or both of the loopers will create a more solid-looking stitching line. Overlock edges with your serger. Stitch two opposite sides, then the remaining sides, leaving long chain stitch tails. Weave tails back under the overlock stitches for 1" (2.5 cm), cut off remaining tail, or apply liquid fray preventer at corners. Allow fray preventer to dry, then cut off tails.

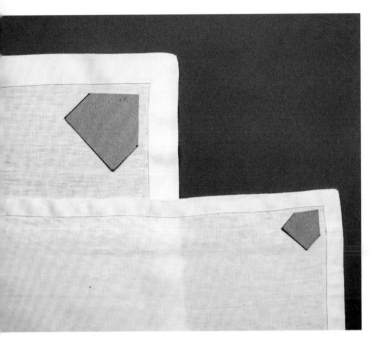

Double-folded Mitered Hem

A generous 1" (2.5 cm) double-folded mitered hem linen napkin is the grande dame of table fashions and will lend any meal formal elegance. A ½" (1.3 cm) double-folded mitered hem napkin is excellent for everyday use and is a simple way to showcase favorite fabrics.

You may miter the corners of napkins using the method for a square tablecloth (page 289). However, especially if your fabric has considerable bias give, like many linen fabrics, you may find it easier to make very square mitered corners using the following method:

First, you will need to fashion a template from piece of card stock.

How to Make the Template

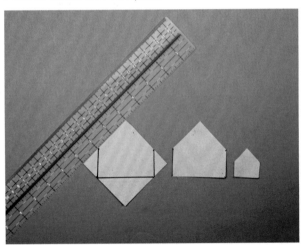

To make a napkin with a 1" (2.5 cm) double-folded hem with a mitered corner, cut a square of cardstock measuring 3" × 3" (5 × 5 cm). Turn the card stock square like a diamond. Measure in and draw a vertical line 1" (2.5 cm) in from each of the side corners of the rhombus.

To make a napkin with a ½" (1.3 cm) double-folded hem with a mitered corner, cut a square of card stock measuring 1 ½" × 1 ½" (4 × 4 cm). Turn the card stock square like a diamond. Measure in and draw a vertical line ½" (1.3 cm) in from each of the side corners of the rhombus. Connect the two lines with a single horizontal line. Cut along all three lines to form a pentagon "house."

How to Make Mitered Napkins

1 **Place the "roof"** of the template into each corner of your napkin.

2 **Trace around the template** with temporary marking tool.

3 **Fold each corner in half** along the true bias and pin.

4 **Stitch** along the marked lines. Backstitch at the beginning and end of your stitching line (contrasting thread used to show detail).

5 **Trim a scant ⅛"** (3 mm) from the stitching line. Notch the outer corners and clip the inside corner.

6 **Turn the corner fabric** under once. You will notice the L-shaped seam on the napkin's right side.

7 **Tuck in the top** of the L-shaped seam again to form a mitered double-folded corner. Create crisp corners with the aid of a point turner.

8 **Press** the resulting double-folded hem beginning at the corners and moving toward the center of each napkin side. Edgestitch very close to the fold.

Glossary

A

Armscye: The opening in a bodice to accommodate the sleeve.

B

Batting: A nonwoven polymer, natural cotton or bamboo material in sheet form used to give sewn items volume and insulating properties.

Baste: To stitch together with long, loose, temporary stitches. Basting can be used in fitting and to hold pieces temporarily together. Baste stitches are removed once the garment is complete.

Beeswax: Beeswax refers to either natural beeswax or, more commonly, a paraffin substitute, through which sewing thread is passed to strengthen the thread and ease stitching in hand sewing.

Bias: Bias refers to any direction on the fabric that is neither on the grain nor perpendicular to it. A "true bias" refers to a 45-degree angle from the fabric grain.

Bias tape: Bias tape is a strip of fabric cut on the true bias. Most often, the long edges are pressed toward the center. Bias tape is used as trim and to bind edges. Being cut on the bias allows materials to curve without puckering.

Binding: Material used to encase raw edges.

Blind hem: Hemming by machine or hand using tiny, almost invisible, stitches.

Blocking: Most often used with knit or crocheted items, blocking uses heat and moisture to set the stitches and bring the item into its final dimensions. Washing an item will return it to its original shape and the item will require blocking again. Blocking may be done only on natural fibers. See "killing" for shaping items made from synthetic fibers.

Bodice: That portion of the garment covering the torso.

C

Casing: A tunnel of fabric through which something such as elastic, a sash, or tie is fed.

Clapper: A pressing tool made of hardwood that may be used with an iron. A clapper is placed over a pressed area to hold in the heat and solidify the seam or fold. A clapper is especially useful for pressing fabrics that cannot be ironed directly by holding the heat of the steam into the fabric.

Clip: Making small cuts along the edge of a seamline to accommodate curving the fabric or to ease at corners.

Closure: The area on the garment that opens and closes for dressing. Also called opening.

Convertible collar: A collar without a stand that may be worn buttoned up or worn open to expose lapels.

Custom backing: A fusible reinforcing material such as polyester tricot is bonded to the reverse side of a decorator fabric to increase durability.

Cushion wrap: A nonwoven polymer material that is used in upholstery. It is often wrapped around rectangular foam pieces to give the cushion a rounder form. Cushion wrap is also known as poly wrap or upholstery batting. It is sometimes referred by different trade names, such as Dacron or Terylene.

D

Dacron: A trademarked name commonly used to describe a nonwoven volume-adding polyester cushion material used in upholstery. Dacron is also referred to as cushion wrap or upholstery batting.

Dart: A tucked fold of fabric tapered to a point used to give a garment shape.

Dart tuck: A fold of fabric partially stitched in place and allowed to release into a pleat. Usually, a dart tuck is an inverted dart.

E

Ease: (1.) To draw the fibers or threads of the fabric closer together than when they were woven or knit. Easing should not result in puckers or gathers but, rather, be a construction of the fibers. (2.) The give in the fabric or garment needed for dressing ("dressing ease").

Edgestitch/Edgestitching: To stitch a line right along the edge of a garment, usually along an enclosed seam.

Enclosed seam: A seam concealed within the garment.

Eye: The hole in a needle through which thread is fed.

Eyelet: (1.) A small round hole, either stitched or punched through the fabric with a small metal grommet. (2.) A
type of embroidered cotton faric, traditionally white with white stitching.

F

Favoring: Rolling one fabric edge over another to conceal a seam underneath, for example, on a shirt collar.

Finger press: Pressing a seam flat or creasing fabric with your fingers or with a wooden finger press.

Finish: (1.) To finish refers to the practice of preventing fabric edges from raveling. Examples include, stitching a line of overcast stitches along the fabric's edge, pinking the fabric edges, or stitching a line of zigzag or straight stitches near the fabric edge. It can also include the practice of stitching the seam allowances together once the seam has been stitched. (2.) A fabric's finish refers to chemical processing done after weaving to lend the fabric additional properties, such as repelling water or reducing wrinkling.

Fly: The material on a garment which conceals an opening.

G

Grade: To grade a seam allowance means to reduce bulk in the seamline by trimming away one seam allowance close to the stitching line.

Grain, grain line: In woven fabrics, the grain is the warp, the longwise yarns that the weft (crosswise yarns) are woven over and under. Generally, it is parallel to the fabric's selvedge. However, if the warp was askew during weaving, and the warp yarns are not perfectly perpendicular to the weft, then the grain will not be parallel to the selvedge: Such fabric is considered "off grain". Similarly, if the warp and weft are at perfect 90-degree angles, but the print is askew, the fabric is also considered "off grain". The grain line is the corresponding direction to which a pattern piece is to be placed during layout. The warp is stronger and should carry more weight, therefore, the grain line on a pattern generally follows a vertical line down the body. While knit fabrics do not have a grain in the true sense, the grain line is parallel to the ribs, perpendicular to the courses.

Gusset: Often a triangular or diamond-shaped piece of fabric added to create shape or add ease, for example, in the armscye.

H

Hair canvas: A traditional interfacing material used in tailoring jackets and in millinery. Hair canvas has a percentage of goat's hair, which is particularly suited to grip the fibers of the fabric it rests against.

Hand: In sewing, hand is the term used to indicate the tactile properties of fabric, for example, the material's smoothness, stiffness, softness, draping qualities, and so on.

I

Ice wool: A loosely woven, fluffy wool-blend filling fabric used in tailoring.

Inset: Piece of fabric or trim contained within the construction of a garment for fit or decoration.

J

Jump hem: A jump hem is formed when a small pleat is folded along the bottom edge of the lining before it is sewn to garment outer hem allowance. That fold is called a jump pleat.

K

Killing: Adding heat and moisture to synthetic fibers in a very controlled manner. Killing melts the fibers in a specific way to achieve a final form and dimension. Killing is similar to blocking of natural fibers, however, killing differs from blocking in that once a synthetic item is killed, it can never return to its original shape.

L

Lap: An edge that extends over another edge, for example, on a placket.

Lapel: A lapel is the outward-facing edge above a jacket closure below the collar.

Layout: The arrangement of sewing pattern pieces on the fabric to be cut. Often, sewing patterns will suggest the layout for different views, sizes or fabric widths.

Lining: Lining is added to garments to retain shape and improve wearing properties. Lining is usually a lightweight, slippery material, such as acetate, which allows
for ease of dressing.

M

Mark/Marking: Transferring informational marks, such as notches, darts, buttonhole placement and so on from the sewing pattern to the garment fabric pieces.

Muslin: A plain woven cotton fabric, which comes in a variety of weights. In dressmaking, "a muslin" refers to a test garment sewn from an inexpensive fabric to try out the fit and form before an expensive fabric is cut. "Muslin fitting" refers to basic draping, pinning, marking, and/or baste stitching an inexpensive fabric on a person, dressmaker's form or around an object to create a rough outline pattern.

N

Negative ease: A finished garment that is smaller than the actual body measurements. Negative ease is common in knit fabric designs such as swimwear and dancewear, which require a lot of stretch and recovery.

Notch: (1.) A small cut made into the body of the fabric. A notch, for example, in a corner, can help form a neat, square corner. Several notches in a row along a curved seam can allow the material to turn with the seam. (2.) The marks on a sewing pattern on the seam allowance to be cut and used as a guide in placing pieces. A notch may be either clipped into seam allowance or cut outside it.

Notion: Things required for sewing besides the fabric, sewing pattern, and the sewing machine. Notions include tools, special equipment, closures, thread, tapes, glues, stabilizing products, scissor and shears, measuring and marking devices, and so on.

O

Opening: The area on a garment that opens and closes. Also called closure.

Overedge: An overedge stitch is either a zigzag variation or a serger stitch, where the threads lap over the edge of the material. An overedge stitch helps prevent a fabric edge from raveling.

P

Piece goods: Piece of fabric sold by the yard.

Pin fitting: Using straight pins to determine the right placement of seams or darts once the garment fabric is rough cut. Sewing pattern pieces may also be pin fit to the wearer to determine placement of darts and adjust for different figure types.

Pinking: Cutting fabric with special pinking shears, which have zigzag scalloped blades to prevent raveling.

Pivot: Turning the fabric in a new direction with the needle down and the presser foot in the up position.

Placket: A garment opening, usually lapped, fastened with buttons, a zipper, hooks and eyes, or hook-and-loop tape.

Pleat: An unstitched fold.

Press (v): To solidify seamlines and give shape to the garment. While pressing is commonly done with a hot iron, it may also be done with a wooden finger press or clapper, used either by themselves or in combination with steam.

Prewash/Preshrink: To wash or dry clean a fabric according to the care instructions for that material before sewing. Prewashing/preshrinking removes excess dyes and fabric finishes and brings the material into the form it will take when the garment is washed. Preshrinking prevents seams from puckering and helps the garment retain its original shape once the finished garment is sewn.

R

Railroaded: In decorator fabric, when the design runs from selvedge to selvedge, the design is considered "railroaded". If the design is woven or printed down the length of the fabric, then the fabric is not railroaded.

Ravel: To become unwoven or unwound.

Raw edge: An unfinished edge of fabric.

Release pleat: A small fold of fabric often included in the lining pieces of a jacket to accommodate the different elasticities of lining and outer fabrics.

Release tuck: A stitched fold of fabric used to control fullness or add shape. The tuck may be released on the top, bottom, or both ends.

Right side: In sewing, the side of fabric that will be seen on the outside of the garment. Often marked "RS" on sewing patterns and in sewing instructions.

Roll: Maneuvering one layer of fabric over another slightly to conceal a seam, for example, on a shirt collar.

S

Scant: The fabric taken up by the fold when the item is turned or rolled. Generally, this is approximately a couple of threads under ⅛" (3 mm). However, because each fabric behaves differently, the scant cannot be given an exact measurement. Generally, it refers to the least amount possible in turned or rolled hems. Also "just short of" or "just inside of" when indicating seam allowance widths.

Seam: The stitching together of two pieces of fabric.

Seamline: The line of stitching resulting from seaming fabric together. On a sewing pattern, it is the line representing where the fabric will be stitched.

Seam allowance: The lip or edge material beyond the stitching line in a seam.

Self: In sewing, self refers to the same fabric used as in the remainder of the garment.

Selvedge: The lengthwise edge of a piece of material. The selvedge is parallel to the grain. It is often woven more tightly to accommodate tentering, has fabric information printed on it and/or has tentering holes evident.

Shirting: A type of tightly woven, high thread count cotton or cotton blend commonly used for tailored shirts.

Shank: The link between the button and the fabric, either connected as part of the button or constructed of thread, to create space for the overlapping fabric.

Sharps: Machine or hand needles that have a sharp point intended to cut through fibers.

Slash: A cut into the body of the garment piece to accommodate construction.

Sleeve head: The part of a garment designed to fill the gap between the armscye and the sleeve top, forming the shape of the sleeve cap. Its function is to support the sleeve cap in jackets and coats where a shoulder pad is included. The sleeve head helps to make a nice roll line in a high cap sleeve and prevents the seam allowance from slipping. Finished sleeve heads may be purchased from specialty retailers or you may make your own with just a bit of filler fabric.

Stab stitch: A kind of tack commonly used in drapery making, wherein the needle, instead of going straight through the fabric, is pushed through at a very low angle, almost flat against the material, so that the thread catches the minimum amount of the top layer of the outer fabric and the tacking thread, therefore, remaining invisible from the front.

Stitch in the ditch: To stitch in the ditch is to stitch right along the stitches of the seam, avoiding the fabric as much as possible.

T

Tack: (1.) A series of closely spaced stitches intended to hold something securely in place. A bar tack is a series of very closely spaced small zigzag stitches used, for example, to hold belt loops in place. A triangular tack is three sides of straight stitches, often used for pocket corners. An arrowhead tack is a couture reinforcing technique, which results in a decorative threaded triangle. A French tack is a string of chained thread used to loosely tether linings to garment outers. (2.) To tack is the same as to baste: to add long, loose temporary stitches before final stitching.

Taper: Cutting or stitching at an angle, usually to reduce the size or meet an adjoining edge.

Tension: The amount of pull placed on the machine's threads.

Timing: A sewing machine's timing refers to the needle-to-hook relationship and the precise interaction required to make consistent, even stitches at all sewing speeds.

Topstitch/Topstitching: An additional line of stitching added along the seam allowance to hold the seam allowance in place, and, in some instances, to reinforce a seam against tearing open. Topstitching can also be a decorative design element to emphasize the seams and shapes within the garment.

Transfer: Marking garment pieces to be sewing with instructional and placement marks found on the sewing pattern.

Trim: To cut away excess material.

Trimming: Ribbon, rick-rack, tassles, appliqué patches, or similar decorative items added for ornamentation.

Tuck: A fold stitched in place. Folds of fabric stitched partially in place and then released to form soft drapes or pleats are also called tucks or dart tucks.

U

Understitch: To stitch a line close to the edge of an interfacing to keep it in place and prevent it from appearing on the face side, for example, around a neckline.

V

Vent: A lapped slit, often found on blazer and suit coat back hems, as well as straight-fitting skirts.

Valance: A decorative drapery found along the tops of windows and canopy beds. It is intended more for decoration and to conceal drapery hardware than for privacy.

W

Warp: In woven fabrics, the stretched longwise yarns over and under which other yarns are woven.

Weft: In woven fabrics, the crosswise yarns that are woven over and under the weft.

Welting: A thick edge piping used in upholstery.

Welted: Welted refers to pockets with small, thin flaps of fabric that fill the pocket slit or buttonhole. Pockets may have one or two welts.

Welts: Welts are small flaps of fabric that fill a pocket slit or buttonhole.

Wrong side: In sewing, the reverse side of the fabric, which will not be seen. Most construction and marking is done on the fabric wrong side. Often marked "WS" on sewing patterns and in sewing instructions.

Y

Yoke: A horizontal, fitted piece of the garment, usually across the shoulders or hips.

Z

Zipper pin and box: In a separating zipper, the pin is inserted into the box to correctly align the teeth.

Zipper tab: The part of the zipper slider you hold in your fingers to open and close the zipper.

Zipper tape: The fabric part of the zipper to which the teeth are secured.

Zipper slider: The device that moves up and down the zipper and interlocks and divides the zipper teeth.

Zipper tape end: The upper and lower portions of the zipper tape beyond the stops without any teeth.

Zipper stop: Devices affixed to the top and bottom (of nonseparating zippers) to prevent the slider from coming off the chain.

Zipper separating mechanism: The device that moves up and down the zipper and interlocks and divides the zipper teeth (also known as the slider).

Zipper chain: The continuous strip of interlocked teeth.

Zipper teeth: The individual bits that comprise the zipper chain.

Index

About the Author

Nancy Langdon is the author of the best-selling book, *Sewing Clothes Kids Love* (CPi, 2010) and designs a line of sewing patterns under the name studio TANTRUM/Fledge. Very much a product of the "mend-and-make-do" generation that came before her, Nancy understood from an early age that it was better to make it yourself than to buy it from the store. With a master seamstress for a mother and a sewing machine always at the ready, Nancy grew up knowing that if there was a certain dress, shirt, jacket, or skirt she wanted, all she had to do was ask. Her early years were spent sifting through decades of sewing patterns, standing very still for fitting sessions, and paying close attention as her mother explained French seams and bias cuts.

As Nancy started her own family, she relied on that well of knowledge, along with a good dose of autodidacticism, to sew for her loved ones and her home. Nancy found sewing a good fit for her, as it marries logical, analytical, and objective thinking with intuitive, subjective, and creative thought processes to make beautiful, useful, unique items. Nancy collaborated with Sabine Pollehn of Farbenmix to produce a line of sewing patterns that have become very popular in Europe.

Nancy is proud to be an ambassador for sewing, which has brought much more than beautiful, useful garments and home décor items into her life. Sewing has also become Nancy's source of community, empowerment, enrichment, and life-long learning; for that, she is most grateful.

Acknowledgments

We wish to thank Hans-Gerd Swafing, Swafing GmbH for providing much of the fabric featured in this book.

Swafing GmbH
Bentheimer Str. 175
48529 Nordhorn, Germany

Thank you to Sabine Pollehn and Farbenmix.de for providing notions and sewing patterns.

Farbenmix.de
Olympiastr. 1
Gebäude 12, Eingang 8
26419 Schortens, Germany

We extend our thanks to Hanne Bemenberg and the firm Freudenberg Vliesstoffe SE & Co. KG for information on interfacings and interlinings.

Freudenberg Vliesstoffe SE & Co. KG
Fliselina
69465 Weinheim, Germany